Internet
for Parents

Karen Strudwick, John Spilker and Jay Arney

Resolution Business Press, Inc.

Bellevue, Wash.

Internet for Parents

Karen Strudwick, John Spilker and Jay Arney

Published by
Resolution Business Press, Inc.
11101 N.E. 8th St., Suite 208
Bellevue, WA 98004
Phone: 206-455-4611
Fax: 206-455-9143
E-mail: rbpress@halcyon.com

Manufactured in Canada

Library of Congress Cataloging in Publication Data
Main entry under title:

Strudwick, Karen
Internet for Parents
ISBN 0-945264-17-8

Acknowledgments

We would like to thank the many parents, teachers and other interested individuals and organizations from around the world who offered support, suggestions and stories for the content and direction of this book. Your electronic mail, letters, phone calls and personal contacts confirmed we were on the right track, and inspired us throughout the months of research and writing. In particular, we would like to express our deep gratitude to Carol Rice, Judy Nelson and the staff of the Bellevue (Wash.) Regional Library; John Newsom, Steve Means and Silvia Loomis of the Bellevue School District; Sandy Barnes, Frances Spilker, Ruth Kinchen, Bill Holt, Dug Steen, and Kirt Smith; and, especially, Skyla Loomis for a job well done.

About the Authors

Karen Strudwick and John Spilker are principals in Resolution Business Press, and co-editors of *Northwest High Tech,* a guide to the computer industry. In addition, Karen has worked as a copy editor at the *Seattle Post-Intelligencer* and the *Seattle Times*, and as a freelance reporter for news organizations including the *Vancouver Sun* and Victoria *Times Colonist.* She holds a journalism degree from Ryerson Polytechnical Institute in Toronto.

John is a former business editor of *The Anchorage Times* and was a labor reporter in British Columbia. He has written extensively about the computer industry. John is a Ryerson journalism graduate, and also holds a history degree from Concordia University in Montreal.

Jay Arney is a freelance advertising copywriter and technical writer who has worked in the software industry. He is a graduate of Amherst College in Massachusetts, where he majored in English.

Preface

Internet for Parents is for parents (and grandparents) who are thinking about getting plugged into the Internet but aren't sure why they should or how they can. It's also for families who are already connected but aren't sure what to do next. In short, it's for people who want to prepare themselves and their kids for the 21st century, and the new methods of research and communications that are increasingly being used at work, at home and in school.

Like you perhaps, I had heard about the Internet for some time. So had my co-authors: John Spilker, who's also my husband and business partner, and Jay Arney, a freelance writer with whom we've worked on various projects for several years. But none of us was in a position to connect to the Internet until early 1994 when access finally became widely available to small businesses and home-computer users at moderate rates.

We used online services such as CompuServe and America On-line to tap into computer hardware and software support groups and for corporate electronic mail. But until very recently, these services were separate from the international network of networks we know as the Internet, and offered only limited access, if any, to the Internet. We weren't satisfied — we wanted to be *on* the Internet.

Why we got connected

For professional reasons, John and I felt badly left out of the information loop. In 1990, one of our books, *Northwest High Tech*, received a rave review on an Internet discussion group. We were flooded with orders from places in the United States and Europe that we'd never heard of. It seemed everyone had read the review-except us. Our need for the Internet didn't diminish. A year later, we were editing a dictionary about the UNIX operating system and wanted to check relatively obscure details about technology and events. The Internet is based on UNIX, yet ironically we couldn't tap into it to find the information we knew it could provide.

What's more, as the parents of a four-year-old — who, like all others his age, never stops asking "Why?"—John and I realized we couldn't afford to ignore the opportunities the Internet offers to help a child learn and develop.

How we got connected

The process of getting connected wasn't simple. In our area, unless you worked for the government or a huge corporation, or attended a university, you were out of luck. But once access to the Internet became available to the general population in 1993, we jumped at the chance to hook up.

While John had a fair amount of computer experience, he found the Internet software that was available difficult to use. The Internet provider wasn't much help. John did figure out many of the problems. And fortunately, one of the authors of *UNIX: An Open Systems Dictionary* (the book we were working on) was able to answer some crucial questions. In all, it took us three days to accomplish what can now be done painlessly in less than 15 minutes.

But once connected, these difficulties quickly faded from memory as we began to explore the Internet's ever-expanding territory.

What we've found on the Net

You don't just get connected, you get hooked on the Internet. You become part of a lively community that seems to be operating in parallel with your "real" life. You may never meet any of the people there face to face or touch any of the books or research materials you find online, but they all become a part of your daily life. And as you'll see in this book, the Internet can save you a lot of time and hassle as life becomes more and more hectic and our responsibilities-to career, family and continuing education-snowball.

Take our experiences, for example.

At one point, John had to write an article about Microsoft Corp. and its various business deals. He turned to the most up-to-date and well-briefed source he could find: the Internet. There he found the full texts of Bill Gates' speeches, marketing discussion papers, and other current and unedited information, all immediately available. He didn't have to leave the office or play telephone tag.

Another time, after installing the Windows NT operating system on the office computers, John discovered our Hewlett-Packard scanner wouldn't work. He contacted both Microsoft and H-P, but neither had an answer. Finally he posted a query to an Internet discussion group. Within 48 hours, an H-P computer technician in Sweden messaged him back, with a simple solution involving a $20 cable.

It's not just for work, work, work

A devout hockey fan, he also discovered a mailing list devoted to this sport. Based in the United Kingdom, the list provides daily reports on games from members around the world, even in such unlikely hockey haunts as South Africa!

I became an avid e-mail user and member of a myriad of mailing lists on topics ranging from early childhood education and school networking technology to running a public library and home schooling.

In my personal life, however, the Internet took on an even more important role. I have a rare vision disorder called retinitis pigmentosa (RP) and have found an Internet "support" group on that subject. Before the Internet, I had met very few people with RP; now not only am I in daily contact with the 200-plus members of this electronic mailing list around the world, but I have relatively easy access to resources, including people, that help make my life easier. In late 1994, a member in Turkey recently diagnosed with RP joined the group in search of information not readily available there, as well as the support and friendship of people who would understand the daily challenges of RP. The group, which has no officers, office or dues, sends out a free daily digest of news and comments submitted by those who particpate through e-mail. A member in France, who got the list going, continues — voluntarily — to keep us in line and on topic.

Even at the age of four, our son Stephen has benefited from the Internet. After trips to Yellowstone National Park and Mount St. Helens National Monument, he wanted to know all about geysers and volcanoes. A search on the Internet brought him pictures of the latest volcanic activity around the world, and gave us a refresher course so we could better explain seismic activity in simple terms. Whenever we bring him to our office now, he wants us to find the latest news and pictures of a *Jurassic Park*-like exhibition that's touring North America.

He still talks about how he e-mailed his wish list to Santa. Just in case you're wondering, Posty (the mail elf) did reply.

So, what's the deal?

Our intent in *Internet for Parents* is to show you *why* it's important to get connected, and given that the technology is changing and making it easier, how to do so. Through the more than 700 resources we profile, as well as the many true stories we recount about the experiences of people — like you, perhaps — who use the Internet, we try to give you many ideas about what to do once you're logged on.

But we don't just want you to read about the Internet — we want you to *do* it! And do it with your family so you all get the most out of your Internet experience. To that end, we've tried to keep things short and sweet, and make it simple for you to try out what we talk about in this book through the software package that's included and the online access that it gives you to all the resources we mention.

So, give it a shot — and see you online!

Karen Strudwick
Co-author
Internet for Parents
Resolution Business Press
E-mail: rbpress@halcyon.com

Contents

Part I

Why use the Internet?

Chapter 1 shows how some families are using the Internet for educational and family purposes. *Chapter 2* explains how many schools are successfully using this technology to give students new opportunities in the Information Age. However, some schools are being left behind on the Information Superhighway, and in some cases informed parents must drag a reluctant school system onto the Net. No one wants to see his or her child left behind.

internet@home

Surfing Alaska-style

The Teel family explores the Net together.

When the temperature dips to 10 below in Chugiak, the Teels go surfing. Not in Hawaii, as most Alaskans would, but on the Internet.

"Since we put our family home page on the World-Wide Web, we've 'met' many wonderful people from Italy to Canada," says Susan Teel, who now not only maintain the Teel Homeschool Page and Internet Alaska's K-12 & Homeschool Web pages, but also designs home pages for others. "We're able to share our lives and the state of Alaska in a great new way."

Susan and husband Matthew, a computer consultant, decided to get connected to the Internet in October 1994. They wanted to make use of the online resources they'd heard so much about in home-schooling their children—Sarah, 11; Caleb, 10; and Ricky, 4.

They indeed found activities and information they couldn't have accessed in any other way: pen pals for the kids from all over the world, hourly satellite images of the weather over Alaska, the latest NASA space pictures. Plus, says Susan, "the support and resources of the mailing lists and newsgroups have brought us a wealth of information."

In fact, the Internet has become as important to her as it has to the kids. "In the wintertime especially, I find myself confined inside with only the kids to talk to. They're wonderful, but they're not adults, and I crave some communication and interaction. The Internet lets me communicate with friends, relatives, and other home-schoolers around the country, as well as visit interesting Web sites."

✔ **The Teel Homeschool Page**
   http://www.alaska.net:80/~mteel/homesch/homeschl.html

✔ **Internet Alaska's K-12 and Homeschool Home Page**
   http://www.alaska.net:80/~steel/

Chapter 1

The Internet and your family

● ● ● ● ● ● ● ● ● ● ● ● ● ● ● ● ●

This chapter will show you

✔ That the Internet is a revolutionary tool for communication and learning—a tool no parent can afford to ignore.

✔ That a home Internet connection can help your kids continue their learning outside the classroom, while providing you with valuable parenting resources as well.

✔ That your Internet connection will pay for itself time and again, putting your family in touch with people and resources you couldn't find any other way.

● ● ● ● ● ● ● ● ● ● ● ● ● ● ● ● ●

Every generation or so, a new technology shows up and makes the world seem smaller. The telephone, the automobile, air travel, commercial radio and television, satellite communication—each of these creations, in its way, pulled everyone a little closer to the global campfire. And to this list of technological revolutions, we can now add the Internet.

The Internet places more and more of the world every day within reach of your family's computer. For no more than the cost of your monthly cable bill, you can access resources — informational articles, learning tools for kids, news, books and magazines, software — that can enrich you socially and financially. And you and your kids can carry on conversations, and forge friendships, with people you may never meet in person.

There's no doubt that the Internet is here to stay. It's already changing the way government and businesses operate, and it will soon transform the way your kids are educated. In this book, we'll show you how you can get up and running on the Information Superhighway (it's probably easier than you think). Then, we'll point you to some of the valuable resources the Net already offers for you and your family.

Families power the Internet revolution

It seems as though we all woke up about a year ago and found this Information Superhighway staring at us from the morning paper. In fact, what we now call the Internet is a quarter-century old. So who's responsible for this sudden "arrival" of the Net?

To a large extent, people like *you* are. Regular people with families.

For its first twenty years, the Internet was the province of government workers, college professors and students, and large corporations with government research contracts. Using the power of a mainframe computer, people could exchange electronic mail (e-mail) and access databases. The information available online was character-based (text only), primarily technical in nature, and generally difficult to access.

Clamor grows to get on the Net

Throughout the 1980s, as personal computers (PCs) spread steadily into businesses, schools, and homes, the Internet remained unknown to most. But the popularity of commercial networks such as CompuServe and America Online clearly indicated that the general public *would* use electronic mail and online information tools. And when the Commercial Internet Exchange (CIX) was formed in 1991 to make Net connections widely available to PC owners, the public's response was rapid.

To become palatable to the general public, the Net had to become easier to use — and almost immediately, it did. The software program *gopher* first allowed users to browse online information using convenient "menus" reminiscent of the Apple Macintosh and Microsoft Windows operating systems. The Net got even more user-friendly with the advent of the *World-Wide Web*, a graphical online environment that took advantage of high-speed PCs and modems.

Computer expertise not necessary

With these new tools, you don't have to be a computer expert (or work with one) to navigate the Internet. As a result, millions of families have gotten connected. Almost without exception, Internet service providers (the companies that connect businesses and homes to the Net) report more activity in evening hours than during the day, indicating that households are more likely to be *surfing* the Net than are businesses.

It's no coincidence that PCs are selling like never before. The computers being manufactured today offer powerful 486, Pentium, and PowerPC processors, with a high-speed modem as standard equipment. And most of these machines are being sold to home buyers — another indication that families are embracing the Internet and are likely to drive its development.

What your family stands to gain

Worldwide, millions of parents and kids have discovered the possibilities of the Internet. Why exactly has the Internet become so popular so rapidly?

A direct line

It provides a direct line to people, places, and organizations that most people simply can't access through any other channel. Without the Internet, many of us would never get to places like the Louvre museum, the Library of Congress, and NASA's archives — or give our kids the opportunity to ask questions of scientists, artists, and business and government leaders.

For example:

✔ Kids electronically tour the Smithsonian and other museums on rainy afternoons.

✔ Parents and teachers exchange frequent e-mail about kids' progress in school — rather than meeting once a year for a conference.

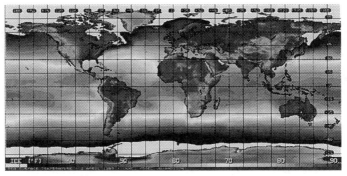

This satellite map of world ocean temperatures is available on the Internet from the University of Wisconsin

✓ Parents e-mail messages and photos of their kids to family members who live too far away to visit frequently.

A powerful research tool

The Internet brings a powerful research tool right into your home. On the Net, you can explore the information servers of universities, libraries, government agencies, and nonprofit organizations worldwide — using powerful search tools to find the information you need quickly. You can also ask questions of experts in every subject. And though relatively few "e-texts" (electronic documents) are available in their entirety, you can access library catalogs and find out where a particular book or article is available.

For example:

✓ Students writing research papers about other countries get information from servers (and even people) in those countries, from online magazine articles and photographs, and from libraries.

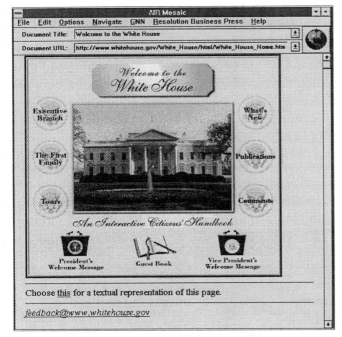

Families can visit the White House anytime ... at its home page on the World-Wide Web.

✔ Many universities and colleges post their catalogs and admission requirements on the Internet. Parents and kids go straight to these folders to research schools and find courses they can take. Some universities even allow you to earn a bachelor's or master's degree online, using e-mail to exchange assignments and comments with instructors, and enabling parents constrained by work or family responsibilities to continue their education.

✔ Kids and adults download (copy to their own computer) free software, electronic texts of literary classics, photographs, and other useful or interesting materials.

Hard-to-find resources

It offers you resources you won't find in a library or in the media. Imagine being able to view satellite weather films for any part of the world. Or clicking an onscreen button to hear the Croatian national anthem. Or performing a knifeless frog dissection from your desk.

For example:

✔ High-school students download satellite photographs from NASA to illustrate science projects.

✔ Parents home-schooling their kids find teaching tools, including complete lesson plans in several subject areas, that they can download and use at no cost.

Contact with different cultures

Through the Internet, you are exposed to different cultures, languages, and beliefs. The Internet spans the world, and it brings you in contact with fascinating people and places. This contact will not only expand your horizons, but also help you and your kids better understand and participate in the developing global economy.

For example:

✔ Kids correspond with pen pals around the world using electronic mail.

internet@home

Busy Mom juggles career and family with the Net

Silvia Loomis juggles a career, continuing education, and family life every day. And she relies on the Internet to help her keep all those balls in the air at once.

"I would say that I use it a minimum of three hours a day," says Silvia, a Chapter 1 Remedial Reading Instruction Assistant with the Bellevue (Wash.) Public Schools.

She counts on the Internet to save her time and money. Through e-mail, she stays in touch with colleagues as well as family back east. "Now we 'talk' at least twice a week."

Using FTP (File Transfer Protocol), a method of copying files from a distant computer to your own machine, she keeps her software cache up to date by pulling down upgrades as well as free and low-cost programs. Through the World-Wide Web and gopher, she finds resources she can use in teaching, many of which aren't available at her public library.

Silvia avoids rush-hour traffic on Interstate 5 by taking the Information Superhighway instead. "I'm taking classes at the University of Washington that are done over the Internet," she explains.

From home, she e-mails questions and assignments to her on-campus instructor, who responds quickly with answers and grades. "It's been great. It saves me all that commuting time and parking fees, and allows me to be home with my family."

Silvia's 14-year-old daughter Skyla is using the Internet to plan for college and a career. Skyla is considering becoming a doctor, and she's corresponded with a medical student at the University of Washington through a Usenet newsgroup to learn more.

"We're also starting to collect information from colleges and universities for Skyla," adds Silvia. "Many of them have World-Wide Web sites. We don't need to order scads of catalogs if they don't look like they'll meet our needs."

✔ Classrooms (and sometimes families) create their own *home pages* (sites) on the World-Wide Web to show the rest of the world what they're doing.

Find free help and advice

You now have the opportunity to join literally thousands of discussion groups, most for no more than the cost of the Internet connection. On the Net, you and your family will learn new approaches to work, school, and hobbies from like-minded people around the world. And you'll make a lot of new friends.

For example:

✔ Over 100 parents around the world post messages each day to an Internet parenting discussion group. They're getting answers to questions ranging from day care to bedwetting.

✔ One parent in a rural community turned to several Internet discussion groups for advice, and got plenty, when he and other frustrated parents hit a brick wall in dealing with their local school district.

Why connect now?

Hardly a day goes by when you aren't hit with another story about the Information Superhighway — who's getting on, how fast it's growing. If you're like many of the parents we've talked to in preparing this book, you wonder if you've already fallen behind in the Internet race.

Don't despair. You aren't yet roadkill on the Information Superhighway. But it's true that some 80 million people worldwide already have access to the Internet at home, school, or work, and that figure is growing by at least a million users every month. If the Internet isn't in your public library and your kids' schools already, look again in six months.

Parents often ask us, "Why should I do this now and not wait a while? Won't it be cheaper next year?" Well, here are four good reasons to stop waiting and become part of the Internet now:

The CIA home page on the World-Wide Web offers the full text of the agency's Factbook filled with background reports on countries around the world.

✔️ **It's already easy** to get an Internet connection and start "surfing." Many of the Net access tools (such as Mosaic, the World-Wide Web browser) let you simply point and click on objects using the mouse, just as you do a Macintosh or Windows program.We'll talk more about connecting to the Internet, and using Mosaic and other tools, in following chapters.

✔️ **Monthly connection charges** are within the reach of most families, usually between $10 and $30 per month.

✔️ **Although the amount** of information on the Internet is growing by leaps and bounds, it's already a remarkable resource. Each day that passes without an Internet connection means lost opportunities for you and your children.

✔️ **By starting on the Net** now, you give your kids a leg up on tomorrow's technology. Very soon, basic Internet skills — the ability to use a computer, send e-mail, access on-line databases, and speak the language of the Net — will be essential for high-school and college students and will be required for many careers.

Reality check

Before we move on to explain just what the Internet consists of and how you can use it, let's answer some questions a lot of parents are asking about the Net.

Q **Just what is and what isn't available through the Internet?**

A Let's start with what isn't available. Classified government documents aren't. Individual and corporate tax returns aren't. Many government agencies are putting their public documents online, but the process has only begun, and not all of the information is complete or easy to navigate. And although many libraries have placed their card catalogs online, not all the actual books, periodicals, and video and audio materials are available in electronic form. Certainly the files you keep on your own computer aren't available to anyone on the Internet.

What is available? Free or low-cost information from governments, universities, businesses, and nonprofit organizations. Thousands of discussion groups. News from around the world. Software of every kind. Hundreds of new resources are added to the Internet each day.

Q **Couldn't I just buy information on CD-ROM instead of hooking up to the Internet?**

A Sure you could. And many of the CD-ROM products on the market are colorful, informative and educational. But they quickly become dated, and they restrict you to a single source. The Internet offers a much broader selection of material from a far greater variety of sources than CD-ROM publishers could ever afford to do. What's more, the Internet's resources are frequently, if not continually, revised and expanded, and you can often take your questions directly to the authors of these materials.

Q **Will the Internet and other online technologies replace schools?**

A Not any time soon, and probably never. The Internet is a research and communications tool that will supplement libraries and bring people together, but it can't provide the guidance and support a human teacher can.

Q **Can my high-school student download a term paper and put her name on it?**

A That's unlikely. But she will find ideas for papers and projects, and research materials she can incorporate into them..

Q **Can kids use the Internet on their own?**

A For preteens, the answer is no. Parents will generally have to assist their children in logging on to the Net and finding materials.

Teenagers can learn how to access and navigate the Internet without a parent's supervision. However, parents should be cautious, because not everything that's on the Net is suitable for young people.

Q **I've heard that people on Internet discussion groups can be rude to newcomers or to people who present dissenting opinions. Is that true?**

A While the practice of *flaming* (insulting other users) hasn't entirely run its course, it does seem to be decreasing. Most Usenet newsgroups and mailing lists—especially those addressing a serious subject—now frown on that sort of rudeness. Also, discussion groups designed for kids tend to be moderated by adults, so unfriendly or inappropriate messages don't get distributed.

Q **Will using the Internet cost me a lot of money?**

A The charge for Internet service should run you anywhere from $10 to $30 per month. If you can find an Internet service provider within your local calling area, you shouldn't have to pay any long-distance charges for the time you spend on the Net. Of course, you do need a computer and modem, but you can easily find a fully equipped system today for under $1,500.

Q If my child's school will be hooked up soon, why would we need access to the Internet at home?

A Although many school systems are now starting to incorporate the Internet into their curricula, there are several roadblocks to full Net access in the classroom. First, most teachers have little or no Internet training themselves and aren't able to instruct kids in using it. Second, many schools have outdated equipment that can't take advantage of the newer and more powerful features. Third, most schools don't have enough computers to allow any one child access to the Internet for more than a few minutes a day.

With an ordinary computer—either a Macintosh or a PC with the Windows operating system—and five to ten hours of Internet self-training, most parents will find themselves ahead of their school system.

Q Do I have to be a computer wizard to hook up to and use the Internet?

A Not anymore. You can purchase self-configuring software that should get you up and running in a half-hour or less. The programs you need to access information on the Internet are Windows- or Macintosh-based and require no programming skills.

In our school district in Bellevue, Wash., even kids at the elementary level use electronic mail to converse with adult mentors at Microsoft Corp. in neighboring Redmond. This example is being repeated across the country, and it's a clear sign that kids aren't intimidated by the Internet. If they aren't, their parents shouldn't be, either.

The flip side: Porn on the Net

Like any other medium, the Internet has flaws too. You've probably heard that kids can be exposed to inappropriate information on the Internet. In fact, Congress is now facing a move to censor the Information Superhighway. You're probably wondering if your child will see or read unsuitable material if you get hooked up to the Net.

Without supervision, that's possible — just as kids can run into inappropriate subject matter on television, on newsstands, or on the playground at school. Most experts who've addressed this question feel it's an issue of guidance and trust, one that must be considered by each parent individually.

Buyer beware

The Internet is rooted in the belief that information should be freely exchanged. That means it's home to certain materials: explicit language, frank discussion of sexuality and other sensitive issues, racist and sexist opinions, pornography — that many parents probably won't want their kids exposed to.

In the interest of free speech, a few university servers have even deliberately included these types of materials, albeit with a "buyer beware" warning attached.

Although schools and public libraries have searched for ways to limit access to controversial materials on the Internet, there's no clear-cut solution yet.

Some material self-destructs

By and large, it's not easy to find such information on the Internet unless someone tells you where it is or you're an experienced user. One parent we interviewed, for example, pointed out that if you know how to use a World-Wide Web search tool like Lycos, you can simply plug in the word "erotica" to find a list of materials related to that subject.

Ironically, the success of such searches can actually lead to the downfall of sites that offer this type of information. If too many people try to access the servers hosting the information, they can overload the system. The systems administrators there may then simply remove the "popular" material to avoid a major computer crash.

Not much fun

Regardless, says Stacy Sherman of the University of Hawaii, "Most of (the pornographic material) is written in story form so the child would have to read through the story to get the idea instead of just glancing at pictures at a newsstand."

Kids who do find sites with pictures may have to download and then decode the files before they can view them.

"That's a pain in the butt and beyond the scope of your average 12-year-old," says Stacy, who concedes kids could learn to do it if they were really motivated.

Fear of Usenet

Some parents fear the alt.* Usenet newsgroups, which discuss a broad mix of topics, from raccoons to sex. Most Internet service providers, however, don't carry the more controversial news-groups.

But some providers — such as the one used by Steve Savitzky, the father of a 9-year-old in California — do: "Apart from the pictures, which are mostly pretty tame, and a few stories, which are mostly so badly written as to be unreadable, there's little actual pornography in alt.sex.*," Steve says.

For some, it's not an issue

For the most part, the parents we interviewed believe kids are un-likely to stumble onto something that's highly inappropriate.

"The Internet is new and the news shows have to have something to alarm people with. Stories about children and pornography and pedophiles get (high) ratings," says Stacy, at the University of Hawaii.

Adds Brian Harvey, a former high-school computer science teacher and now lecturer at the University of California-Berkeley: "This is a non-issue." Like many other people, he's more concerned about what kids watch on television. "If you think primetime is bad, check out the daytime talk shows."

So what do you do?

If your kids are young (preteens), you'll generally be assisting them when they're exploring the Net. For older kids, you'll want to discuss with them what you consider appropriate and why—just as you discuss any other moral or ethical issue.

Bear in mind as well that the user base of the Internet is changing. Two years ago, the majority of Net surfers were young adults with young—adult sensibilities. Today's users represent all ages and beliefs, and most longtime Net users will tell you that the online frontier is becoming more civilized every day. Notes Stacy at the University of Hawaii: "I think a person comes across more foul language in public than on the internet."

Sandy Barnes, the mother of four children who have Internet access at their Seattle-area schools, adds the school district has decided against a Usenet newsfeed. "They feel that they can avoid much objectionable material that way. I am not sure that that accomplishes their goal, but I have seen that the Web has cleaned itself up quite a bit just by attrition."

For those who do want their kids to be able to use the Internet but also want a tangible means of restricting what they can find on it, there may be a software solution. Companies like California-based SurfWatch Software, Inc., now offer programs that enable parents and teachers to limit access to inappropriate material on the Internet. SurfWatch, for example, blocks such material from being viewed on the computer it's installed on. It costs $49.95, and for about $6 per month the company offers a service to automatically block new sites that come online and contain doubtful material.

For more information on this topic, see:

✔ **Americabn Civil Liberties Union**
   gopher://aclu.org:6601/

✔ **Children Accessing Controversial Information mailing list**
   e-mail: caci-request@media.mit.edu
   Message: subscribe

✔ **Electronic Frontier Foundation**
   http://www.eff.org/

✔ **Information Highway Parents Empowerment Group**
   htp://home.netscape.com/newsref/
   newsrelease29.html

✔ **Net Nanny**
   phone: 800-340-7177

✔ **Solid Oak Software, CYBERsitter**
   phone: 800-388-2761

✔ **SurfWatch Software**
   http://www.surfwatch.com/

internet@school

Parents can play a part

Some educators foresee the day when parents will use the Internet to play a more active role in their kids' school life.

Pat Ridge is one of them. He is director of the Community

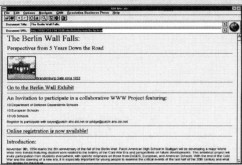

Patch's home page

Learning Network at Patch American High School in Stuttgart, Germany, a school for U.S. military and civilian dependents. Patch was the first school in Europe with its own World-Wide Web server. With a full Internet connection since March 1994, it boasts a

home page on the Web that is chock full of student research and papers on topics ranging from the 50th anniversary of D-Day to the fall of the Berlin Wall.

Since April 1995 CompuServe's European arm has been offering its subscribers full Internet access as part of their regular subscription. This, Pat says, has brought "scores of parents" to Patch's Web site.

"Many of the parents of my students have CompuServe at home, and they can now connect to the school's Web site and look directly at their daughter's or son's work in a multimedia format from the comfort of their own den," he explains.

"This has startling implications. Within a few years, a great many parents will be able to take part vicariously in the school's educational program through telecommunications."

✔ **Patch American High School**
   http://192.253.114.31/Home.html

Chapter 2

Aa Bb Cc Dd Ee Ff Gg Hh Ii

The Internet in schools

● ● ● ● ● ● ● ● ● ● ● ● ● ● ● ● ●

This chapter will show you

- ✔ That the Internet will play a key role as schools strive to meet higher educational standards.

- ✔ How teachers are using the Net as an interactive learning tool for kids.

- ✔ The role you can play in increasing the use of the Internet in your son's or daughter's school.

● ● ● ● ● ● ● ● ● ● ● ● ● ● ● ●

Slowly but surely, the world's schools are making the Internet part of the educational process. Despite budget cuts in many parts of the country, surveys show that more than one-third of the kindergarten through grade 12 (K-12) schools in the United States already have at least one computer connected to the Net.

In remarks to a conference of teachers and administrators in early 1995, U.S. Secretary of Education Richard W. Riley envisioned a future in which technology will enable teachers and parents to communicate electronically, making sure that concerns about students don't fall through the cracks. "Families working together at a computer may become what sitting around the fireplace, listening to the radio, was 50 years ago," Riley said.

In this country, schools have a compelling reason to use the Internet: rising educational standards. After years of study and debate, Congress in 1994 passed the Goals 2000: Educate America Act, setting tough goals for schools.

The new law focuses especially on turning out graduates better qualified for the increasingly technical requirements of the job market. To achieve this aim, schools are required to increase the use of technology in the classroom, and the Internet fits the bill perfectly.

But the main reason schools are using the Internet is that it's a powerful teaching tool. Today's kids, perhaps reflecting their generation's love of video games, seem to respond well to the interactive technology of the Internet — they genuinely enjoy exchanging electronic mail with students in other countries or using the World-Wide Web to do research for a paper. The Net also provides a resource for teachers, who can find ideas for enhancing their lessons or improving their teaching techniques.

How schools use the Net

As we've discussed, it will be a few years before most school children are cruising the Net daily. Even though many schools have established Internet connection, most don't yet have enough computers (or trained teachers) to make e-mail or the World-Wide Web a fixture in the classroom. So far, most of the Internet's benefit to K-12 education has been the materials it provides for *adults*. Teachers can share ideas with their peers via e-mail, download lesson plans, and do research to enhance their knowledge of a subject before introducing it to their students.

Already, however, many K-12 classrooms (especially those at private schools or in more affluent public school districts) have found ways to put kids on the Net.

Here are a few examples:

✔️ Students from 36 schools around the world, including the United States, are using the KIDLINK Math Pen Pal program to discuss how the math they learn in the classroom applies to their daily lives. For example, kids can monitor daily temperatures in their area, or the prices of goods at local stores, and compare results with their peers in other countries.

✔️ Arbor Heights Elementary School in Seattle has created its own home page on the World-Wide Web. The page offers online editions of the schools's student and parent-teacher newspapers, information about Seattle (prepared by students), and an e-mail feature that allows parents to contact teachers directly. This last feature — parent-teacher e-mail — is being adopted by many schools in the hope of increasing communication between schools and homes.

✔️ After studying the structure of stories, a sixth-grade class at Hillside Elementary in Cottage Grove, Minnesota, worked together to create an introduction to a story about a character called Buzz Rod. Each student then composed a unique ending to Buzz Rod's story. The class posted their endings, along with graphics and biographical information about the writers, on the school's World-Wide Web site.

✔️ A school librarian in Colorado posted an e-mail message to an international teachers' discussion group seeking a pen pal for an 11-year-old student. While pen-pal requests are

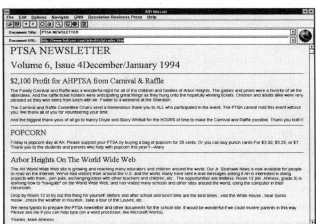

Through the home page at Arbor Heights Elementary, parents and teachers use e-mail and online newsletters to keep in touch with one another.

common on the Internet, this one was unusual: the student was a native Korean who had been adopted at age 4 and now wanted to learn more about her country of birth.

✔ Students connected to Canada's SchoolNet are able to chat with their peers around Canada (and in other countries) in real time, using a multi-user environment. Kids type in their messages and, even as they do so, begin receiving responses — much as in a normal conversation.

The Web's the way to go

For K-12 schools, the vehicle of choice for cruising the Internet (or publishing on it) appears to be the World-Wide Web, which is relatively easy to use and offers graphics, sound, and movies. In the fall of 1994, the Clearinghouse for Networked Information Discovery and Retrieval (CNIDR) estimated that more than 100,000 K-12 users in the United States were accessing the Internet in just one way alone: through World-Wide Web browsing programs.

We also recommend the Web for families, and we discuss it in detail later in this book. The majority of the Internet sites listed in the *Resources* section are Web sites.

How many schools use the Net?

A government report released in early 1995 shows that 35 percent of 1,500 K-12 public schools nationwide have Internet access. The findings are contained in *Advanced Telecommunications in U.S. Public Schools, K-12,* commissioned in 1994 by the Department of Education's National Center for Education Statistics in cooperation with the Federal Communications Commission and the Department of Commerce.

The study paints a picture of teachers and administrators primarily using e-mail to contact colleagues and track down resources on the Internet. Access to the Net is far more widespread in secondary schools than at the elementary level, and it's twice as likely to be available in schools with more than 1,000 students. Those students, though, don't always get access to it.

Snapshots: Schools on the I-way

Big and small, many schools around the world have found their way on to the Internet. Just what two of these are doing there is the focus of the following accounts, in which teachers and students share their views. If you'd like to take a look at some other school sites online, use the *Schools to see on the Web* list that follows these stories to get started.

McFadden, Wyoming

Little school does big things on the Net

66 *To be honest, it's hard to imagine how we got along without telecommunications or, more specifically, the Internet.* **99**
—Jim House, teacher

Internet Crossing

McFadden Elementary may be 50 miles from the nearest library in Wyoming, yet all five of its students have the educational resources they need at their fingertips.

"The Internet lets us make friends and find people who are interested in the same things we are," says Jenae Bosler, a fifth-grader at the school in the Rock Creek valley, just north of the Snowy Range Mountains and the Medicine Bow National Forest. "Also, sometimes we don't have the books that we need to find information for reports, and the Internet helps us with that."

This "one-room schoolhouse" — actually located in a 10-room school building left over from days of

larger enrollments — boasts seven computers, a laser disc player, and a satellite dish. Using the dial-up SLIP account of their teacher Jim House, the school's two fifth-graders and three third-graders regularly turn to the World-Wide Web, gopher, FTP, and Usenet newsgroups to find information about topics they're studying.

"When we did our unit on the weather, we were able to download daily weather maps for our area or for any area around the world," Jenae says. "That was neat. I also like to visit the Web sites that have museums and things like that."

"To be honest, it's hard to imagine how we got along without telecommunications or, more specifically, the Internet," observes Jim.

It's easier for the students at McFadden Elementary and their teacher, Jim House (previous page), to find information by logging on to the Internet than to pile into the "school bus" (above) for a 50-mile ride to the nearest library in rural Wyoming.

When Jenae wanted to meet kids from other parts of the world, she took the e-mail route. "I think it's faster and easier (than regular mail). When I was looking for a pen pal, I just told the mailing list what I was interested in and soon I heard from kids from all over the world."

Now she has pen pals from Romania, Australia, Arkansas, and Massachusetts. She learns about life where they live, and in turn tells them what it's like to be growing up near McFadden, one of the oldest company-owned oil camps in the United States, where gophers and mule deer now outnumber the town's human population.

But Jenae isn't using e-mail only to socialize — at least not as far as her teacher is concerned. "My two fifth-graders come in every morning and check their messages. I've incorporated that time into their reading and language arts. It's a chance to apply all of the things they've learned in English and spelling," Jim says.

Isolated from his colleagues, Jim uses e-mail himself to find out what's going on in education, technology, and other topics that interest him. Also, he points out, "Many of the resources that are available to us are available only through the Internet. Through the Internet, my kids have been able to take part in projects, and I've been able to download plans and research a variety of topics."

Stuttgart, Germany

Students discuss the value of the Net

❝ *I think the Internet is one of this century's greatest achievements for mankind. It has made the transfer of information almost instantaneous.*❞ *— Sara Uriona*

Patch American High School, in Stuttgart, Germany, was the first in Europe to get on the Web. So what have the kids there done? How did they do it? And what do they themselves think about the Internet? Four students at Patch offered essays describing their experiences and their views. They have been using the Internet as part of their curriculum, and have even helped to set up the World-Wide Web server at their school, which is attended by children of U.S. military and civilian personnel.

● ● ● ● ● ● ● ●

For educational purposes the Internet provides opportunities available never before.

Sara Uriona, Grade 12

This is my second semester in the Internet class. I have learned more about using search tools, HTML formatting, and a little bit about downloading programs. As an assignment I have spoken with people in Antarctica using CU-SeeMe (video-conferencing software), and then continued on for several weeks having a dialog with one of the scientists there using e-mail. This was very interesting and an enforcement as to what the Internet can do.

Another assignment that turned into an enjoyable experience instead of just something to get done was creating a page for our Web server. There is a section on the server for information on the school's athletic teams. However, I found that no information had been added after a few short things about last year's teams. This has opened up a new avenue of ways to help the school. So far I have updated the information to include one of the winter teams and will write pages for at least one more team while encouraging others to do the same.

This quarter I should also be learning more about downloading programs, transferring information between different programs, and switching back and forth between using Macintosh and DOS-compatible machines.

I think the Internet is one of this century's greatest achievements for mankind. It has made the transfer of information almost instantaneous, as well as communication. For educational purposes the Internet provides opportunities available never before — such as a high-school biology student interested in a career in anatomy being able to check out the (World-Wide Web) page containing the Visible Human in California. Before this, that same student would have had to wait until medical school to be exposed to the same thing. In college a student would have access to libraries worldwide to facilitate research and give more to think about, which in turn expands the way the student thinks — the purpose of attending college.

The advantages for an elementary school are the least evident and the most important. The earlier a child is exposed to computers and the Internet and associated therewith, the more comfortable and capable the child will be later on when the knowledge is necessary.

Businesses are in constant communication and have the information for buying or selling commodities at their fingertips 24 hours a day. In past times, this same information would have had to wait days or weeks before being available to the people who had to make a decision — until a golden opportunity had been missed. For governments the advantages are very similar to those for nearly all citizens with much less frantic work.

As I stated before, the Internet is one of mankind's greatest achievements.

Angela Stevens, Grade 9

You will no longer have to go to the library and check out 20 books to do a report.

During the past semester, I have been involved in a lot of Internet-related activities. As a daily activity, I downloaded or copied items from the Internet and put them in the bulletin boards I maintain (i.e. Space: The Final Frontier, Food for Thought). I also gave a presentation to the Director of the Department of Defense Dependent Schools, Ms. Lillian Gonzales, and the wife of the SACUER Commander. I hope to take part in a joint German-American Teacher's Seminar to learn more about the World-Wide Web, and to teach others about it.

I think that the Internet will have a big impact on the government and business. For one, we will soon be able to write directly to Congressmen and the President. You won't have to wait six months for the "snail-mail" message to reach the Senate.

The only drawback on the Internet is the fact that it is wide open to hackers and other people who operate illegally on the World-Wide Web.

Educationwise, the Internet will definitely be a big help. You will no longer have to go to the library and check out 20 books to do a report; you can use the Internet's search capabilities to find what you need.

I think that the Internet is a great tool if it is used correctly.

Joel Borden, Grade 12

It's the place to be.

I have been using the Internet since August (1994) when school started. I have learned how to use the World-Wide Web, TELNET, FTP, IRC, gopher, and lots more. All the parts of the Internet tie in closely to each other. I have learned this in this class. The world's eyes are just starting to be opened to the Internet. CompuServe now has Internet access. In the last year lots of people have gotten on the Internet. It's the place to be.

It is very interesting learning about what it is like to live in Antarctica and to actually get the firsthand experience from someone who is actually living there.

Jason Smith, Grade 11

I have been taking this Internet class since the beginning of the year. It has been a very interesting and educational course. I had an option of Pascal (a computer programming language) or the Internet class. I chose the Internet class and it has been the best.

I especially like CU-SeeMe. I have talked to many people throughout the world. There is a man in New Orleans that I have talked to several times. It is totally amazing that you could be talking to someone and see them at the same time when you are thousands of miles apart from each other. Plus there is very little delay between each picture or wording that is passed through the cables. It is also interesting that the message from you, to them and back takes only one second or less to travel all those miles.

Last semester I took part in a conference with BBN (Bolt, Beranek and Newman, an Internet service provider) in November. That was a little interesting. Since then, I have worked on the Berlin Project, but that too has slackened off. Since the beginning of the second semester, I have been writing to Terry Trimingham in Antarctica. We write to each other whenever we can. I think I am the only student in the Internet class that has kept in contact with her. It is very interesting learning about what it is like to live in Antarctica and to actually get the firsthand experience from someone who is actually living there. As for the rest of this semester, I don't know what I will be doing. New things pop up all the time in this technological world and you can never tell what will happen next. You can't even tell what projects will be coming up too.

✔ **Patch American High School**
http://192.253.114.31/Home.html

Schools to see on the Web

Special thanks to John Clement of the Clearinghouse for Networked Information Discovery and Retrieval for his suggestions.

✔ Ralph Bunche School   Harlem, New York

Features a newspaper written by grade 4 to 6 students and grade 7 to 9 students at Adam Clayton Powell, Jr., Junior High.
http://Mac94.ralphbunche.rbs.edu/

✔ Hillside Elementary   Cottage Grove, Minn.

Features research papers by students in grades 3 to 6 who have used the Internet as their primary resource.
http://hillside.coled.umn.edu/

✔ Captain Strong Elementary   Battle Ground, Wash.

Features the Salmon Project, designed by third-graders to teach other students about Pacific Northwest salmon.
http://hillside.coled.umn.edu/

✔ Boulder Valley School District   Colorado

Features *Vocal Point*, an electronic newspaper (complete with images and animations) created by district students.
http://bvsd.k12.co.us/cent/Newspaper/Newspaper.html

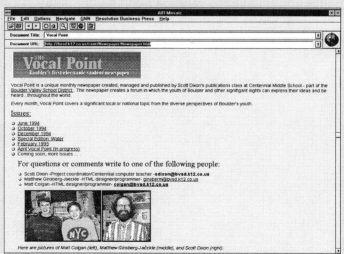

The home pages of the Boulder Valley School District, above, and Arleta Elementary School, top of facing page.

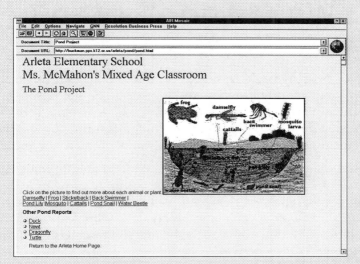

✔ Arleta Elementary School   **Portland, Ore.**

Features a Pond Project, with graphics and reports from kids of different ages on flora and fauna.
http://bvsd.k12.co.us/cent/Newspaper/Newspaper.html

✔ Claremont High School   **Claremont, Calif.**

Features reports, tables, and a QuickTime movie of a math and computing project done by the school's "Knot Dudes."
http://bvsd.k12.co.us/cent/Newspaper/Newspaper.html

✔ American School   **Tokyo**

Features stories by journalism students, including a look at the life of a 600-pound disco-dancing sumo wrestler.
http://bvsd.k12.co.us/cent/Newspaper/Newspaper.html

✔ Highland Park Elementary   **Austin, Texas**

Features student research in botany, including a Trees of the World project.
http://bvsd.k12.co.us/cent/Newspaper/Newspaper.html

✔ University Park Elementary   **Fairbanks, Alaska**

Features stories and pictures of life in Alaska, including suggestions on what to do when it's 40 degrees below.
http://www.upk.northstar.k12.ak.us/

Why schools aren't on the Net

So what's holding back those schools without access? By and large, it's a question of money and logistics. The schools responding to the government survey on *Advanced Telecommunications in U.S. Public Schools, K-12,* pointed to limited funding, lack of (or poor) equipment, and too few access points in the school building.

The good news is that most schools are at least trying to find their way to the Information Superhighway. Roughly three-quarters of them now have computers with some type of telecommunications capabilities, as well as cable and broadcast TV hookups. What's more, some two-thirds of the schools are planning to install or upgrade to a wide-area network, bringing the Internet a step closer.

Finding the on-ramp

The decision to offer or expand access to the Internet in schools is most often made at the district level. In the recent government study we cited above, over 80 percent of those schools with a telecommunications plan of some sort said it was part of a districtwide effort. Even when the plan was developed by a single school, state or region, nearly 90 percent said that any expenditures still had to get the green light from the district.

Of course, that's not too surprising when you consider that nearly half of those schools with a wide-area computer network (and possibly some Internet access) rely on regional administrators to help develop their telecommunications programs. Only a third reported teachers or others taking charge.

While a growing number of teachers support the concept of using the Internet, many school districts have been hesitant. School administrators often feel that their district doesn't have the money to set up the infrastructure and keep it going, and that parents wouldn't support such spending because they don't understand the technology and how it could help their kids. It may be up to you to change their minds.

Snapshots: Getting schools connected

More and more schools may be taking the preliminary steps to connect, if not actually getting connected to the Internet. But in many areas it is going to take a concerted push from parents like you to ensure that these plans are implemented sooner than later.

In the debate over schools' access to the Internet, bear in mind:

✔ **Children in school systems** that have wide Internet access will develop important computer and research skills needed for post-secondary studies and future job opportunities.

✔ **Children enrolled in schools** with Internet access will be able to develop their own network of friends and contacts worldwide, a potentially invaluable resource in our ever-shrinking world.

✔ **Many educational programs** offered on the Internet are geared to classrooms, not individuals. You may not want your child to miss out on these opportunities and contacts.

An expert's view

Getting families involved

Carol Hyatt is an advocate of involving families in education through the use of technology. She chairs the Consortium for School Networking Parent Committee, and is actively involved in numerous other efforts to better equip schools across the United States for the 21st century. Below she summarizes her views and advice to parents who want to help their local schools get connected to the Internet.

Internet and education

Now that many families have access to a computer and modem, online communications can help more parents become informed and involved in what their children's school and PTA are doing. Many parents are reluctant to leave their children and attend meetings, but still care deeply about their children's education. Online communication provides an excellent way to reach out to more people and to do a better job of involving those who are interested but unable to attend meetings.

There are many resources and people within this learning community, and elsewhere, to support you in your efforts to use technology to become more involved in parent-teacher-administration-learner relations.

There is a wealth of information of interest to parents already online, but parents are likely to be unaware that it exists. Teachers, parents and other school system staff generally have little time available to help build parental awareness of what resources are available to them, but there may be a PTA technology committee in your community that can help parents learn about and make use of existing resources. If no technology committee exists, perhaps you could suggest to the PTA president or to the principal that such a committee be created.

If you know of parents in your school community already using the Internet, please share with them the information about the National Parent Information Network and the Consortium for School Networking (CoSN) parents discussion forum. Encourage

Some parents don't have much interest in school politics, but want to contribute in other ways to their child's education.

them to help your school community by writing an occasional article for the school newsletter, making a presentation to other parents or perhaps serving as a mentor to one or two interested parents, students or teachers. If they have questions or concerns, urge them to join the CoSN Parents discussion forum and to learn from those of us who have already begun sharing information about how to make effective use of whatever technology we have.

Some parents don't have much interest in school politics, but want to contribute in other ways to their child's education. A parent or grandparent volunteering to become the subject of their child's or grandchild's oral history project can be a wonderful way to become involved. Helping your child or grandchild remember their lineage in connection with a genealogy project is another terrific way. Becoming a mentor to your child's class around a civil rights project is, if you were intimately involved in the movement, yet another idea for contributing. No doubt there are dozens of other ways to get "closer to the action."

Talk to your child's teacher about your desires. There are many resources and people within this learning community, and elsewhere, to support you in your efforts to use technology to become more involved in parent-teacher-administration-learner relations.

To learn more, see:

✔ **National Parent Information Network**
   http://www.prairienet.org/htmls/eric/npin/npinhome.html

✔ **Consortium for School Networking**
   http://cosn.org

✔ **Discovery Learning Community**
   http://ericir.syr.edu/Discovery/

This article originally appeared online in the gopher of the Discovery Learning Community, a project of the Discovery Channel. It is reprinted with permission of the author.

Mother crusades for the Net in schools

❝ *I thought that it might be a good fit to use my (newfound) expertise with the Internet tools with the school district.***❞**
— Sandy Barnes

With her four kids attending three local schools, Sandy Barnes had good reason to get involved in 1994 when her Seattle-area school district began connecting its schools to the Internet one by one.

"The district has had a high commitment to technological tools and was already setting up an extensive network," she explains. "Very few of the adults I talked to were familiar with Net resources, but almost everybody was interested. I thought that it might be a good fit to use my (newfound) expertise with the Internet tools with the school district."

Parent Sandy Barnes offers some hands-on tips during a family Internet Night, which she helped organize at a Seattle-area school.

Sandy first encountered the Internet when her husband, a technical writer, decided to log on for research purposes in late 1993. Soon she was doing her own surfing. She began passing along her growing Internet knowledge and skills at Friday Forums held at a local school, in which community members are invited to teach students, giving teachers time for planning.

Among other projects, Sandy went on to conduct family Internet Nights at the middle school, help an elementary-school class find pen pals, and work with two high-school students who were setting up a World-Wide Web site for the school district.

Despite frustrations with newly installed equipment, Sandy remains positive about her involvement at the school. She adds: "I had students who were interested, who knew what they wanted and got a lot out of their session. I had a group of them who returned to my classes and built on their expertise. They would show up whether they were signed up or not!"

She hopes more parents—and teachers—will get involved with Internet activities at the school. While many teachers are enthusiastic about Net access, others have been slow to embrace the new technology—with good reason. "They're very busy, and it takes a fair investment of time to become proficient. It's not always clear how (the Internet) fits into the classroom," Sandy points out.

Nonetheless, a number of district teachers are getting involved. Now the district's greatest challenge seems to be figuring out what to do with its Internet access, Sandy says.

"I think the most compelling use is direct communication, but it takes a lot of attention to figure out who to communicate with and what form this communication will take."

She points to the many collaborative classroom projects, which use e-mail to connect students in diverse geographic areas, as one way for schools to begin using the Internet.

Sandy now maintains the Adoption Information Exchange, a Web site that provides adoption resources, and is uncertain whether she will continue her involvement with the school district. But, she says, "This area is changing so fast that I'm sure that there will be new Net projects initiated by teachers in the near future."

✔ **Adoption Information Exchange**
   http://www.halcyon.com/adoption/

Sunnybank Hills, Queensland

Father rolls up his sleeves

Internet and education

Canterbury College has more than 100 PC and Macintosh computers for its 800 students, and will be joining several other schools in Queensland in going online.

Peter Quodling is quite willing to do his part in building the Information Superhighway. He believes the Internet will be an integral element in the education of his six-year-old son, Andrew.

Technical director for Innovation Consulting, an Australian computer consulting firm in Sunnybank Hills, Queensland, Peter has covered his bases at home. "Andrew has been using computers since the age of 2," Peter says. "He was classified as gifted in the first week of first grade (in 1994), and I'm about to give him his own laptop computer tied into our household LAN (local area network)."

But that's not all. Peter has offered his services to help get his son's school connected to the Internet. Canterbury College already has more than 100 PC and Macintosh computers for its 800 students, and will be joining several other schools in Queensland in going online.

He believes the Internet will be an integral element in the education of his six-year-old son, Andrew.

Back at home, Andrew is rapidly learning how to get around on the Internet himself. Of course, Peter says, Andrew's schooling doesn't yet require detailed reports and research projects, so "he's not a heavy browser per se. But he has on occasion asked me about things, and we've headed off to browse Lycos or one of the other Web walkers. So he's learning how and where to go look for things."

Andrew already knows how to get to the "good stuff," his dad says, like the Web sites for Power Rangers and Sega of America.

Stuttgart, Germany

Making the world the classroom

*B*ill *Dyer first got involved as a community volunteer in helping Patch American High School in Stuttgart, Germany, get connected to the Internet. "I was familiar with networking and telecommunications and the school was in need of some expertise so I decided to help them learn about the Internet," explains Bill, who has a background in computer sales and information management. His involvement grew into working for the school as a technology consultant and helping to create its Internet servers.*

Q   **What do you see as the major problems to schools getting connected to the Internet?**

A   For most schools it is a lack of equipment, phone lines, expertise, and support. We have seen many schools with enthusiastic staff and students, but one of the above always seems to be a major hurdle. This is why we are trying to create partnerships with other schools and universities to help bring the Internet to a greater number of K-12 schools.

Q   **If a parent wants his or her child and the child's teachers to have access to the Internet at school, what concrete steps can that person take to help or spur on the school or school district in that direction?**

A   We have seen parent support as a major force in getting the schools online. We have formed a technology committee with parents, students, and staff to voice their concerns and goals to the district office. This focus has helped accelerate the installation and integration of technology in the classroom.

Q   **Tell us about your school and how it got its Internet access.**

A   Patch is a Department of Defense Dependent School (DoDDS) that serves the dependants of military and civilian parents stationed overseas. It is connected to the Internet through the Defense Simulation Internet (DSI), a high-speed worldwide military network for doing computer simulations and war games. Congress mandated that money be spent on four DoDDS pilot schools to test the effect of having high-speed communications, and to use existing military technology for educational uses. ... After that we quickly realized the potential of the Internet for education and started to actively take advantage of it.

Q **How long has your school been connected to the Internet?**

A We have had a full Internet connection since October '93. The school has been using Internet e-mail since 1988.

Q **How were the students involved?**

A The students at Patch are actively involved in the World-Wide Web server. More than 100 students have contributed pages or graphics to the server over the last 14 months. Our server has grown to 180 MB with over 558 HTML pages and 1,400 GIF and JPEG images. Our server has transferred over 500,000 documents and 9 gigabytes of data since March 22, 1994. The average traffic on our server is 4,000 to 5,000 hits (number of times the page is accessed) per day.

Q **What do the kids like to do the most on the Internet?**

A The kids enjoy having their work published online for the world to see. They also enjoy getting mail from people all over the world and using CU-SeeMe video conferencing software to see and talk to them. This type of modern interaction allows students to communicate ideas in a quick and effective manner. Our juniors and seniors also enjoy doing research on the Internet for term papers. They also enjoy taking virtual field trips to different countries and research universities in the U.S. to find out admission and financial aid information.

Q **What are some things they can do on the Internet that they couldn't otherwise?**

A It allows the students the opportunity to have their work seen by a larger audience than through conventional means. It allows them to get up-to-date information on a huge range of subjects from experts worldwide. The Internet has helped make the world the classroom for these students.

✔ **Patch American High School**
http://192.253.114.31/Home.html

Michigan

Teacher-to-be has plans for the Net

❝ *To be able to ask people for help, to get information on topics of interest, and to obtain software and support — these (benefits) just aren't available by any other means to the extent they are on the Internet.* **❞** *— James N. Perry II*

It's the fall of 1997 and James N. Perry II has just started his first teaching job. He has everything he needs to begin: a blackboard, chalk, and, of course, one computer and an Internet connection for every five of his kindergartners. Today, he'll begin by logging on to the Internet so the kids can join a collaborative project with students overseas.

Yes, it's only make-believe in 1995. And James, 21, is still attending Michigan State University. But he's taking steps to make his dream a reality — inquiring about upgrading his home computer; and making the most of classes, conferences, books, magazines, and the various services of the Internet itself, via MSU's system, to find out all he can now about using networking with young students.

"Slowly but surely, I'm getting better informed about (the Net)," says James, who's majoring in Child Development and expects to receive his teaching certificate in 1997. "By the time I start up my own class, I hope to have a lot of it down and ready to implement."

He's excited about the possibilities.

"Slowly but surely, I'm getting better informed about (the Net)."

"Even though young children may not be able to read and write, they can still (communicate) with others around the world. They can learn firsthand about how people live in other countries, or even in other parts of our own state, which can be quite different. Pictures as well as text can be transmitted. This would expose the children to new things, which is part of what learning is all about," he says.

James also recognizes the Internet's value as a tool for professional development and contact. "To be able to ask people for help, to get information on topics of interest, and to obtain software and support — these (benefits) just aren't available by any other means to the extent they are on the Internet."

Part 2

What is the Internet, and what do I need to surf it?

In this section we look at the nuts and bolts of the Internet. *Chapter 3* describes the Internet and its history, *Chapter 4* looks at the hardware and software you need to get connected, and *Chapter 5* outlines how the Internet works.

internet@school

Students turn to the Net for answers

Sometimes the people you find on the Internet are as amazing as the information itself.

But the information they were looking for wasn't the type to be found in a textbook or magazine article.

The student journalists working on *The Lowell*, the school newspaper of San Francisco's Lowell High, needed current information about the Russian space program. But the information they were looking for wasn't the type to be found in a textbook or magazine article.

They decided the best way to find it was on the Internet. After all, the global network had proven to be a reliable source in the past, providing information for a computer literacy class, a report on American democracy, and even ideas and contacts for *The Lowell*.

So, using their school's Internet link, the students posted a series of tough questions on *sci.space.shuttle*, a Usenet newsgroup. Here are a few of the things they wanted to know:

What joint ventures, if any, had been seriously discussed by NASA and the Russian space program? What was involved in getting American Norm Thagard aboard the Mir space station? How did NASA and the Russian space program compare in terms of facilities, technology, funding, and experience in space? How were current Russian efforts to find customers for commercial launches going?

In quick time, the students received four responses, including details from a Lockheed engineer and a NASA representative.

Could the student journalists have obtained this information in any other way?

"That's not really likely," says Sherwin Lee, the paper's technology editor.

"The Lockheed engineer requested anonymity because he isn't supposed to talk to the media."

Chapter 3

Aa Bb Cc Dd Ee Ff Gg Hh Ii

What is the Net?

● ● ● ● ● ● ● ● ● ● ● ● ● ● ● ● ●

This chapter will show you

- ✔ What the Internet is and how it got started.

- ✔ Who's behind the Net, who's getting on board, and how that may help you.

- ✔ Why you get access to all of this information free.

- ✔ How the Internet fits in with commercial online services like America Online and CompuServe.

● ● ● ● ● ● ● ● ● ● ● ● ● ● ● ● ●

We hear about the Internet every day now. But the concept is so nebulous that the news media generally don't even try to explain what it is—they just tell you what it's doing. Exactly what the Internet is, and how it moves information around, remain mysteries to most. We hope this chapter clears up that uncertainty for you.

So, what is the Internet?

- It's a worldwide network of computers connected by telephone, high-speed data and satellite links.

- It brings together millions of private individuals and people in government, the academic world and business, enabling them to communicate and share information.

- It's a flexible system that is inexpensive to connect to. Anyone can post information on the Internet or make resources available without acquiring permission.

- It allows all types of computers to communicate through a common language or protocol.

- The Internet lets users access its services through a common set of communication tools.

- It's always changing, with new uses are continually being found for it.

- It's not owned by anyone.

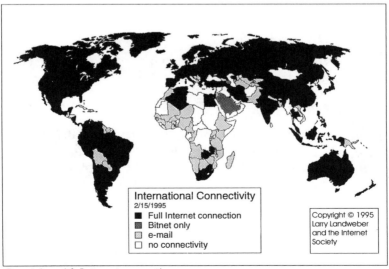

Countries with Internet connections

● The Internet is a hands-on tool and not a passive form of entertainment like television. It doesn't come into your living room; you must go to it.

● The Internet consists of many worlds, or communities. It's not a single entity.

Let's look at these points in more detail.

1. It's a network of networks

The Internet is a worldwide network of computer networks. It is a flexible and low-cost way of connecting computers around the world through a combination of telephone lines, high-speed data-cables and satellites. All told, the Net consists of more than 3 million computer systems connecting some 20 to 40 million users around the world, and that number is growing by about 10 percent per month, according to figures by the Internet Society.

Over 70 countries have some form of connection to the Internet, from Russia to Mexico to South Africa. In most of these nations, average people find it difficult or impossible to get connections. Outside of the United States, Canada, and most of western Europe, the Internet is now restricted to people in government, universities, and large corporations. But that situation will undoubtedly change.

Fortunately for Americans, this country offers the world's most widespread access to the Internet. Connections are available through national as well as local providers, meaning that almost anyone with a phone can get up and running on the Net.

Despite the fact that the Internet is growing and doing all sorts of wonderful things, you can't go out and take a look at it, or for that matter even find an accurate map showing its exact routes. In reality, it's a collection of communication lines that crisscross the United States, span oceans and interconnect several other countries.

2. The Net is a global meeting place

While the Internet technically is a network of computers, in reality it's a place where people meet and come together. It is one of the most remarkable systems of communication. It allows users to keep in touch with old acquaintances, make new ones, conduct research, and spend countless hours just surfing from place to place around the world.

3. The system is flexible

The Internet was designed as a military communications network that could survive a nuclear war. But over the years, it has evolved into a network that can accommodate anything from interactive coloring books to home banking. This flexibility is due to the technical soundness of the network, which was designed by some of the finest minds in the computer industry.

4. Computers "speak" one language

All computers connected to the Internet, regardless of their size, must "speak" a common language, or protocol, called TCP/IP. This can be accomplished by installing a relatively simple software program that lets a computer speak TCP/IP while, at the same time, running all the software it normally operates.

By using a common language, computers connected to the Internet can find one another as well as share information. In addition, the system allows the operators of computer systems to decide what they will make available to Internet users. For example, a university system may allow everyone to access the library catalog but deny access to student records.

This acceptance of a common protocol was rather remarkable for the computer world, which is prone to infighting. Computer users tend to identify with their computer systems with a religious fervor, as was demonstrated in the "holy war" that broke out a few years ago between the two major UNIX camps. Despite the fact they were using the same operating system, each felt their variation was morally superior to the other's.

5. Computers use same applications

While TCP/IP allows computers on the Internet to speak the same language, it doesn't deal with the question of how information can be stored on a computer and accessed by a wide audience or how individuals can communicate with each other through the network.

To deal with these issues, a number of Internet *services* have been developed over the past 25 years along with a number of software programs to utilize these services. Most of the computers offering services on the Internet are UNIX systems and are called *servers* while the tools to access these servers are available for just about every computer system, especially those running the Microsoft Windows or Macintosh operating systems.

The oldest such service is e-mail. The standard for this service defines the structure of an electronic message, an addressing scheme, and the mechanics of an electronic post-office system. For users, a number of e-mail programs have been developed for just about every type of computer ever created. This means a Windows user can easily send an e-mail message to a Macintosh user via the Internet, probably through a number of UNIX systems, without a hitch.

Other popular Internet services include:

- ✔ **FTP** A way of transferring software between computers
- ✔ **Gopher** A menu-driven system for presenting information
- ✔ **TELNET** A tool to *log on,* or connect, to computer systems and view information stored in databases and other files
- ✔ **Usenet** A worldwide network of discussion forums
- ✔ **World-Wide Web** A multimedia system of presenting information

Recent additions include:

- ✔ **CU-SeeMe** (see you see me) A video-conferencing system
- ✔ **Internet Phone** A phone system that works over the Internet

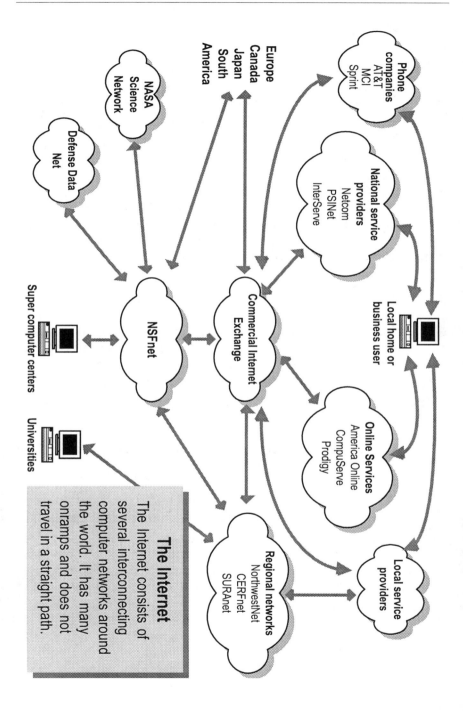

Phone
companies
AT&T
MCI
Sprint

National service
providers
Netcom
PSINet
InterServe

NASA
Science
Network

Defense Data
Net

Europe
Canada
Japan
South
America

Local home or
business user

Super computer centers

NSFnet

Commercial Internet
Exchange

Online Services
America Online
CompuServe
Prodigy

Universities

Regional networks
NorthwestNet
CERFnet
SURAnet

Local service
providers

The Internet
The Internet consists of several interconnecting computer networks around the world. It has many onramps and does not travel in a straight path.

6. More uses for the Net in the works

As more people connect to the Internet, more uses for the Net are being developed. Some are refinements of existing services, such as home banking and shopping via the World-Wide Web, while others involve the development of new technology or protocols, such as the Internet Phone or the CUSeeMe video-conferencing system. Other developments, such as virtual reality, are in the works.

7. No one owns the Internet

Perhaps the most unique feature of the Internet is that no one owns or controls the network. Some parts are owned by government agencies and private interests, but the Net does not fall under the total control of one group. This explains why the Internet is growing so fast, and new technology and features are being added at breakneck speed, making the Net sometimes seem chaotic.

But you aren't a freeloader!

Many Internet users are under the mistaken belief that the National Science Foundation underwrites all Internet use. Not true. The foundation subsidizes the NSFnet, which connects universities and research centers. Most individuals connect to the Internet through Commercial Internet Exchange (CIX) providers, which are self-supporting.

8. You must go to the Internet

The Internet is not a passive form of entertainment. It doesn't come blasting into your living room. Instead, the user must be curious enough to venture into new worlds, and generally possess some skills, such as the ability to read and type.

The Internet is somewhat similar to a bookstore or library. You must have an idea of what you are looking for, even if you're only browsing. The Internet definitely is not for everyone.

9. Virtual worlds in different orbits

Because the Internet offers such variety, it's different things to different people. Most users tend to find or create many virtual worlds for themselves. For some, it's a place to find people who share similar interests while for others it's a place to maintain old friendships. Some users see it as a research tool while others use it to explore new places.

A quick history of the Net

Now that we've taken a look at what the Internet is, let's see how it got started.

Have packets, will travel

In the early 1960s, the Rand Corp., a Cold War think tank, looked into developing a communications network that could survive a catastrophe as severe as a nuclear war. A postwar America would need a communications network that would link cities and military bases, and would operate without any central command. After all, who knew what would be left? Moreover, who knew how much of the network would be operational after such an event? Such a system would have to be decentralized, and designed to operate even if parts of it were blown to smithereens.

To create such a network, data would have to be broken into packets. A message of 5,000 characters, or letters, could be broken up in several packets. Each packet would contain a mailing address, return address, and mailing sequence. Packets would then be transferred from one computer system to another. If one system broke down, the packets could be rerouted through another computer system until they reached their final destination, and were reassembled into the original message. This system of *packet switching* became the foundation of the TCP/IP protocol, which we'll look at a bit later.

The packet concept was mulled over for several years until in 1969 the Pentagon's Advanced Research Projects Agency decided to fund a trial project.

The beginning: ARPANET

ARPANET (Advanced Research Projects Agency Network) was an attempt to link major research institutions using incompatible computer systems. In today's terms, the ARPANET's goal of connecting four organi-

 zations — the University of California at Los Angeles, Stan-

ford Research Institute, the University of California at Santa Barbara, and the University of Utah — was modest. But the network experiment worked, and by 1971, 23 computers were connected to ARPANET. Two years later, the first international connections were extended to the United Kingdom and Denmark.

Over the next 20 years, the development of new technologies like electronic mail and the creation of other network services (including the Users Network, or Usenet) laid the foundation for organizations to more easily exchange messages and data electronically.

The explosion

In 1986, the National Science Foundation (NSF) — with help from the Department of Energy and NASA — created the National Science Foundation Network (NSFnet), a "backbone" system connecting several regional networks nationwide. NSFnet at last brought widespread Internet access to universities, colleges, and research institutions across the United States. Educators and students began to take advantage of the Net's research and communication capabilities.

The cat was out of the bag. Anyone who had access to the Internet or e-mail in college quickly found that they missed these technologies when they arrived in the working world.

CIX: The on-ramp for most of us

Until 1991, NSFnet rules made it next to impossible for most businesses and individuals to connect to the Internet although many were clamoring for access to the Net. So that year the NSF encouraged the creation of the Commercial Internet Exchange (CIX).

Originally, CIX (pronounced "kicks") consisted of three networks developed by corporations — General Atomics' CERFnet, Performance Systems International's PSInet, and UUNET Technologies' AlterNet. More than 100 other CIXs have since appeared. You can find CIXs not only in the United States but in Russia, South Africa, Japan, and most Western European nations. In fact, the CIX network is now handling most of the traffic on the Net.

Unlike the NSFnet system, which uses a central "thruway" to pass data between regional networks, the CIXs around the world are all interconnected. If you send e-mail from Seattle to Miami, the message crosses many CIXs until it reaches its destination. It doesn't touch the NSFnet.

The CIXs vary widely in size. Some, like US Sprint and PSInet, offer service across the country and maintain nationwide networks. Others are confined to a single community, and simply sell service to individual users and small businesses. Some of the regional networks connected to the NSFnet have become CIXs so they can reach a broader commercial market.

Other components of the Internet

These major networks also form part of the foundation of the Internet but, for the most part, aren't accessible by ordinary users:

- ✔ **Defense Data Net (DDN)** Serves U.S. military installations.

- ✔ **Corporation for Research and Educational Networking (CREN)** Links some 1,400 educational institutions around the world through Bitnet, a network that offers primarily e-mail service to its members and transmits data more slowly than the Internet.

- ✔ **Energy Sciences Network (ESnet)** An energy research network connecting 19 sites, financed by the Department of Energy Office of Energy Research.

- ✔ **NASA Science Network** Links NASA installations around the world. (NASA also has resources that are available through regular Internet connections.)

Some key players on the Net

As you surf the Net, some names will pop up more often than others. Here's a list of agencies, companies and organizations you may encounter.

Government agencies

NSFnet The National Science Foundation operates the network that connects major research centers in the United States. Its influence over the Internet is declining as commercial companies provide more and more of the network's infrastructure.

http://www.nsf.gov/

CERN The Center for European Nuclear Research, based in Geneva, Switzerland, sponsored the development of the World-Wide Web in 1989 and now figures prominently in the W3 Consortium, a group of organizations conducting further development of the Web.

http://www.w3.org

NASA The National Aeronautics and Space Administration has taken full advantage of the Internet by making many of its resources available to the public.

http://www.nasa.gov/

Organizations

CIX The Commercial Internet Exchange organization represents over 100 service providers in the United States and abroad. Most Internet traffic now flows through CIX lines.

http://www.cix.org/

Electronic Frontier Foundation The EFF is the civil liberties association of the Internet, promoting freedom of expression, privacy, and global access.

http://www.eff.org/

Internet Society This international group promotes and develops new Internet technologies.

http://info.isoc.org/

InterNIC Society InterNIC is dedicated to providing information on using the Internet. InterNIC is financed by General Atomics, AT&T, and Network Solutions.

http://www.internic.net/infoguide.html

Major universities and research centers

NCSA Based at the University of Illinois, the National Center for Supercomputing Applications created Mosaic, the original World-Wide Web browsing program. It also maintains a list of new Web resources.

http://www.ncsa.uiuc.edu/SDG/Software/Mosaic/Docs/whats-new.html

Carnegie-Mellon University This Pittsburgh, Pa., university has been the source of many notable contributions in computer science. People doing research will be impressed with the university's search tool, Lycos, which finds information on the Internet.

http://lycos.cs.cmu.edu/

Major businesses

America Online, CompuServe, and Prodigy The "big three" commercial online services all now offer some sort of Internet access.

AT&T, MCI, and US Sprint The three major long-distance telephone companies all offer (or plan to offer) Internet connectivity.

CommerceNet This nonprofit organization is bringing the Internet to just about any business that wants it in the Silicon Valley area of northern California. Ultimately, CommerceNet will be a virtual "mall," letting consumers shop through online catalogs.

http://www.commerce.net

Microsoft Recent versions of Microsoft's Windows operating system come bundled with software for connecting to the Internet. The company also sells HTML software (for publishing World-Wide Web pages), plans to offer multimedia and Internet services through partnerships with cable television providers, and has started its own online service.

http://www.microsoft.com

CompuServe, America Online join the act

Before access to the Internet became so readily available, home and business computer users looked to commercial online services, such as America Online, CompuServe, and Prodigy, for communication, research and entertainment purposes. But with the advent of the Internet, the role of the commercial services is changing rapidly. For millions of people, these online services are the on-ramp to the Internet.

What is an online service?

Commercial online services differ in many respects from the Internet. Each commercial service is run from a central computer system that is usually housed under one roof. Users connect directly to that system by telephone. The services either operate or contract a telephone network that can be reached locally from just about every community in the United States. CompuServe also has access in many European countries as well as Japan.

The online services provide users with proprietary software programs that are generally easy to install and use. When they say you can be up and running in less than 15 minutes, they mean it.

The cost of using online services varies, and is likely to change. Some currently offer a fixed monthly rate of under $15 but charge extra for premium services. Others offer several hours of service for less than $15 per month but charge several dollars per hour for additional use.

Easy to navigate

Because these services are centralized, they're easy to navigate, much easier than the sprawling Internet. Each has complete control over what it offers, and designed these offerings with the end-user in mind. Everything—all the software you need to access what these services offer, such as an e-mail program and news-reader—comes bundled in a single package, although you generally can only use one program at a time.

Each commercial service also boasts several exclusive features — such as moderated conferences with celebrities, electronic versions of certain periodicals, and online tutorials for new users — which you won't find on the Net.

But there are disadvantages

Many online service users find they outgrow the service quickly — something we can attest to. After the novelty wears off, there isn't much you can do with the service.

Part of this problem is due to the rigid structure of each service. Nothing can happen on a service without the service's approval. A library can't decide one day to make its card catalog available to service users. Nor can a company set up its own area like it can on the Internet. Moreover, forum discussions may be censored if the service deems a topic to be outside of its standards of conduct.

Other users find that the monthly service charges add up quickly. In our own case, we dropped all services except CompuServe, which has a wide selection of computer-related forums operated by all major software and hardware vendors (the cheapest way of getting direct support for most computer products). We also use several of the news services CompuServe offers.

Online services make the transition

With the public's attention shifting to the Internet, each of the major commercial services has announced plans to become a full-scale on-ramp to the Net while keeping its exclusive features. In early 1995, CompuServe purchased Spry Inc., the developer of Mosaic in a Box, while America Online purchased Advanced Network & Services, the company that created the Internet's backbone.

For many Internet users, the commercial services may offer the best way to connect to the Internet — especially for people with limited technical knowledge or those who live in areas without local providers.

What about the Information Superhighway?

It's a common misconception, but the Internet and the Information Superhighway are *not* one and the same thing. The two terms aren't synonymous, either, although many people (including your authors), are guilty of using them that way to avoid constantly repeating the word Internet. The Internet is an enormous international network of computer networks, which we've described in detail in this chapter. The Information Superhighway, still only a concept, would encompass the Internet and go beyond what the Internet is and does today.

The term *Information Superhighway* is a metaphor Vice President Al Gore has used to describe his vision of a National Information Infrastructure that will provide U.S. workers and students the tools to become more competitive and ultimately attain a higher standard of living.

Government proposes one route

The NII would consist of interconnected computer networks, televisions, fax machines, telephones and other technologies. Operating at extremely high speed, the NII would enable all types of data, from text to video, to be transmitted more easily than currently possible. It would dwarf the Internet, offering all the information and services you now find on the Net plus new ones that we haven't even heard of yet. It would offer people from all walks of life, in all types of occupations, of all ages, a way to communicate, learn, do business, and perform many other tasks electronically, interactively, and at an affordable price.

The private sector would take the lead in managing this enormous network, according to the Information Infrastructure Task Force (IITF) and Advisory Council on the NII *(http://iitf.doc.gov/NIIhome.html)*. Private companies currently invest about $50 billion annually in the U.S. telecommunications infrastructure, and that type of investment would continue to be encouraged. The federal government—which now spends about $1.2 billion a year to promote development of the information technology needed for the NII—would continue to assist in funding research and development, as well as promoting the use of the NII.

Cable, phone companies have other ideas

The TV cable companies have a similar vision of an Information Superhighway, but theirs, of course, advances a network based on interactive television, offering information, communications and services brought to homes, businesses and other places through cable. The phone companies also would like to bring the Information Superhighway to you over the phone lines.

Why is all this stuff available to me?

Many users, awestruck by the range of resources available free of charge on the Internet, wonder why so many organizations are being so *nice*. The answer is simply that for many companies and government agencies, the Internet is the easiest and most cost-effective way to reach the public. A commercial Net connection starts at about $200 a month-about the cost of mailing 1,000 brochures.

Companies can use the Internet to advertise (often by providing free information or entertainment as an attraction) as well as to provide customer support for their products or services. For example, more than 10,000 people each month download software upgrades from Microsoft's Internet servers.

Government agencies and nonprofit organizations use the Internet to stay in the public eye. The Field Museum of Natural History, for example, can reach thousands of people who can't visit personally but want a glimpse of its fascinating holdings, and NASA can provide researchers and space buffs with photographs from Shuttle missions and the Hubble space telescope. Though neither the museum nor NASA charges for these services, both use the Internet to increase their public presence—an important concern for any organization that depends on government and private funding.

Is the information on the Internet really free?

The Internet was created by the military, and adopted by government and educational organizations, as a means of sharing information and research with few restrictions and at no cost. This tradition of cost-free sharing has become an essential part of the Internet's credo. It's tied to another tradition: for everything you receive, you should give something back to the Net.

Even commercial businesses seem to follow these customs, probably realizing that they have more to lose (in the form of public goodwill) by breaking them than to gain. So, to attract people to their Internet sites, businesses generally try to offer useful information at no charge. And even though you can place orders at many Internet sites, you're never compelled to buy.

internet@home

What prompted you to get connected to the Net?

❝ **Initially it was just** idle curiosity, and the fact that the new computer we bought (in September 1994) came with a modem. I read a fair amount about the Internet before I ever connected, and it sounded interesting. But I didn't really have a very good idea of what the various resources (gopher, World-Wide Web, FTP, etc.) were like or what was available until I actually started exploring. ❞

Steve Burr
Phoenix attorney and Webmaster of Kids' Web
http://www.primenet.com/~sburr/index.html

❝ **I have always** been involved with computers and data processing since my college days in the 1970s. I first became interested in the Internet about 18 months ago because my husband decided to get a shell account at a local provider to communicate about technical issues. I started with a blank UNIX prompt. The first 10 times all I could get was a weather report; after that I stumbled onto an organic recipe newsgroup via TRN (a type of UNIX newsreader program). I knew there must be more and just kept at it. That was before Lynx (a text-only browsing program) or much Web stuff. It was an exploration for me, and I had the time, tools, and interest at that time. ❞

Sandy Barnes
Seattle-area mother of four school-age children
Webmaster of Adoption Information Exchange
http://www.halcyon.com/adoption/

❝ **The reason we** initially connected to the Internet was to get software updates, shareware, and freeware. I (had been) connected to the Internet through Bellevue Public Schools, but it was—and still is—a limited connection. I could see the wonderfully tantalizing software names, but wasn't able to download them. ❞

Silvia Loomis
Chapter 1 Remedial Reading Instruction Assistant
with the Bellevue (Wash.) Public Schools

Chapter 4

What you need to get started

This chapter will show you

- ✔ What kind of computer and software you'll need to access the Internet.

- ✔ What to look for in an Internet service provider.

- ✔ Some of the technical terms you'll come across as you make your first Internet connection.

Just a couple of years ago, connecting to the Internet could be a mystifying and expensive process, as your authors discovered firsthand. Fortunately, that's not the case anymore. Recently, everyone who sells Internet-related products and services — including hardware manufacturers, software publishers, and service providers — has been racing to make Net access easier and cheaper.

If you choose the right hardware, software, and service provider, you should be up and running on the Internet within a few minutes.

Hardware

The hardware requirements for connecting to the Internet are a moving target, so we have included three possible scenarios for IBM-compatible PC users.

Here are a few things to bear in mind. Connecting to the Internet at the moment doesn't require an exceptional system. Just about any IBM-compatible PC that runs the Windows or OS/2 operating system, or any Macintosh computer, is adequate. A PC that runs only MS-DOS may pose problems when it comes to finding software. Since we believe World-Wide Web access is crucial in using the Internet, a modem of 14,400 bps or faster is mandatory.

The hardware requirements for connecting to the Internet are changing rapidly as new Internet services are introduced. Multimedia computers are essential if you plan to take advantage of new services, such as the Internet Phone and Internet Radio. Faster processors will undoubtedly be needed to handle virtual reality and other complex graphics services when they are eventually released.

On top of this, new operating systems, such as OS/2, Windows NT and Windows 95, require lots of memory. OS/2 and NT require at least 16 megabytes, and operate more smoothly with 32 megabytes, while Windows 95 can get by with half that. It is always possible to operate with less memory, but the speed will suffer dramatically. We believe memory is more important than processor speed.

Computer

Minimum PC configuration

- ✔ 486-25 MHz SX or better
- ✔ 4 MB of RAM (8 MB recommended)
- ✔ 200 MB or larger hard drive
- ✔ Color monitor
- ✔ Mouse

✔ Microsoft Windows or Windows 95

✔ 14,400 bps internal or external modem

Standard PC configuration

✔ 486-66 MHz or Pentium

✔ 8 MB of RAM (16 MB preferable)

✔ 500 MB or larger hard drive

✔ Color monitor

✔ Mouse

✔ Microsoft Windows or Windows 95

✔ Multimedia (CD-ROM and sound card)

✔ 14,400 bps or faster internal or external modem

Power-user configuration

✔ Pentium processor

✔ 16 MB of RAM (32 MB preferable)

✔ 1 gigabyte or larger hard drive

✔ Color monitor

✔ Mouse

✔ Windows NT or OS/2

✔ Multimedia (CD-ROM and sound card)

✔ 28,800 bps internal or external modem

Sample Macintosh configuration

✔ 68040 (the least expensive) or Power Macintosh

✔ 4 MB of RAM (8 MB recommended)

✔ 200 MB or larger hard drive

✔ Color monitor

✔ Mouse

✔ System 7.x operating system

✔ Internal or external modem (see the next section)

Modem

In Internet terms, the most important component of your computer system is the modem, the piece of hardware that connects your computer to the telephone line. A good modem will cost you anywhere from $60 to $200.

Downloading information from your Internet service provider to your computer always takes time. To shorten the down time between requesting information and receiving it—and keep your kids from fidgeting—get the fastest modem you can afford. We recommend at least a 14,400-bps (bits per second) unit with V.32bis (a data compression standard). A 28,800-bps modem is better, but some Internet providers aren't yet capable of handling that high a transfer rate, so be sure to ask yours.

Some providers are better equipped to handle certain brands of modem than others. If you have a choice, you're generally safer to stick with the more popular brand names, such as Hayes, U.S. Robotics, Intel, and Practical Peripherals. Ask your provider if you're not sure.

ISDN: A high-speed alternative

Some local telephone companies offer access to the *Integrated Services Digital Network (ISDN)*, which allows data transfers at a minimum speed of 64,000 bps-at least two times faster than the fastest modem. California, especially in the San Francisco area, is at the vanguard of ISDN access for two reasons. First, it is located near Silicon Valley, home to the world's largest concentration of technology companies. Second, the state of California is trying to alleviate traffic problems by urging companies to have employees work at home and connect to their workplace by computer.

ISDN may play a significant role in the near future because it will allow phone companies to transmit video and other complex data over phone lines. In some areas, people are already using ISDN to access the Internet, but there are drawbacks.

First, not all Internet service providers are equipped for ISDN connections, whether or not the local phone company offers them. Second, prices for ISDN service can be outrageous. And third, you need a special ISDN card instead of a modem, and those cards cost over $300 at press time. Your Internet provider should be able to explain the pros and cons of ISDN in your area.

Cable companies jump on the bandwagon

Many parts of the United States may soon be able to connect to the Internet through cable television at unbelievable speeds. Tele-Communications, Inc. (TCI), the largest cable TV provider in the United States, says it will offer access to the Internet at 10 million bps (300 times faster that the fastest modem) through its cable network. A special modem will be required to link a computer to the cable wire. Monthly fees are expected to be in the $20 to $30 range. If this service does materialize, more people will connect to the Internet, and new applications will be found to take advantage of this speed. We can't wait for this to happen.

Software

Finding software to connect to the Internet is now simple. If you purchased a copy of this book with *Mosaic in a Box* (see page for more details, please see page 381), you will have all of the major components: the software necessary to connect to the Internet, a World-Wide Web browser, and an e-mail program. Most people will find this package more than adequate to get a feel for the Internet. This package connects only through the Spry/CompuServe Internet system. However, if you want to connect to the Internet though a different on-ramp, here are the software tools you must consider.

If you are completely new to the Internet, we recommend that you purchase a package such as Internet in a Box (available for Windows only), which is simple to install and supported by just about every Internet service provider. It includes all the software you need and automatically configures your system to work with a choice of several regional and national Internet providers.

Here are the programs you'll need for full Internet access:

Essential tools

✔ TCP/IP software

✔ Dialer

✔ World-Wide Web browser such as Mosaic

✔ E-mail program

Useful tools

✔ Newsreader

✔ Gopher

Advanced-user tools

✔ FTP (File Transfer Protocol)

✔ WAIS (Wide Area Information Server)

✔ TELNET

Will shareware do?

Some people balk at buying software in retail stores when there's so much shareware (low-cost software you can try before you buy) and free software available. But for easy access to the Internet, you really should consider a retail software package.

There are some fantastic free and shareware programs for the Internet. We use a couple of them on our Windows NT computer. But they come with little or no technical support, and generally can only be found at FTP sites on the Internet. They should only be used by knowledgeable Internet users.

Service provider

To a large extent, your success with and enjoyment of the Internet depend on the company you choose to provide you with Net access. If you buy a popular Internet software package like Internet in a Box, you'll find informational brochures from several of these provider companies, each claiming to offer the best service at the lowest price. It's important to choose a provider wisely.

Two types of Internet service providers are available: national and local. National providers, such as US Sprint, tend to offer high-quality service at a relatively high cost. These providers offer local phone numbers that you call to make an Internet connection, but they usually charge you an hourly rate. If you get hooked on the Net (and lots of people do), those charges can add up quickly.

Local Internet providers offer service at a flat monthly rate, usually between $15 and $30 per month, which is normally less than you'll pay a national provider. However, the quality of local providers varies greatly. Some offer too few phone lines, making it difficult or impossible to connect during peak hours, and others are understaffed and won't be able to provide quick answers if you have a technical question. You should try to choose an established provider with a reputation for good service.

What you need from your provider

Make sure your provider offers all three of the following services:

✔ **E-mail** Your provider should have an e-mail server that collects your in-mail and forwards your out-mail.

✔ **Usenet** You should get access to the 10,000 or more newsgroups that make up the User's Network (Usenet).

✔ **SLIP/PPP connection** To surf the Internet — that is, explore resources using such services as the World-Wide Web and gopher — you'll need either SLIP (Serial Line Protocol) or PPP (Point-to-Point Protocol), both of which are methods computers use to communicate with one another over phone lines. If you have a choice, take PPP, the newer and faster system.

Some service providers offer only e-mail and Usenet service without SLIP or PPP. Don't be fooled — mail and newsgroups are great, but cruising the World-Wide Web and gopherspace is just as rewarding, especially for kids.

Where to go for help

If you're having trouble finding an Internet service provider, you can get a list of them from InterNIC Information Services, which maintains information about the Internet. Contact:

InterNIC Information Services
General Atomics
P.O. Box 85608
San Diego, CA 92186-9784
Phone: (619) 455-4600
Fax: (619) 455-4640
E-mail: info@internic.net

internet@school

Daycare surfs the Net

At her home day care in Maine, Bonnie Blagojevic and the kids loved to read stories from other cultures. They were "word travelers," making imaginary treks around the world through the pages of picture storybooks.

"The Internet makes the concept of 'world' come alive, as children connect with other children around the globe."

But when the children began to exchange e-mail and do simple projects with real kids from some of the very countries they'd been reading about, those imaginary trips suddenly took on new meaning.

"The Internet makes the concept of 'world' come alive, as children connect with other children around the globe," says Bonnie, a preschool teacher and director of the Sharing Place, a nonprofit day-care center in Orono, Maine. "Exchanging ideas and collaborating on projects are extremely valuable experiences."

Bonnie got connected to the Internet in 1992 when a friend moved to Finland. She'd always wondered whether the books she was reading to the kids were truly favorites abroad as well. Now she had an excuse to get an e-mail account and find out.

Soon her young charges were exchanging periodic e-mail messages and book lists with children in Iceland and Russia.

"The children at my day care have really enjoyed using the Internet," says Bonnie, now administrator of the Early Childhood Education Online mailing list.

"I think they felt quite grown up and special to be communicating with others in this way."

✔ **Early Childhood Education Online**
   gopher://gopher.cic.net:3005/00/listservs/Early-Childhood-Education

Chapter 5

Aa Bb Cc Dd Ee Ff Gg Hh Ii

Surfing the Net

● ● ● ● ● ● ● ● ● ● ● ● ● ● ●

This chapter will show you

- ✔ What happens on a technical level when you cruise the Internet.
- ✔ How to make sense of Internet addresses.
- ✔ The various services available on the Net and the software you need to use them.

● ● ● ● ● ● ● ● ● ● ● ● ● ●

O nce your hardware, software, and Internet provider are squared away, the fun begins. You're ready to use—or *cruise* or *surf*—the Net. Most people find that the best way to learn how to navigate the Internet is just to jump in and do it. But before you get started, here's some background information that should come in handy.

What happens when you connect to the Net?

To most novices, connecting to the Internet seems mysterious and confusing at best. Here's a brief look at what typically happens when you connect to the Internet from a home computer.

After your computer starts, you load TCP/IP. The Dialer program in Internet in a Box or Mosaic in a Box does this automatically. Now the computer is ready to talk TCP/IP to other computers.

Next, you dial your Internet service provider from the Dialer program. The service provider's computer verifies your computer's password, and then assigns it an Internet Protocol (IP) address. Your computer is connected and part of the Internet.

Under the hood

You may wonder how the computers talk to each other through telephone lines. All computers "think" and store information in the form of zeros and ones. The word "dog" looks like 10000100 10010110 10000111 to a computer. However, telephone lines, which were designed to accommodate humans, transmit information in a range of sounds. To make the two incompatible systems work, you need a modem to turn the computer's zeros and ones into sound (just like the beeps made by a fax machine). The service provider's modem converts the beeps back into zeros and ones so that the computer at that end can make sense of the transmission.

Let's see if we got any e-mail

The first thing most Internet users do is check to see if they've received any e-mail. To do this, start your e-mail program, which has been configured to work with the service provider's e-mail post office. The e-mail program asks the post office to send any mail it has received for you since you last checked. The post office obliges.

If you have any outgoing mail, the e-mail program transfers it to the post office. In a matter of seconds, your service provider's post office sends it to the recipient's post office, where it will remain until that person requests it. Because the post office is located on the service provider's computer system, which presumably runs 24 hours a day, friends and family can send you e-mail anytime.

If you travel a lot, you many want to consider signing up with a worldwide service, such as CompuServe, which has local telephone access throughout North America, Europe and Japan. This would allow you to keep in touch with family and friends, not to mention colleagues, when you're on the road.

Now let's do something a little more exciting. Say you want to catch up on the news through the Electronic Telegraph, the World-Wide Web version of the London newspaper. Start Air Mosaic or any other Web browser and point it to *http://www.telegraph.co.uk/* (this is easier than it looks). In a few seconds, the Electronic Telegraph's computer will send the logon information followed by page one, complete with graphics.

How did we get to London and back?

The first thing to remember is that there are *no long distance charges* involved, unless you must dial a long-distance number to reach your Internet service provider.

The request your Web browser makes to the Electronic Telegraph is passed to your service provider's computer system. It helps route the request along the appropriate Internet networks until the request gets to its final destination. The computer at the other end evaluates the request and sends the information back, probably along the same route. The Web browser collects the information and displays it on your computer screen.

A tale of two packets

Remember the packets of data and system of packet switching we mentioned in *Chapter 3*? Well, take a look at what happens to some of those packets on a trip from Seattle, Wash., to London, and then what happens to some packets traveling between two

sites in the Seattle area. The Internet route is fairly direct from Seattle to London, moving the data through the Midwest to London:

Seattle to London

Connection	Network name	IP address
1	blv-e0.wa.com	[204.29.16.254]
2	sl-chi-4-S2/3-T1.sprintlink.net	[144.228.54.49]
3	sl-chi-7-F0/0.sprintlink.net	[144.228.50.7]
4	sl-chi-7-F0/0.sprintlink.net	[144.228.57.46]
5	telegraph-gw.demon.co.uk	[158.152.1.200]
6	demon-gw.telegraph.co.uk	[193.130.188.30]

But it's quite a different story within the Seattle area. The Internet
route from our office in Bellevue, Wash., to the FTP server at Microsoft Corp., about 5 miles away, is long and circuitous, looping
through Chicago. The two computers are on different networks,
which converge in the Midwest:

Within the Seattle area

Connection	Network name	IP address
1	blv-e0.wa.com	[204.29.16.254]
2	sl-chi-4-S2/3-T1.sprintlink.net	[144.228.54.49]
3	sl-chi-6-F0/0.sprintlink.net	[144.228.50.6]
4	sl-chi-nap-H1/0-T3.sprintlink.net	[144.228.56.10]
5	*	198.32.130.227
6	border2-hssi1-0.Chicago.mci.net	[204.70.25.5]
7	core-fddi-1.Chicago.mci.net	[204.70.3.81]
8	core-hssi-3.Seattle.mci.net	[204.70.1.30]
9	border1-fddi0-0.Seattle.mci.net	[204.70.2.146]
10	nwnet.Seattle.mci.net	[204.70.52.6]
11	seabr1-gw.nwnet.net	[192.147.179.5]
12	microsoft-t3-gw.nwnet.net	[198.104.192.9]
13	*	131.107.249.1
14	ftp.microsoft.com	[198.105.232.1]

How TCP/IP works

Now that we've seen what happens during a typical Internet session, let's take a closer look at TCP/IP and find out how it manages the complicated task of acquiring and routing information between computers.

TCP/IP (Transmission Control Protocol/Internet Protocol) is a language, or *protocol*, that computers on the Internet, whether big or small, must speak to communicate with one another.

Many such protocols are available—but some are proprietary and you must pay to use them. TCP/IP, on the other hand, was developed in the early 1970s by the Department of Defense and is a public-domain protocol, so no one pays to use it.

TCP/IP's independence from any particular type of hardware or software system has prompted many organizations to adopt it as the protocol for their internal networks. Thanks in large part to its flexibility and widespread popularity, TCP/IP has also become the single protocol for the Internet.

TCP/IP actually embodies two protocols that have evolved over time. The TCP portion establishes the link between computers exchanging data. In order to prevent one machine from monopolizing the network, it breaks the data into packets, or small units, which usually consist of fewer than 1,500 characters. Regardless of how busy a network is, each connected machine is allowed to transmit its packets.

Each packet includes a header, similar to an address written on an envelope, that indicates its destination and origin. The header also gives a sequence number for the packet, which tells the receiving computer how to reassemble the data. TCP has an error-checking mechanism, so any data that arrives garbled is automatically retransmitted.

The IP portion of TCP/IP simply allows each computer on the network to determine whether a packet it receives has reached its final destination or should be passed along to another computer.

All those odd-looking addresses

In order for TCP/IP to work, all computers connected to the Internet must have an address.

Two addressing systems are used to identify computers on the Internet—one number-based, one mnemonic.

Internet Protocol (IP) addresses

Each computer on the Internet is identified by a unique address composed of four numbers separated by periods. This is the *Internet Protocol (IP) address*, and it might look like this:

198.105.232.1

This address would be pronounced "one hundred ninety-eight dot one hundred five dot two hundred thirty-two dot one."

Your computer is usually assigned an IP address when you log on to your Internet provider's computer. For home accounts, the address generally changes every time you connect, so don't worry about remembering your IP address. In fact, about the only time you'll need to know an IP address is when you're configuring your SLIP or PPP software, which may need the IP address of your provider.

Domain name addresses

Computers are good at keeping track of numbers, but most people aren't. That's why the Internet uses mnemonic addresses, called *domain names*, to make its addressing system more intelligible. The IP address *198.137.240.100* becomes *whitehouse.gov* – the home of the President of the United States. When you want to explore the White House server, you type *whitehouse.gov,* not the IP address.

Your Internet service provider's computer usually maintains a database of domain names and their corresponding IP addresses. Internet programs like Mosaic know where to find this database and how to convert the domain name to an IP address quickly.

Generally, domain names are case-sensitive, and it's a good idea to retype an address exactly as it has been presented to you.

Domain types

Domain types are indicated by the three letters at the far right of a domain name (whitehouse.*gov*). This information tells you a lot about the organization. In the United States, organizations use the following domain types:

COM (pronounced "comm") Commercial organizations—for example, *apple.com* (Apple Computer).

EDU (pronounced "ee-dee-you") Educational organizations—for example, *harvard.edu* (Harvard University).

GOV (pronounced "guv") Government agencies, branches, and departments—for example, *whitehouse.gov* (the White House).

INT (pronounced "int") International organizations—for example, *nato.int* (NATO).

MIL (pronounced "mill") Networks and organizations run by the military—for example, *osd.mil* (Office of the Secretary of Defense).

NET (pronounced "net") Companies or organizations that run networks—for example, *cerf.net* (CERFnet, a California network).

ORG (pronounced "org") Special organizations, usually nonprofit, that represent a special interest—for example, *cix.org* (Commercial Internet Exchange).

Foreign domain names

Foreign countries use slightly different domain-name structures. The address always ends with a code for the country name, such as *ca* for Canada. (In fact, fully qualified domains in the United States could end with *us* – for example, *whitehouse.gov.us* – but Americans have somehow avoided the rule the rest of the Internet world lives by.)

In Canada and some other countries, domain names are differentiated by province or region, not by the nature of the organization. For example, the address for the Alberta (province) Software Society is:

sas.ab.ca

Domain names in e-mail addresses

To send e-mail to a particular user on a particular Internet site, you precede the domain name with an identifier for the addressee and an @ (at) sign. For example, *jspilker@aol.com* is the address of **John Spilker** at **America Online**. This system allows multiple users to have accounts at the post office of a single computer. An e-mail address can't contain blank spaces, periods, or @ signs, which might conflict with the symbols used to separate the elements of the address.

Tools to surf the Internet

Now that we've taken a look at what TCP/IP does, let's examine the tools you need for exploring the Internet.

Surfing, or *cruising, the Net* can mean several things. It can mean sending an e-mail message directly to one person, or browsing a newsgroup and posting a message (to be read by *everyone* who subscribes to that group) if you want to, or tapping into an informational server via the World-Wide Web or gopher. The various Internet tools can operate concurrently, sometimes linking different computers. If a World-Wide Web server is very busy and taking forever to transfer information, you can always start the e-mail program or newsreader program and do other things while your Web browser waits for its data.

Here's a brief explanation of the major Internet *services,* which present different types of information on the Internet, and which you access with different types of software programs. We'll have more information about using some of these services in later chapters.

✔ **E-mail** Electronic mail is the single most widely used service on the Internet. It's the system you use to send and receive messages from other Net users. To use e-mail, you need a post office account (most Internet service providers give you one) and an e-mail software program. Some of the e-mail programs available are AIR Mail (part of Spry's Internet in a Box) and Eudora from Qualcomm Inc. See *Chapter 9* for details.

✔ **FTP** File Transfer Protocol is just that — a protocol that lets you have files transferred to you over the Internet. You can download software, images, sound files, and electronic texts from several FTP archives around the Net. This service is generally used by more experienced Internet users.

✔ **Gopher** Gopher is a software program developed at the University of Minnesota (and named for that school's mascot). When you run gopher, you can "burrow" to thousands of informational servers just by clicking on folders and file names — your screen resembles Windows File Manager and the Macintosh Finder. Gopher files contain only plain text, with no graphics or sound, which is the main reason gopherspace is rapidly giving way to the flashier World-Wide Web. Gopher programs are built into Internet in a Box and other retail packages. Many World-Wide Web browsers also give you gopher access.

✔ **TELNET** The Teletype Network is actually a protocol developed by the Defense Advanced Research Projects Agency that allows you to connect to a computer at another location. That computer (the remote host) lets your computer act like a terminal, or part of its own system. This enables you to access library catalogs. electronic bulletin boards and other information files that some organizations, such as universities, normally only make available to their staff, students and users in their local area. TELNET, a text-based technology, was a forerunner of Internet services like gopher. It is rapidly losing ground to faster and more graphical services like the World-Wide Web.

✔ **Usenet** The Users Network includes more than 10,000 groups of people worldwide who share a particular interest — such as home schooling, Macintosh computers, or tropical fish. On a Usenet newsgroup, you can post your opinions and questions to the group at large. Most Internet service providers have a Usenet server for their customers. See *Chapter 10* for details.

✔ **WAIS** Many servers on the Internet that allow you to search for information by keyword are using WAIS, a networked information retrieval system. A computer that acts as a Wide Area Information Server indexes the data it stores not just by file names, but by specific words in each file. When you enter a keyword, the server hunts for files that come closest to matching what you're looking for. Most WAIS servers now use the Web as their frontend, eliminating the need for a special WAIS client program.

✔ **World-Wide Web** The most rapidly growing service on the Internet is the World-Wide Web, a network of informational servers that features formatted text, graphics, animated "movies," and sound. Some Web sites, or home pages, let you read and post messages, and others let you download files using FTP. The Web features hypertext links, letting you click on a highlighted word to call up more information — even if it's based on another server halfway around the world. Many Internet service providers allow customers to set up a home page on their Web server. Could this make Christmas letters a thing of the past? See *Self publishing on the Web* (page 112) for details.

New Internet services

As more and more people come to the Net, more and more new and innovative services are being developed. Below are some of those that people are talking about. Most use proprietary technology and have not been endorsed as an official standard. However, they may become widely used.

Using the Internet to talk

Internet Phone

This, essentially, is a telephone system that operates over the Internet with no long-distance charges (beyond what you may normally have to pay to connect to your Internet service provider). You need a multimedia PC — that is, a computer that's relatively fast, with speakers, microphones, and a high-speed modem (at least 14.4 Kbps). Versions of this software have been released by VocalTec, Inc. and NetPhone, and though far from perfect, are good enough for most families who want to keep costs down, yet still keep in touch. Future versions are expected to include group-conferencing capabilities. Some educational systems may eventually use it for distance education.

We've tested VocalTec's Internet Phone and been generally pleased with the results. Although it has its drawbacks—you can't speak and listen at once, voices sometimes break up, and there's a noticeable delay while compressed speech travels over the Net—it's more intimate than e-mail and much less expensive than regular telephone service. Using the Internet Phone, John can call his mother in Canada several times a week and not pay a cent in international long-distance charges.

To learn more about Internet Phone, see VocalTec's home page:

http://www.vocaltec.com/

Viewing the Net in 3-D

HotJava

This is a new system by Sun Microsystems that will allow some Web browsers to display three-dimensional graphics. It was still being developed at press time. To learn more about HotJava, see Sun's home page:

http://www.sun.com/

Listening to the radio on the Internet

RealAudio

This software technology from Progressive Networks allows radio stations around the world to broadcast over the Internet. The RealAudio Player works with your Web browser to decode and play audio on demand. Among its earliest supporters are ABC Radio, National Public Radio, the Canadian Broadcasting Corp., and KBS of Korea. With a fast Internet connection, you can listen to news, interviews and other programming you probably wouldn't normally be able to pick up, and surf the Net at the same time. This system could make the Internet a modern shortwave system.

To learn more about RealAudio and stations you can listen to, see:

http://www.realaudio.com/

Part 3

What do you use the Internet for?

The Internet is designed for two major uses: searching for information and communicating with other people. This dual ability sets the Internet apart from television and radio, which are one-way forms of communication, as well as from the telephone, which generally links only two parties who are familiar with each other.

Chapters 6, 7 and *8* look at the World-Wide Web, the newest and most exciting feature of the Internet. The Web has brought various libraries and museums to the Internet and has provided invaluable search tools.

Chapter 9 looks at e-mail, the oldest but perhaps most useful feature of the Internet, while *Chapter 10* examines the Usenet system of discussion forums, which brings together thousands of participants from around the world on every imaginable topic.

You can learn the Net if you're 5

Five-year-old Emma Burr is learning her ABCs and another fundamental skill for the future: how to use the Internet.

A tall order for such a young child? Emma's dad, Steve Burr, doesn't think so. "I take Emma on excursions over the Internet for much the same reason that we read to her when she was an infant," he says. "I want her to begin to be comfortable with and to enjoy a skill that she will need to succeed later in life."

> *... Don't forget that the Internet may appeal to other members of your family, like your own parents.*

Steve, an attorney in Phoenix, Ariz., prefers to read stories from books to Emma and to take her, when possible, to see exhibits at museums rather than visit them online. But he points out how much easier and cheaper it is to access information on the Internet than by hunting for it, for example, in a library.

"I believe that this will be increasingly true in the future and that the ability to share information over computer networks and the Internet will be a crucial skill for Emma's generation. It's close to being one for mine!

"When my three-year-old son Simon is a little older, I'll take him exploring as well," Steve adds.

...or 55

While you may be focusing on your kids, don't forget that the Internet may appeal to other members of your family, like your own parents.

Ask Kyle Cassidy, who teaches Internet skills to K-12 teachers. "I use the Web with my dad, and since I'm 28, it's sort of like he's the kid," Kyle says. "He can't get enough of it, and I'm pleasantly amazed at his wide-eyed glee."

Chapter 6

The
World-Wide Web

● ● ● ● ● ● ● ● ● ● ● ● ● ● ●

This chapter will show you

✔ Why the World-Wide Web is unique among Internet services and why it's becoming the Net's most popular feature.

✔ How you can navigate the Web using Mosaic or another browsing program.

● ● ● ● ● ● ● ● ● ● ● ● ● ● ●

Like the Internet itself, the World-Wide Web (or just Web) is hard to describe to someone who hasn't seen it. It's not a network in the usual computer sense (multiple computers connected to one another), though it operates on the overall Internet network. It's not a software program, but you use software (Web browsers, like Mosaic) to explore it. Essentially, the Web is a concept—a way of making text and graphical information easier to access over the Net.

The World-Wide Web consists of thousands of electronic informational repositories. Web home pages, or sites, are sponsored by government agencies, educational institutions, corporations, non-profit organizations, and even individuals. There's no organizing body; anyone can create a page and make it part of the growing Web.

Graphics, sound, video on the Web

If your previous Internet experience has been exclusively with gopher, e-mail, or Usenet and mailing list groups, you'll be amazed by what you find on the Web. Graphics, sound recordings, and even video clips are available at some sites. And the Web's hypertext links let you click on a highlighted word or phrase and jump to another Web site that might be halfway around the world.

Once you get started with the World-Wide Web, you'll understand why it's becoming the most popular service on the Internet (and why text-only services like gopher and FTP are going the way of the dinosaurs). But beware: the Web can be addictive. You may find yourself spending hours surfing from page to page, learning things you never set out to. Remember to let your kids have a turn!

Why the Web?

If you're still wondering why the Web is so popular, here are a half-dozen reasons:

✔ **It's easy to use.** The Web completely hides the Internet's UNIX understructure, letting you do much of your navigating just by pointing and clicking. If you're a Macintosh or Windows user, you'll quickly get used to the Web's interactive design.

✔ **It looks good.** The Web gives the Internet the look of a magazine, with most pages presenting a combination of text and graphics. A properly designed Web page can be very attractive and a joy to read.

✔ **It contains several powerful searching tools.** At Web sites such as Lycos, you can ferret out almost any piece of information that's publicly available on the Internet. The Web is also compatible with WAIS and other more complicated search tools.

✔ **It cuts down on the software you need.** Today's best Web browsers eliminate the need for separate gopher and FTP software. Some even offer access to e-mail and news-groups. Soon, a good Web browser may be the only Internet software you need.

✔ **It can make you a publisher.** Schools, small businesses, and families can easily design their own Web pages; in fact, you can do most of the work on a word processor. It's a great way to publicize student achievements, products for sale, family photos, or valuable information you'd like to share.

✔ **It's where the online future lies.** The Web is likely to be the host for the cutting-edge online technologies that will appear over the next few years. Electronic shopping malls, online banking, and interactive video are all likely to show up first on the Web.

Sound too good to be true? Well, there is one drawback to the Web. It can be painfully slow at times. If you have a 14,400-bps modem and a good connection, a page of Web text (say, 2,000 characters) should download to your machine in about a second. But if the page contains a photograph, you might wait 30 seconds for the image to arrive.

Designers of Web pages are increasingly using smaller, more com-pressible images to cut down on these delays. But when you start exploring the Web, you'll quickly discover the value of a fast mo-dem.

Picking a Web browser

To use the World-Wide Web, you need a program called a Web *browser,* which translates data coming from Web servers into viewable images on your screen. If you're looking for a definitive list of browsers for the PC, Macintosh or another computer sys-tem, you'll find it on the Web site of the W3 Consortium (W3C):

http://www.w3.org/hypertext/WWW/Clients.html

internet@work

How the Web was woven

Tim Berners-Lee

Research on the World-Wide Web started in 1989 at CERN, the Center for European Nuclear Research, in Geneva, Switzerland. The group, led by Tim Berners-Lee of the Massachusetts Institute of Technology, had three goals: to standardize the presentation of online text, to provide a practical way to transfer graphics over the Internet and smaller networks, and to allow multiple users to participate in online "conferences."

To meet these goals, the CERN team developed a new protocol—HyperText Transfer Protocol (HTTP)—that allowed different types of computers to transfer a wide variety of data, including graphics and text, over the Internet.

They also developed a new method of formatting documents, the HyperText Markup Language (HTML), that allowed documents to be presented in exactly the same manner on PC, Macintosh, and UNIX computers.

Originally, the CERN group's efforts focused on the needs of researchers in high-energy physics (CERN's field). But when the Web was launched in 1991, the system proved so powerful and flexible that researchers in other areas quickly adopted it.

A free software program called Mosaic was released in 1993 by the National Center for Supercomputing Applications (NCSA) at the University of Illinois. It quickly became the most popular tool for browsing Web servers.

A *New York Times* article later that year hailed the Web/Mosaic combination as the "killer application of the Internet." This pronouncement proved correct: by mid-1994, the Web had overtaken gopher and FTP to become the Net's most-used service.

✔ **W3 Consortium**
  http://www.w3.org/hypertext/WWW/Clients.html

Surfing to the Resolution Business Press home page

Once you are up and running with your Web browser, you may want to visit our home page, which contains the latest hypertext links to all the resources listed in *Internet for Parents* as well as the links for *Around the World in 10 minutes*, *Knowledge surfing*, *Surfing with older kids* and *Surfing with young kids*. By going to our home page, you'll be able to directly access the resources and avoid typing in the addresses. Our home page will also include any updates to the resources.

To go to our home page, dial your Internet service provider, log on, and start your Web browser. If you are using Mosaic in a Box, you may first be taken to the Spry home page.

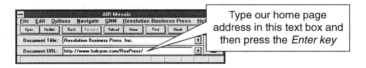

Type *http://www.halcyon.com/ResPress/* in the **Document URL** box and press **Enter**. Please remember to capitalize the *R* and *P* in *ResPress*, but keep the rest of the address in lowercase letters. Once you reach our home page, you may want to add it to your Hotlist for future use (please see page 107 for details).

Click the mouse on <u>*Kids and Parents on the Web*</u>. Once this page loads, select the set of resources you would like to explore. The re-

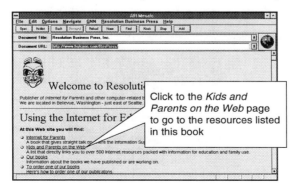

sources will be listed by category and alphabetically. Remember to click on the **Back** button to return to the previous step.

12 essentials for browsing the Web

In this section, we explain the basics you need to know to surf the World-Wide Web. These instructions should work for most browsers, but be sure to check your browser's manual or online help file for specifics.

1. Starting your Web browser

Before you start a browser from Program Manager in Windows or your folder on the Macintosh, you have to load the TCP/IP protocol and log into your Internet provider. Some browsers, like AIR Mosaic in Spry's Internet in a Box, do this for you automatically. Others require you to do these tasks manually.

Once you're logged on to your provider, you can run your browser. Most browsers take you to a particular Web home page by default—usually a page with information about the developers

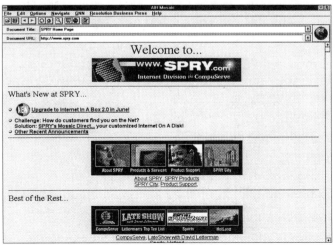

In AIR Mosaic, Spry's home page is the default.

of the browser. (You can easily change the default home page, but wait until you're more familiar with the program and Internet before doing so.) It may take several seconds for the home page to load, depending on how busy the network is. If you were running AIR Mosaic, with Spry's home page as your default page, you'd see something like the image on the previous page.

If Spry isn't your default page, enter *http://www.spry.com/* in the Document URL box at the top of your browser to go to that page.

Now you can follow along with the examples we describe in the steps below.

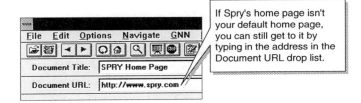

> If Spry's home page isn't your default home page, you can still get to it by typing in the address in the Document URL drop list.

2. Moving to other pages

Let's say you want to look at David Letterman's Top Ten List for a laugh. On the Spry home page, click on the underlined text <u>Late Show with David Letterman</u> or the Letterman graphic.

Click on the underlined text or image to reach the David Letterman page.

Underlined text, and images surrounded by blue or green borders, are *hot spots*. When you click on them, you're transported somewhere else—either to another page on the same server or to a different server entirely.

3. Going back to the previous page

After you read the Top Ten List, you'll probably want to go back to Spry's home page and move on to something else. Click the **Back** ◀ button, which lets you retrace every step you've made.

You'll notice that pages appear a lot faster when you return to them than they do the first time you load them. Browsers temporarily save the text and graphics from past pages on your computer's hard drive, so you don't have to download them again.

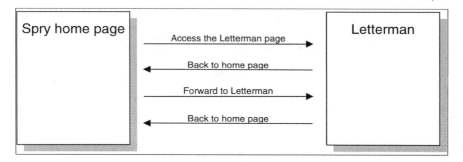

4. Going *forward* to the previous page

Although it sounds like a contradiction, browsers let you go forward to pages you've just visited. Let's say you can't remember Number 9 on the Top Ten List and want to view the list again. Click the **Forward** ▶ button and the page will immediately be displayed.

5. Using the Hotlist to navigate

One of the most useful features of better Web browsers is the Hotlist (some browsers use a different name), which lets you select a new site from a list and move to it. In AIR Mosaic, for example, the default Hotlist is an index of major Web sites, and you can add items to this list or create your own list.

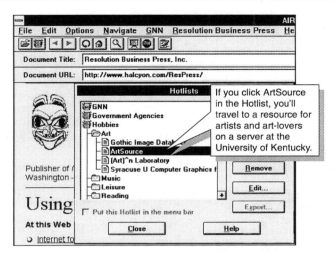

6. Going to a Web site that isn't on the Hotlist

Say you read about a great Web site that isn't on the Hotlist—for example, the page for Resolution Business Press. Its address is:

http://www.halcyon.com/ResPress/

To go to this page, you type the address in the **Document URL text box**. Be sure to type in the address exactly as you see it. URL addresses are case-sensitive, so it's important to get uppercase and lowercase letters right.

7. Adding new sites to the Hotlist

If you find a place on the Web you really like, you can add it to your Hotlist so it's easy to go back to later. In AIR Mosaic, you do this by clicking the **Add** button while you're examining the resource you want to add.

To add *Resolution Business Press* to your Hotlist, click the **Hotlist** button, go to the Hotlist group or folder to which you would like to add this resource and click **Add**. You then will be asked whether you want to create a new *folder* or *document*. A folder is a new sub group while the document option will simply add the resource to the current Hotlist group.

8. Finding text in a document

Most browsers let you search a Web page for a specific word or group of words. In AIR Mosaic, click the **Find** button and enter the words or groups of words you're searching for. The browser will move to that location.

It's also possible to search for files containing specific words

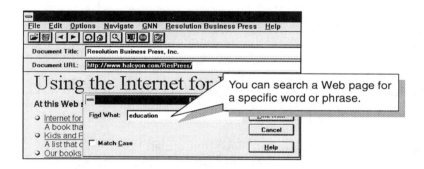

across the entire Internet. See *Chapter 7.*

9. Saving the current Web page to your computer

Most Web browsers let you save the text of the current Web page (but not any graphics) to your computer so you can read it later at your leisure. Some browsers have a simple **Save** or **Save As** button that you click. To save a document in AIR Mosaic, you would:

From the **Options menu**, choose **Load to Disk**. This forces AIR Mosaic to save every page that is loaded on your computer.

Click the **Reload** button. You'll be prompted for a filename. You can keep the default name unless it conflicts with an existing file name. You'll be asked to save every new page that loads to your computer. To stop this, go back to the **Options** menu and choose **Load to Disk** again.

10. Opening a Web page stored on your computer

Once you've saved a Web page to your computer, click the **Open** button and select the appropriate filename, which should end with an .HTM extension. The file will load quickly.

11. Stopping in mid-download

Sometimes you'll move to a new Web page and decide you don't want to wait for it all to load. In AIR Mosaic, you just click the **Stop** button and the download stops. Anything already downloaded remains on your screen. If you simply want to read the text on a page, you can stop the download so you don't have to wait for the graphics.

12. Exiting your browser

Simply go to the **File** pulldown menu and select **Exit.** Don't forget you're still connected to your Internet service provider, so if you want to continue surfing using another service (like e-mail), you can. But if you're finished with your Net session, go to your **Dialer** or other program that connects your computer to the Internet and select **Hangup**.

Possible pitfalls on the Web

The World-Wide Web and its browsing programs aren't perfect, and you can count on running into some problems sooner or later. If you get an error message, it isn't likely to be very helpful. Here are some common Web problems and their probable causes:

✔ **Nothing happens when you try to go to a page.** If the globe symbol in the upper right-hand corner of the screen keeps spinning and nothing appears on the screen, chances are the resource exists but the Web server is extremely slow or overworked. The only solution is to move on to something else and return later.

✔ **The page loads very slowly.** Some Web servers can be extremely slow, and there's nothing you can do about it (except maybe get a faster modem). More often than not, it's because the server is extremely busy or its Web pages have large graphics. Most Webmasters are aware of this problem and are starting to use smaller and less complex graphics.

✔ **FTP errors.** You'll often run into errors when your Web browser attempts to use FTP to download files. This frequently means that the FTP server has reached its login limit and can't handle your request. If the error persists after a few attempts, try using a regular FTP program to transfer the file.

Here are some specific error messages you might see:

✔ **Socket error.** Something has gone wrong with one of the Internet programs on your computer. You may have to reboot your computer.

✔ **Forbidden 403.** You're not allowed to view this page or resource.

✔ **Not found 404.** This fairly common error message generally means that the Web page has been removed. In some cases, the page may have been moved to another location and the Webmaster has neglected to update the hyperlink.

✔ **Internal error 500.** For some unknown reason, the Web server can't fulfill your request. Try again and see if the message reappears. If it does, the Web page may no longer exist.

Changing your default home page

Most Web browsers let you change the default home page (the first page the browser goes to when it loads). To change the default home page in AIR Mosaic, go to the **Options** menu and choose **Configuration**. In NCSA Mosaic, select **Preferences** from the **Options** menu.

In the **Home page URL** text box, enter the name of the new home page you want.

When you become more experienced with the Internet, you may decide you don't want a default home page. In AIR Mosaic, you can deselect the **Load automatically at startup** check box. In NCSA Mosaic, simply remove the name of the home page.

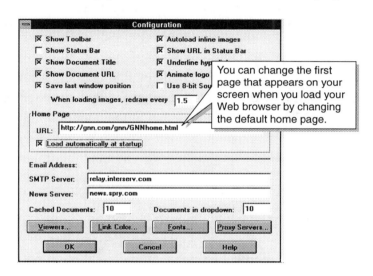

Alternative default home pages

Here are some alternative home pages you can use as your default. Remember to type the address exactly as it appears.

Spry, Inc.

This page (the default in AIR Mosaic) includes a comprehensive Hotlist of Web sites.

http://www.spry.com

Yahoo

Here you'll find a fast, complete, and searchable list of Web sites. A sublist shows you new and popular sites. Be sure to include this site on your Hotlist, even if it's not your default home page.

http://www.yahoo.com

Global Network Navigator

Developed by book publisher O'Reilly and Associates, this page contains a lot of Internet-related information. It tends to be slow, however.

http://gnn.com/gnn/GNNhome.html

EINet Galaxy

This page is maintained by EINet, an Internet service provider. It offers a searchable index of Web sites.

http://www.einet.net/galaxy.html

Planet Earth

This page can be slow, but it offers some interesting links to Web sites. The focus is on science-related resources.

http://teal.nosc.mil/planet_earth/future_unix.html

W3 Consortium Virtual Library

The World-Wide Web Consortium, which has taken over the development of Web standards from CERN, has a list of Web servers divided by subject and country. This page has an academic focus.

http://www.w3.org/hypertext/DataSources/bySubject/Overview.html

Self-publishing on the Web

After you've been using the Web for a while, you may want to try your hand at publishing your own home pages. More and more people—and organizations, including schools—are using the Web in this way to share everything from family photos to favorite hobbies quickly and colorfully.

Michael Bryan Stout is among them. A self-confessed Internaut since 1991, the Seattle sixth-grade history teacher shared the joyous news of the birth of his first child with friends and family via the Web in April 1995.

"Like many Seattlites, my spouse and I are East Coast transplants. We've been using the Web to share photos, laughs, and tall tales with friends and family members spread out literally around the world. Garrett's first home page was online within five or six hours of his birth," Michael explains.

It wasn't all that complicated, either. "The first draft page consisted of three photos I took with a Quicktake camera right there in the delivery room. The text was straightforward—basic height and weight information. Including the uploading time (the time taken to transfer the image and text files from his computer to his service provider's), I probably spent about 20 minutes working on it," Michael recalls.

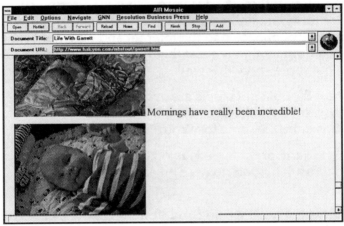

Garrett is a newcomer to the Web

Michael, a Macintosh user, worked with a variety of software for that operating system—Netscape as a Web browser; Gifconverter to handle graphics; Fetch to transfer files; NCSA Telnet to log on to a UNIX system; and Pico as a UNIX editor to write HTML.

"My pages are pretty straightforward. As I learn new tricks, I usually give them a try, but only the worthwhile bells and whistles seem to stick around. I've gotten pretty tired of seeing blinking links," he says.

Whenever he does change a page, he simply sends an e-mail notice to everyone he knows who visits Garrett's page.

What you need to create a home page

Creating a page like this is easier than you might imagine. Here's what you'll need to do it on a small scale:

- ✔ Access to a Web server
- ✔ An HTML publishing tool
- ✔ An understanding of how to transfer files by FTP from your computer to a Web server
- ✔ Publicity for your home page

More and more Internet service providers are offering customers free space for home pages on their Web servers (computers that are continually connected to the Internet and dole out Web pages to other computers that request them). Check with yours to see if you can get some space this way.

Several good publishing tools are available free of charge. Microsoft has developed a free add-on for Word for Windows and Novell has done the same for WordPerfect for Windows.

We've found the pre-release version of the Word add-on straightforward to use. But you do need a basic knowledge of style templates.

Once you've finished writing and designing your pages, you must transfer them from your computer to your service provider's computer. Unfortunately, this isn't easy to do the first time, especially if you aren't familiar with UNIX. Your provider should furnish you with information on where and how to create your own subdirectory. To transfer the files, you must use FTP client software, such as Network File Manager in Internet in a Box. Test all your pages to make sure the hypertext references and image files have been properly transferred.

To publicize your page, include a reference to it at the bottom of your e-mail and Usenet messages. Most e-mail and Usenet programs allow you to create a *signature file* in which you can insert this information for frequent reuse.

If you want greater publicity, especially in the case of a school or organizational home page, you can send announcements to these widely read home page announcement lists:

✔ **NCSA What's New**
http://www.ncsa.uiuc.edu/SDG/Software/Mosaic/Docs/whats-new.html

✔ **Yahoo**
http://akebono.stanford.edu/yahoo/new.html

✔ **comp.infosystems.www.announce**
Usenet discussion forum

The fun doesn't have to stop there. Michael, for example, wants to add video capabilities to Garrett's home page. "I've been trying to talk some of my cousins into loading up CU-SeeMe (videoconferencing software). I'd love to include a videoconferencing gateway through the Web."

✔ **Garrett's home page**
http://www.halcyon.com/mbstout/garrett.html

internet@home

Family is caught in the Web

"Can you imagine a 5-year-old taking much interest in a gopher menu or an Archie search?" Steve Burr asks rhetorically.

The father of a preschooler, Steve quickly recognized the potential of the World-Wide Web, the Internet's fastest-growing feature, after he got an Internet account in the fall of 1994.

"It's the most valuable for Emma because its graphical interface makes it ideal for a young child. In fact, she's really too young for anything else at present. There are already many sites on the Web designed specifically for young children and many more that they can enjoy with an adult's assistance," Steve says.

Steve and Emma should know. They're the Webmasters of Kids' Web, an annotated index of their favorite haunts on the Web.

An attorney in Phoenix, Ariz., Steve will only admit to spending "too many" hours per day on the Internet. But he points out, "(The Web) is also the most valuable (feature of the Internet) for me because it has the most entertaining, interesting and useful material on the Internet."

✔ **Kids' Web**
   http://www.primenet.com/~sburr/index.html

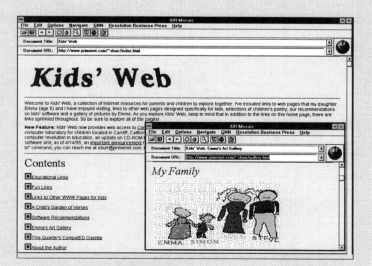

Chapter 7

Researching on the Web

● ● ● ● ● ● ● ● ● ● ● ● ●

This chapter will show you

✔ How to use a Lycos query to locate a particular piece of information on the Internet.

✔ Other useful search tools you can try.

● ● ● ● ● ● ● ● ● ● ● ● ●

T he Internet consists of thousands of servers around the world, but there's no master registry or card catalog with all these resources indexed and cross-referenced. To make it easier to find needed information on the Net, several universities have created innovative search systems — called *spiders, robots,* or *worms* — on the World-Wide Web that maintain lists or databases of resources.

These systems are programmed to wander across the Internet frequently and make note of the resources available at various sites, storing their findings in a database. You design a query (a request for information) using keywords, and the spider returns the names and addresses of appropriate records. Some spiders even let you search for specific words in documents stored throughout the Internet—a capability you don't get from library microfiche catalogs.

Because spiders maintain their own databases, queries can take less than a minute to perform. And like most Internet resources, spiders are available free of charge.

● ● ● ● ● ● ● ● ● ● ● ● ● ● ● ●

Lycos: One smart spider

If we could give an award for the most useful site on the Internet, it would go to *The Lycos Catalog of the Internet* (*http://lycos.cs.cmu.edu/*), a search tool developed by Michael L. Mauldin, a research scientist at Carnegie-Mellon's Center for Machine Translation in the School of Computer Science. Named for a wandering species of spider, Lycos hunts for information across the Internet, with particular emphasis on the World-Wide Web.

Since it came online in July 1994, Lycos has cataloged more than 3 million of the estimated 4 million documents on the Web and has responded to more than 9 million search requests. According to Carnegie-Mellon University, the system is used by more than 175,000 people each week. So popular and useful is this search tool that it has been licensed by Microsoft Corp.

Michael L. Mauldin

and Library Corp., and will be included in their software services.

The Lycos database adds hundreds of new resources everyday, and you'll find it responds quickly to new informational needs. For example, almost immediately after the massive earthquake in Kobe, Japan, in January 1995, Lycos had compiled a list of Internet resources dealing with the disaster.

Lycos simplifies the search for information in many ways:

Finding financial sources

Whether you're monitoring the markets or trying to get tax information, you can probably do it on the Net. Here's a sampling of what's out there, accessible through the World-Wide Web. You can use a search tool to find more.

✔ EDGAR Dissemination Service

Electronic filings with the SEC by public companies, and materials from the U.S. Patent and Trademark Office.

http://www.town.hall.org/

✔ Small Business Administration (SBA)

Contacts and training aids for people interested in starting, financing or expanding a business.

http://www.sbaonline.sba.gov

✔ Foreign Exchange Rates

Federal Reserve Bank of New York's 10 a.m. EST exchange rates for major foreign currencies.

gopher://una.hh.lib.umich.edu:70/00/ebb/monetary/tenfx.frb

✔ Stocks and Commodities
Federico Brown, Internet Interactive Marketing

Daily petroleum prices, stock market quotes, information about national incomes and economic news.

http://www.onr.com/stocks.html

✔ Internal Revenue Service (IRS)

Information about filing income tax returns and access (with special viewing software) to forms you many need.

http://www.ustreas.gov/treasury/bureaus/irs/irs.html

✔ Financial Services, Security APL

Track a stock; check the current level of the Dow Jones Industrial Average; and monitor some markets.

http://www.secapl.com/cgi-bin/qs

✔ J.K. Lasser's Home Page

Provides tax information alerts and answers to many frequently asked questions about taxes.

http://www.mcp.com/bookstore/jklasser/jklhome.html

✔ **Instead of jumping** from one Internet computer to another, you can perform your information searches solely on the Lycos server.

✔ **You can search** by keyword. Lycos reads pages on the World-Wide Web and keeps track of the 100 most important words on each page.

✔ **The items in resource lists** are ranked by their probable value to you. Lycos gives precedence to resources that contain your keywords in titles or headings, and it also considers the number of times keywords appear in the document text.

✔ **Lycos uses hypertext**, so you can go directly to a suggested resource just by clicking on its name in the list. If the resource doesn't provide what you want, you can return to the Lycos resource list and try another.

Lycos does have some drawbacks. For one thing, it's so popular that it can be hard to get into, especially during the day. Also, · you can't force Lycos to search for an exact text string, or series of words, such as "Bob Dylan". Instead, Lycos will search for all documents that contain both the word "Bob" and the word "Dylan" (not necessarily together), followed by documents containing either "Bob" or "Dylan". Finally, you won't be able to find out about every Internet resource; some haven't been found for one reason or another, and some sites have asked Lycos not to list them.

Despite these quibbles, you'll find that Lycos is an invaluable tool for finding out what the Internet has to offer.

Finding news on the Net

Who says you can't keep up with current events and world affairs when your nose is glued to a computer monitor? The Internet rivals the best newsstands and libraries in its eclectic mix of newspapers, magazines and other periodicals.

✔ **Newspaper Services Accessible on the Internet**
Steve Outing of Planetary News, Inc.

Describes and links to online dailies and weeklies worldwide, indicating how to access and subscribe to them electronically.

http://marketplace.com/e-papers.list.www/e-papers.internet.html

✔ **Commercial News Services on the Web**
University of Florida

Points to the online offerings of newspapers from around the world. Most provide sample articles and allow searches.

http://www.jou.ufl.edu/commres/webjou.htm

✔ **Popular Mechanics**

Includes lots of information about technology taken from the magazine's pages plus searchable archives and online forums.

http://popularmechanics.com/

✔ **Create Your Own Newspaper (CRAYON)**
Jeff Boulter

Lets you create and receive online a customized newspaper, drawn on a daily basis from various Internet sources.

http://sun.bucknell.edu/~boulter/crayon/

✔ *Time* **magazine's Daily News Summary**

Offers a daily roundup of national and international news events tied to related articles on each topic in *Time*'s database.

http://pathfinder.com/time/daily/time/1995/latest.html

How to perform a Lycos query

To do a query in Lycos, follow these steps:

1. In your World-Wide Web browser, type the following address:

    http://lycos.cs.cmu.edu/

If all goes well, you should enter the Lycos main-menu page.

2. On the main menu, you can choose from several Lycos servers. You're usually best off selecting one of the servers where you can set the number of "hits" — that is, instruct Lycos to return more than the 10 references it normally defaults to.

3. Type the keywords you want Lycos to search for. For example, if you want information about fish in the St. Lawrence Seaway, type *St. Lawrence Seaway fish*. The best strategy is to use only a few keywords in your first query, then add more if you get too many resources.

Making a query more precise

There are two ways you can make queries more or less precise:

✔ **Exact matches**. To force Lycos to search for an exact word, add a period to the end of the word. In one search we tried, the keyword *law* (no period) returned 7,184 resources, in-

You can set the maximum number of resources you want Lycos to list when it answers your query.

cluding *lawbooks* and *Lawrence,* while *law.* (with a period) returned 999.

✔ **Enlarge-prefix matches**. If you want Lycos to do a more extensive search of a prefix, add a dollar sign ($) to the end of the word. For example, *law$* returned 12,363 possible matches, including *lawn* and *lawsuit.*

4. If the server allows, you can use the **Max-hits box** to enter the maximum number of *hits* (listed resources) you want returned. For example, enter 100 to instruct Lycos to return no more than 100 of the best resources with information about the subject.

5. Click the **Start search** button to have Lycos begin its hunt. This can take several minutes to complete, depending on how busy the server is.

> **Note:** Make sure your computer receives the entire list before you try to go to any of the listed resources. Otherwise, an error will appear at the bottom of the resources list, and you may have to press the **Reload** key to restart the query.

When the search is complete, Lycos gives you a list of available resources, complete with abstracts and hypertext links. Resources are listed in descending order according to their probable usefulness.

6. To view a resource, click on the hypertext link (usually the address of the resource).

7. From any resource, you can return to the Lycos resource list by pressing the **Back** button.

8. To start a new search, keep pressing **Back** until you return to the Lycos search page.

Finding libraries online

With the Internet, you don't have to wait for your city library's doors to open when you need information in a hurry. Whether you're looking for a book or an answer to a pressing question, here are some doors to try online:

✔ On-line Books Page, John Ockerbloom

An index and links to the full texts of thousands of books, as well as information from book catalogs

http://www.cs.cmu.edu:8001/Web/books.html

✔ Stumpers-List

Archives of answers to difficult questions, based on exchanges among professional librarians and researchers.

gopher://crf.cuis.edu:70/11gopher_root2%3A%5Bstumpers-l%5D

✔ Library of Congress Home Page

Electronic resources, including historical collections, online exhibitions, and legislation information.

http://lcweb.loc.gov/homepage/lchp.html

✔ Internet Public Library, University of Michigan

A round-the-clock public library on the Internet, including an experimental reference desk.

http://lcweb.loc.gov/homepage/lchp.html

✔ WWW Virtual Library

Access to resources, arranged by subject by specialists.

http://www.w3.org/hypertext/DataSources/bySubject/Overview.html

✔ CARRIE: An Electronic Full-text Library

The University of Kansas' full-text materials, a reference section, and a link to a comprehensive world news service.

http://history.cc.ukans.edu/carrie/carrie_main.html

✔ Library Catalogs Accessible on the Internet

Yale University's worldwide list of libraries that have made their catalogs accessible to Internet users.

gopher://libgopher.yale.edu:70/11/

More spiders, robots, and worms

If Lycos doesn't point you to the resources you need (or if it's too busy to get into), you can try some other Internet search tools. For a complete list of current spiders, robots, and worms, check the List of Robots page:

http://web.nexor.co.uk/mak/doc/robots/active.html

The WebCrawler

The University of Washington's WebCrawler works a lot like Lycos. Go to the WebCrawler search page and you should see a form something like the one below. Just enter the word or words you're searching for and WebCrawler will return a list of possible resources.

http://webcrawler.cs.washington.edu/WebCrawler/Home.html

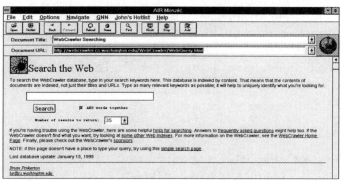

The WebCrawler's search page is similar to that of Lycos.

The World-Wide Web Worm

This is a very fast search tool with flexible options. Developed at the University of Colorado at Boulder, it searches only the Web.

http://www.cs.colorado.edu/home/mcbryan/WWWW.html

Other information sources on the Net

Keyword searches aren't the only way to locate information quickly. Other servers on the Internet offer subject indexes, news articles, and even a complete encyclopedia.

W3C: Searching by subject or country

The World-Wide Web Consortium (W3C), an offshoot of the Center for European Nuclear Research's World-Wide Web project, offers both a subject index of Web servers (mostly academic ones) and a registry of servers by country. For some countries, such as France, the locations of servers are plotted on a map.

http://www.w3.org/hypertext/DataSources/Top.html

Grolier's Encyclopedia

The complete *Grolier's Encyclopedia* is available online. To access it, you'll need a TELNET client, such as AIR Telnet. Go to the Grolier's Home Page on the Web, then click the hotlink to access the *Grolier's Encyclopedia*. Your TELNET program should start and connect you to the University of Maryland server. This resource can be busy and hard to access.

http://gagme.wwa.com/~boba/grolier.html

Time magazine

If you're searching for basic articles about current events, *Time* may be your best bet. This major weekly news magazine — as well as some of its sister publications, such as *People* and *Entertainment Weekly* — is available on the Web, and you can search back issues by keyword. This is an extremely popular Web site, so it can be slow.

http://www.timeinc.com/

Yahoo

The best subject index is Yahoo, which lists over 30,000 resources by topic. The resources are searchable. Everyone should have Yahoo on their hotlist because it's the easiest way to learn what's available on the Web and other Internet services. Its lists of *What's New?*, *What's Cool?*, *What's Popular?*, and *A Random Link* will point you to some fascinating Web sites you normally wouldn't think about visiting.

http://www.yahoo.com

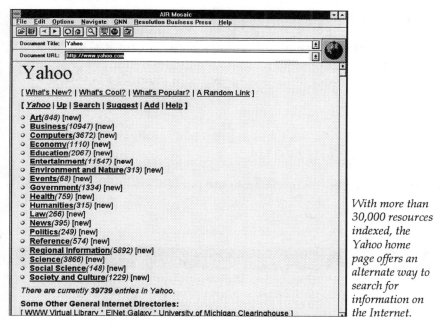

With more than 30,000 resources indexed, the Yahoo home page offers an alternate way to search for information on the Internet.

Researching topics for school projects

Knowing how to use search tools and which specific corners of the Net have the "best" information are fine. But if you're using the Net with your kids, you'll have to put those two skills together at some point in helping them do research for projects. We used several tools and sources to find information on four diverse topics as a way of illustrating how you might conduct your own search.

Project I:

Invasion of Haiti

Current events and world affairs are part of any curriculum. The recent invasion of Haiti could be a topic that your youngster might need information about for a social-science class.

Resource	How it can help
Lycos	A search of the Lycos database found over 500 Internet resources on the subject. Among them were transcripts from White House press conferences, State Department briefings, news stories in the San Francisco Chronicle, position papers by various political parties around the world, and images of Haitian paintings on display at a Virginia art gallery.
Yahoo	A search of Yahoo reveals a few resources including a special feature on Haiti at Amdahl Corp.'s server.
Perry-Castaeda Library Map Collection	This server at the University of Texas at Austin has several maps of Haiti, including maps of the capital city, Port-au-Prince.
CIA Server	Background information on Haiti is available on the CIA Web server. This includes economic information, political history, geographic information and a simple map.
Time magazine	A search of the Time Warner server turned up 60 articles published by Time Warner publications, including several by Time magazine.

Resource	How it can help
Usenet forums	These discussion groups deal with Haiti: *alt.current-events.haiti* *clari.world.americas.caribbean* *soc.culture.caribbean*

Project 2:

The 1964 Alaska earthquake and earthquakes in general

For many people, especially those on the West Coast, earthquakes are never far from mind. The largest earthquake in the United States occurred March 28, 1964, when a quake measuring 9.2 in magnitude on the Richter Scale rocked Prince William Sound, Alaska. Here are some online sources about this subject.

Resource	How it can help
Lycos	A search of Lycos on the words "Alaska earthquake" returned 60 resources, including photographs of the aftermath of the earthquake and a U.S. Geological Survey (USGS) map of major earthquakes in Alaska between 1786 and 1987. Another search of Lycos using the word "earthquake" returned 999 resources, including a link to the USGS Web server. This provided a TELNET link for online information, which led to a list of the 10 largest earthquakes recorded in the United States.
Carleton University	The university has a list of the most recent earthquakes, and its Web server can link to an appropriate map at the Xerox PARC map server.
Yahoo	A search of Yahoo turns up several resources, including the USGS' regional Web servers, which list the location and magnitude of the most recent earthquakes. Also included here are several resources on the Kobe, Japan, and Northridge, Calif., earthquakes.

Resource	How it can help
Usenet forums	*alt.disasters.earthquake* *ca.earthquakes* (California earthquakes) *sci.geo.earthquakes* (Good place to pose questions on earthquakes) *alt.culture.alaska* (Could ask Alaskans their recollections of the earthquake)

●　●　●　●　●　●　●　●　●　●　●　●　●　●　●

Project 3:

American Civil War

One of the most fascinating and important periods in the history of the United States is the Civil War. And on the Internet, you can find not only diaries, photos and historical documents of that time, but connect with people who have taken time to study this chapter in history.

Resource	How it can help
Lycos	A search of Lycos on the words "civil war American" returned over 500 resources. Included were the Library of Congress collection of over 1,000 Civil War photographs, and a Civil War resources page by history buff Bryan Boyle. There also were *Letters from an Iowa Soldier in the Civil War*, a collection of letters written by a soldier to his fiancee, and the *Valley of the Shadow*, a look at the American Civil War from the perspective of two neighboring communities on opposite sides of the conflict.
Usenet forums	*alt.war.civil.usa* (Good place to ask questions on the Civil War)
Electronic libraries	*Project Gutenberg*: This online library contains electronic texts of speeches by Abraham Lincoln, and Civil War-related novels such as *The Red Badge of Courage*. *English Server*: Its history section contains a Civil War reading list. It also features speeches by Abraham Lincoln.

Project 4:

Space Shuttle

NASA has jumped on the Internet bandwagon with greater gusto than perhaps any other government agency. You can find information on just about any aspect of the space program, from photographs of Mars to up-to-date material on a current Space Shuttle mission. For those interested in the next-generation Space Shuttle, NASA has posted information on the X-33 and X-34 programs at: *http://rlv.msfc.nasa.gov/rlv_htmls/rlv1.html*

Resource	How it can help
NASA World-Wide Web	You could spend hours exploring this Web site. It has links to the various NASA facilities around the United States. If a Shuttle mission is under way, check *Today at NASA*. Pictures and background information should be available on the Shuttle vehicle, crew, and mission logo. *http://www.nasa.gov*
Other space agencies	NASA has a list of the space agencies of other countries that are on the Internet, including the European Space Agency and the Brazilian National Institute for Space Research. *http://www.nasa.gov/nasa/other_agencies.html*
Yahoo and Lycos	Both returned several hundred resources when searching for "NASA". These are good places to look for specific information that may slip through the indexes at the NASA Web server.
Time magazine	A search of the Time Warner server turned up 60 articles published by Time Warner publications, including several by *Time* magazine.
Usenet forums	*sci.space.news* *sci.space.policy* *sci.space.science*

Linking kids worldwide

KIDLINK, now one of the best known sources of student pen pals and projects on the Internet, began as a simple experiment.

"It was a provocation from my wife," says its founder Odd de Presno, a Norwegian journalist and computer book author.

In late 1989, she asked Odd what he could do to help organize activities for a Children's Cultural Week in Arendal, Norway, in May 1990. "I proposed a cross-Atlantic chat between kids."

Odd de Presno

With help from Nancy Stefanik in Washington, D.C., Odd arranged an e-mail exchange on the SciNet conferencing system in Canada. That May, 260 kids from Norway, Canada and the United States swapped stories and made friends electronically.

"This event was so successful that I decided to go for it, to create a global network for kids from age 10 to 15," says Odd. "The kids in this age bracket are very much into getting friends. In the process, teachers have discovered what a unique opportunity this is for the educator."

KIDLINK is a free service and doesn't have a precise count of how many youngsters use it. However, more than 30,000 children from 66 countries have answered the set of four personal questions required to join the network.

"The kids of today can reach out and 'touch' new friends in other countries in a very real way," Odd points out.

"They are able to build real friendships, and to start constructing a personal network this way. With today's society so complex, having a global personal network is increasingly important."

✔ **KIDLINK**
http://kidlink.ccit.duq.edu:70/0/kidlink-general.html

Chapter 8

Aa Bb Cc Dd Ee Ff Gg Hh Ii

Things to do on the Web

● ● ● ● ● ● ● ● ● ● ● ● ● ● ●

This chapter will show you

✔ A sampling of the many places you can visit around the globe via the World-Wide Web.

✔ Educational and entertaining activities you can find for your youngsters on the Web.

✔ How to find new home pages on the Web.

● ● ● ● ● ● ● ● ● ● ● ● ● ● ●

Now that you know how to get around on the Web, let's take a quick tour of the world. It will take about 10 minutes, and you won't need any shots before you go.

To simplify the tour, go to the home page of Resolution Business Press (*http://www.halcyon.com/ResPress/*) and click <u>*Kids and parents on the Web*</u> which will lead to all of the tours of the Web listed in this section. This will save you typing in URL addresses and alert you to any updates. For more information, please see page 103.

Around the world in 10 minutes

First stop on the I-Way
The Pacific Northwest

Our Web server is located in the rainy Seattle area—home to major international corporations such as Boeing and Microsoft, a million espresso bars, grunge music, and the baseball stylings of Ken Griffey, Jr.

Many visitors to the Northwest take a side trip to Mount St. Helens, about 150 miles south of Seattle. This volcano blew its top in 1980, and the U.S. Geological Survey has a Web site tracing the disaster. If you have time, take a look at the *Slide set* of the eruption.

http://vulcan.wr.usgs.gov/photo_list.html

Down the West Coast
California dreamin'?

It wouldn't be fair to bring you to the West Coast and skip California. Our tour stops at Yosemite National Park, one of many places to see.

http://woodstock.rmro.nps.gov/wro/nps/yosemite/

If you like visiting national parks, take a look at the National Park Service home page, where you'll find the *Visit Your National Parks* section, which leads to a directory of national parks with home pages.

http://www.nps.gov/

Click to Washington, D.C.
1600 Pennsylvania Avenue, please

Now let's jump across to the East Coast and visit the White House in Washington, D.C. You may sign in by clicking the Guest Book image. If you'd like to e-mail the President or Vice President, click *Speak Out!* and follow the instructions.

http://www.whitehouse.gov

Surfing with young kids

The following resources are suitable for preschool-age children. To go directly to these resources, visit the Resolution Business Press home page *(http://www.halcyon.com/ResPress/)* and select _Kids and parents on the Web_. This will avoid the need to type in the following addresses. Please see page 103.

✔ Carlos' Coloring Book Home Page

Color simple pictures with the click of a mouse.

http://robot0.ge.uiuc.edu/~carlosp/color/

✔ Global Show-n-Tell

Kids worldwide show off their favorite possessions.

http://emma.manymedia.com:80/show-n-tell/

✔ LEGO Information

Try some of these projects and games with our set.

http://legowww.homepages.com/

✔ Mr. Potato Head

Create different versions of this character onscreen.

http://winnie.acsu.buffalo.edu/cgi-bin/potatoe

✔ Theodore Tugboat's Online Activity Center

Read an interactive story and color.

http://www.cochran.com/tt.html

✔ WWW Virtual Keyboard

Click the keys onscreen to hear different notes.

http://www.xmission.com:80/~mgm/misc/keyboard.html

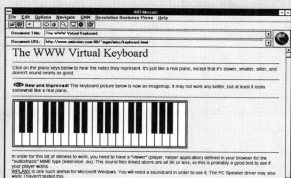

You can tinkle the keys at the WWW Virtual Keyboard home page.

Faster than the Concorde
A taste of Paris

It's time to cross the Atlantic and see what's happening at the Louvre in Paris . If you'd like to view some of the paintings on display, scroll to the bottom of the page and click the *Famous Painting* exhibition. Then click the *Artist Index* and pick an artist. Don't forget to take the *Visit Paris* tour mentioned on the home page.

http://mistral.enst.fr

Next stop
Marvels of Moscow

From France, let's travel east to a building that used to be off-limits to most Westerners, the Kremlin in Moscow. Click the *Begin the excursion* hot link to start the tour. This server can be slow, but it's worth the wait.

http://www.kiae.su/www/wtr/kremlin/begin.html

Iceberg country
From the top of the world ...

The Arctic Home Page is the creation of a student in Norway. It's a nice example of what one person can publish on the Web.

http://www.stud.unit.no/~sveinw/arctic/

Brrr! This place is really cold
... to the bottom of the world

Now let's surf to the opposite pole. The Gateway to Antarctica server is maintained in New Zealand.

http://icair.iac.org.nz/

The I-Way narrows
On to Africa

Africa is the continent with the fewest links to the Internet. Most of the Net servers are based in the country of South Africa. Let's pay a quick visit to Cape Town, a city that's applying to host the 2004 Olympic Games.

http://www.aztec.co.za/aztec/capetown.html

Let's click to Asia
On this budget, we can stop in Japan

Did you know that Tokyo is hosting a World City Expo in 1996? The Expo's home page will give you details about the event.

http://www.tokyo-teleport.co.jp/english/wcet96/0-a.html

Last stop
And finally, some R&R in Australia

We've done a lot of traveling, so let's relax on the home page for several Australian resorts on the Great Barrier Reef . To check the weather conditions Down Under, click to the *Satellite Photo of Australian Weather*.

http://peg.apc.org/~austresorts/home.htm

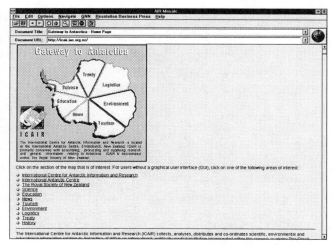

The Gateway to Antarctica server provides information about research and the environment around the South Pole.

Surfing with older kids

The following resources are suitable for school-age children. To go directly to these resources, visit the Resolution Business Press home page (*http://www.halcyon.com/ResPress/*) and select _Kids and parents on the Web_. This way, you won't have to type in the addresses. For more information, see page 103.

✔ Earth Viewer

An interactive map shows where it's currently day and night around the world, plus some other views of the earth.

http://www.fourmilab.ch/earthview/vplanet.html

✔ Field Museum of Natural History

Dinosaur lovers can find 3-D pictures, sounds, animations, and lots of reading material.

http://rs6000.bvis.uic.edu:80/museum/

✔ Froggy Page

A collection of just about everything on the Internet about frogs: images, clip art, sounds, fables, songs, and so on.

http://www.cs.yale.edu/HTML/YALE/CS/HyPlans/loosemore-sandra/froggy.html

✔ Interactive WWW Games List

Choose from *Tic Tac Toe, Hangman,* or other games that you can play onscreen.

http://einstein.et.tudelft.nl/~mvdlaan/texts/www_games.html

✔ KidPub

Read stories by kids of all ages. Kids can add a sentence or two to a collaborative online story.

http://en-garde.com/kidpub/intro.html

✔ Mammoth Saga
Swedish Museum of Natural History

Kids can explore a virtual exhibit on the Woolly Mammoth and other prehistoric mammals.

http://www.nrm.se/mammweb/mamintro.htm

✔ Science at Home, Los Alamos National Lab

Find ideas for hands-on science activities. using inexpensive materials found around the home.

http://education.lanl.gov/SE/RESOURCES/Science.at.home/Welcome.html

✔ Sea World/Busch Gardens Animal Information Database

Hypertext and images show how animals from around the world live.

http://www.bev.net/education/SeaWorld/homepage.html

✔ VolcanoWorld

Take a look at color photos of volcanoes, many taken from the Space Shuttle, or take a "virtual field trip" to the Kilauea volcano.

http://volcano.und.nodak.edu

✔ Wild Adventurers

Build and view a map of the migratory paths of wild animals, from gray whales to sandhill cranes.

http://ics.soe.umich.edu:85/IAPMain

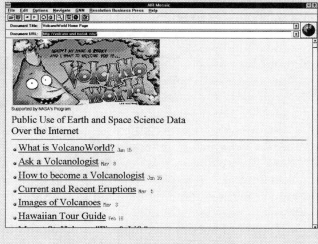

Take a virtual field trip or view photos at VolcanoWorld's home page.

Knowledge surfing

The World-Wide Web is more than an easy way to travel to exotic destinations. It's also a place to find information and exhibits you won't easily run across anywhere else. Now that you've recovered from cyberlag and playing with the kids, let's take a look at some of these.

Newspapers on the Net
All the news that's fit to download

The World-Wide Web gives you access to more news, more quickly, than newspapers and other conventional news sources. When the cruise ship *Estonia* sank in the Baltic Sea in 1994, it took two days for the major wire services to get their reports into North American papers—but detailed reports were available on the Web from Baltica News within hours. A university in the Netherlands keeps tabs on sources of current-events information.

http://www.cs.vu.nl/%7Egerben/news.html

Through the Web, you and your family will have a choice of newspapers to read over morning coffee. We routinely read the London *Telegraph* and the St. Petersburg (Russia) *Press*. Also, take a look at our *News on the Net* list on page 121.

Weather reports
Will it rain tomorrow?

Purdue University has constructed a Web server that pulls together weather information from several sources. You can quickly get a weather forecast and satellite picture for any area in the United States.

http://thunder.atms.purdue.edu/

Worldwide ocean temperatures
How cold was the Pacific last month?

The temperatures of ocean waters reflect-and affect-weather around the world. The University of Wisconsin provides a satellite map of ocean temperatures that's just about suitable for framing. You can compare the most recent image with one from six months or a year ago. If you've ever wanted to see El Nino firsthand, this is the place.

gopher://gopher.ssec.wisc.edu/11/mcidas.d/other.d

Earthquake reports with maps
Where the last one occurred

If you live on the West Coast, you're constantly aware of the earthquake threat. Several offices of the U.S. Geological Survey make available over the Internet a list of recent earthquakes in their region. Carleton University in Ottawa has gone a step further-linking the Survey's data with a Xerox Corp. map server so you can see where quakes have happened. You may be surprised by the number of earthquakes that occur each day.

http://www.civeng.carleton.ca/cgi-bin/quakesShuShu

Library of Congress
Civil War photographs

Do you have an ancestor who fought in the American Civil War? You may find his picture in the Library of Congress' huge archives of Civil War photographs, which is searchable by name, city, or keyword. This photographic database makes a fascinating afternoon escape.

http://rs6.loc.gov/cwphome.html

This picture of John L. Burns, the "old hero of Gettysburg", with gun and crutches, is one of hundreds of high-quality Civil War photographs on the Library of Congress Web server.

Shuttle news
The latest on the space program

You don't have to wait for a PBS special to find out what's happening with the U.S. space program. Just surf to the Today at NASA home page. If there's a shuttle mission under way, this page will provide details (and sometimes pictures).

http://www.hq.nasa.gov/office/pao/NewsRoom/today.html

Finding the latest Web sites

Hundreds of resources and home pages are added to the Web every day. To make sure you don't miss a great new site, stay in contact with these "what's new" lists.

The official registry
NCSA What's New

The National Center for Supercomputing Applications, in conjunction with O'Reilly and Associates, maintains a Web page with descriptions and direct links to new resources on the Web and elsewhere. This list is updated three times a week, and you can also browse previous lists.

http://www.ncsa.uiuc.edu/SDG/Software/Mosaic/Docs/whats-new.html

Hundreds added each day
What's New on Yahoo

Yahoo (Yet Another Hierarchical Officious Oracle), an index of more than 30,000 World-Wide Web resources by subject, maintains a catalog of its newest listings. As many as 100 new listings are added each day. Yahoo was created by David Filo and Jerry Yang, electrical engineering PhD candidates at Stanford University. In the spring of 1995, the two were invited to move Yahoo to the server run by the developers of the Netscape Navigator Web browser. They also received venture financing to continue their master index.

Yahoo founders Jerry Yang and David Filo

http://www.yahoo.com

Web info on Usenet
comp.infosystems.www.announce

Every day or two, this Usenet newsgroup announces the latest additions to the Web. Many of the new listings are unique and do not show up on Yahoo and NCSA What's New. To use this moderated discussion group, you must have a news reader, such as AIR News, and subscribe to *comp.infosystems.www.announce*.

Teacher finds a new tool

Bonnie Blagojevic got started on the Internet almost by accident. An education professor at the University of Maine invited her to sit in on some lectures, one of which was about the Internet.

"One of the strongest resources we have is each other, and the Internet can help us use this resource."

"That was my first exposure to the fact that the Internet even existed," she recalls.

E-mail quickly became part of her own teaching program with the youngsters at the day care center she operated in her home.

"The Internet impacts my life daily," says Bonnie, who logs on for 15 to 20 hours per week. "I moved quickly from knowing nothing about the Internet to jumping in with both feet: exchanging e-mail, joining (mailing) lists, doing some projects with the children, doing freelance writing, and, more recently, making presentations on the value of using the Internet."

Now director of The Sharing Place, a day care center in Orono, Maine, she also is one of the listowners (or organizers) of Early Childhood Education Online, a mailing list dealing with issues in early-childhood education.

"Equally as important in my eyes as having the children use the Internet is the need for early educators-caregivers, teachers, and parents—to realize the potential of the Internet to manage information and help us maximize the often minimal resources available to us professionally.

"One of the strongest resources we have is each other, and the Internet can help us use this resource."

✔ **Early Childhood Education Online**
   gopher://gopher.cic.net:3005/00/listservs/

Chapter 9

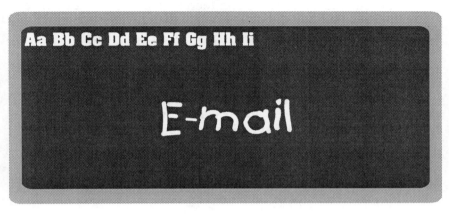

●●●●●●●●●●●●●●●●

This chapter will show you

- ✔ How to use electronic mail to send and receive messages over the Internet.

- ✔ Specific steps for using mailing lists.

- ✔ How to put your kids in touch with Internet pen pals around the world.

●●●●●●●●●●●●●●●●

I n the past two chapters, we've explored the range of informational materials available on the World-Wide Web. But for many people, accessing the information on the Web isn't the sole reason they use the Internet. Instead, they focus on the Net's power to *bring people together*.

At the "global meeting place" of the Internet, you can keep in touch with old friends and reach out to new ones. In this chapter, we'll show you how to do this through the oldest and most widely used service on the Internet: e-mail.

For example:

✔ Through e-mail, you can keep in touch with friends, family members, and business acquaintances who have accounts on the Internet or on a commercial online service with access to Internet e-mail. You can send not only text messages, but also photographs and even voice mail.

✔ Kids of all ages can find Internet pen pals from around the world. It's a good way for kids to learn about other cultures, develop their writing skills (possibly in a language other than English), and become proficient with the technology of e-mail. Several Internet sites post pen-pal requests.

✔ Many schools with Internet connections are encouraging parents to keep in touch with teachers via e-mail. It's a fast, informal way to keep a closer eye on your kids' education.

E-mail is quick and easy

When you send an e-mail message, you'll generally know in less than a minute whether it's been delivered to the other person's mailbox. Also, people seem to respond faster to e-mail than to regular, hand-delivered mail (which Net users often call *snail mail*). To reply to someone's letter by hand, you have to handwrite or print out the letter, put it in an envelope, stamp and address the envelope, and carry the envelope to a mailbox. To reply to an e-mail message, you just type your response and click a **Send** button.

For the three authors of this book, e-mail has become an integral part of daily life, and we'd hate to give it up. At work, e-mail just makes more sense as a communication tool than playing long-distance telephone tag with associates. Most of the interviews in this book, and even much of the correspondence with book printing companies, were conducted by e-mail. And last year, John and Karen included their e-mail address on their annual Christmas letter and discovered that about 10 friends have e-mail accounts. They now keep in touch with these people on a regular basis, just a few sentences at a time.

What you need for e-mail

Once you're connected to the Internet, there are only two things you need to send e-mail:

- ✔ **An e-mail post office account**. Most Internet service providers give you one when you sign up.

- ✔ **An e-mail software program,** such as AIR Mail in Internet in a Box. Another popular program is Eudora from Qualcomm, Inc.

How e-mail works

When you send an e-mail message, it gets transferred to your Internet service provider's post office, which is a program running on a fairly powerful computer. Most post offices immediately send the message to the post office of the recipient. If your post office can't find the other post office, or if the recipient's name is incorrect, the message is immediately returned to your mailbox.

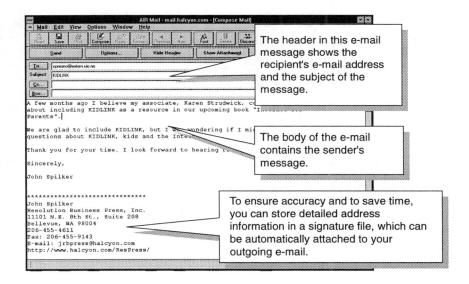

The header in this e-mail message shows the recipient's e-mail address and the subject of the message.

The body of the e-mail contains the sender's message.

To ensure accuracy and to save time, you can store detailed address information in a signature file, which can be automatically attached to your outgoing e-mail.

A quick guide to Netiquette

"Netiquette" means etiquette for the Internet. Folks who use the Internet have developed some accepted rules of courtesy which you should be aware of. Here are a few:

E-mail

✔ **Be brief.** Keep your messages concise, and make sure that you include only what is necessary of someone else's message.

✔ **Be polite.** Sending insults online is known as "flaming," and is unacceptable. If someone sends you something inflammatory, take a few minutes before responding—or better yet, don't respond.

✔ **Be correct.** Proper English is especially important in a purely written forum. A sloppy message on the Internet sends the same signals as wearing shabby clothing in a crowd.

✔ **Be direct.** Most humor (especially sarcasm) doesn't work very well online. Be sure to include some type of disclaimer when you're just kidding—you'd be surprised at what people take seriously.

Newsgroups

✔ **Read the FAQ.** There is almost always a frequently asked questions document for any discussion group. Reading it before posting a message will save you the embarrassment of asking something obvious.

✔ **Use the subject line.** People will decide whether or not to read your article based on your subject line, so make it specific and concise.

✔ **Restrict your audience.** If you're asking for local fieldtrip ideas, you don't need to be talking to Kenya, so don't post your message to the whole world.

From Internet for Teachers by Teachers, by Douglas R. Steen, Mark Roddy PhD, Derek Sheffield and Michael Bryan Stout (Resolution Business Press, 1995).

Otherwise, it's deposited in the recipient's mailbox and remains there until that person logs on and retrieves his or her mail. You can usually send an e-mail message to any recipient in the world and get it there within a few seconds.

Sending and receiving e-mail

Sending a message by e-mail is a straightforward process. Through your e-mail program, you can create a new message or reply to a message that has been sent to you, among other options. All you have to do is click on the appropriate menu item, and the e-mail program will present you with a form on your screen.

For a new message, you simply fill in the recipient's e-mail address, the subject of your message, and then write your message. For a reply to a message, it's even simpler. The program will automatically fill in the recipient's e-mail address and subject line; all you have to do is write a response.

For the most part, e-mail messages look pretty crude. To keep message files small and minimize the time it takes to transfer them, most programs limit you to about 64,000 characters in length, with plain ASCII text (no boldface, italics, or underlining) and no variation in the size of the characters.

In content, e-mail messages tend to be more informal than regular letters. However, you'll find that most people try to stick to the point, and keep them short and fairly precise.

When you've composed your message and are ready to send it, simply click the **Send** button. In seconds, your e-mail will be on its way to the recipient.

E-mail shortcuts

As you grow more familiar with your e-mail program, you'll probably want to take advantage of some shortcuts it offers. One is the *address book*. In this, you can save the convoluted-looking e-mail addresses of all those you correspond with. Then whenever you need to write to someone, just look up their real name in your address book, and instruct the program to plug that into the address line of your e-mail.

The other handy feature is the *signature file*. Instead of typing your name, e-mail address, postal address and any other similar information at the end of each e-mail you send out, you can keep all the pertinent details in a sig file, and instruct the program to attach the file to outgoing e-mail.

Incoming e-mail messages are queued up in your e-mail program's in box. Your program will use a symbol to identify those messages that you haven't read. If you leave it on while you're surfing the Web, for instance, the program will also alert you whenever new mail arrives.

How to find people to write to

We feel quite confident you won't lack people to correspond with by e-mail. In fact, you may be amazed at all the people you already know who are using it. Many people, from teachers to insurance agents, now routinely include their e-mail addresses on business cards and other stationery. As you use the other services of the Internet, such as the World-Wide Web, you will also fill up your address book with useful contacts and sources of information.

Finding a friend's address

If you want to send e-mail to someone you know is on the Internet but whose address you don't know, there's good news and bad news.

The good news is that there is a white pages directory of e-mail addresses. It's called *whois*, and it's on the InterNIC World-Wide Web server:

http://www.internic.net/ds/dspgwp.html

The bad news is that *whois* isn't very complete. While it includes most e-mail addresses for university employees and for government and military personnel, it has very few for customers of commercial service providers. These providers aren't generally tapped into the system, probably out of a combination of reluctance and laxness.

In summary, if you really need someone's e-mail address, you're probably going to have to call him or her and ask for it.

How to send photos or other files with your e-mail

If both you and your recipient have e-mail programs that support binary-file attachments or MIME (Multipurpose Internet Mail Extensions), you can attach additional files to the messages you send. Here are a few possibilities:

✔ **Graphic files**. You can scan a photograph and send it with your message, or attach almost any ready-made image file — even movie files.

✔ **Sound files**. Many programs for multimedia computers let you record speech and other sounds, and you can send the sound files by e-mail.

✔ **Word processor files**. If you don't want to be confined to plain ASCII messages, format your text in a word processor and send along the file.

In general, if you can store a file on a computer, you can attach it to an e-mail message. Just remember that your recipient will need to be able to open the files you send, either through his or her e-mail program or another application.

Getting ready to send a photo

If you want to scan a photograph and transfer it by e-mail, both you and your recipient will need an e-mail program that supports MIME or binary-file attachments. You'll also both need a program that lets you view images, such as the popular freeware program Lview31. (Most scanners provide image viewers, and you can also use a retail imaging program. Although commercial word processors and desktop publishing programs usually let you open image files for displaying or printing, the choice of image formats is generally limited.)

When you scan the photograph, use the screen (lowest) resolution to keep the file small. If your software allows, use the JPEG image format (file extension .JPG or .JPEG), which produces the smallest compressed files with a minimal loss of image quality. Here's a comparison of the file sizes for the same photograph stored in various image formats:

File format	File size (bytes)
Original scan	513,322
Windows BMP	513,322
TIFF (compressed)	358,970
GIF (compressed)	88,063
JPEG (compressed)	44,367

Attaching a photo or other file to an e-mail message

To attach a file to an e-mail message and send it, follow these steps:

1. Open your e-mail program and create a normal message, with the address of the recipient and a subject line if you want one. In your subject line or the main body of the message, you may want to include a description of the file you're attaching.

2. Attach the file to the message. Some programs call this feature *Attach Document*.

3. When you're finished, press the **Send** button.

On the receiving end, e-mail programs vary slightly in how they handle attached files. Some automatically place attachments right into a certain directory, as specified by the recipient program. In others, such as AIR Mail, a screen icon indicates that a message has an attachment, and the user can either open the attachment directly or save it to disk and open it later.

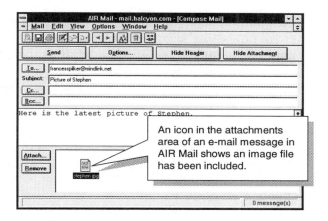

An icon in the attachments area of an e-mail message in AIR Mail shows an image file has been included.

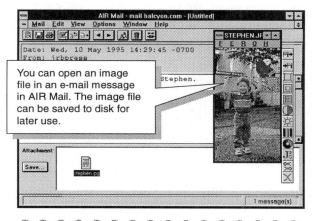

You can open an image file in an e-mail message in AIR Mail. The image file can be saved to disk for later use.

Mailing lists: Mass e-mail

Shortly after e-mail came into existence, organizations realized that this new technology provided the power to disseminate information quickly and cheaply to a large audience. The education-related Bitnet network developed LISTSERV, a group of programs allowing IBM mainframe computers to run automated e-mail newsletters, or mailing lists. This technology allows messages to be e-mailed to hundreds or thousands of subscribers. These mailing lists are commonly called *listservs*.

The concept behind listserv is simple. List members, or *subscribers*, communicate with one another by sending e-mail to a central computer. That computer either e-mails each message to all subscribers or assembles a newsletter summarizing the most important messages (usually on a daily basis) and e-mails it to all subscribers. Some lists are moderated by a list official who weeds out irrelevant or inappropriate messages, but most are unmoderated.

While Usenet (described in *Chapter 10*) is a better technology for large discussion groups and has overtaken listservs in popularity, listservs are still widely used in academic circles and in small groups who carry on very focused discussions. But listservs become less effective as the number of participants increases. When there are too many messages, it's hard to weed through them to find the most relevant materials. (John and Karen joined one mailing list in which messages arrived faster than they could delete them.)

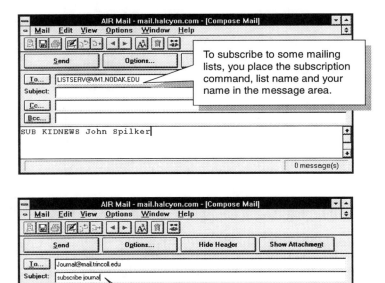

Using a listserv

To use a listserv, about all you need to know is how to subscribe and unsubscribe. The procedure is roughly the same for every listserv (and not that much different for those using other mailing programs, like Majordomo and Mailserver).

Remember that listservs are run by computers and don't always work smoothly. If you make a mistake, the listserv computer will usually tell you by e-mail how to correct the error or, at least, where you can locate an online document that can help you.

Subscribing to a listserv

In your e-mail program, type the following:

Address	listserv@someuniversity.edu
	Replace someuniversity.edu with the domain name address of the listserv computer.
Subject line	Leave blank
Body of message	subscribe ListName FirstName LastName

Many computers maintain several listservs, so you often must specify which one you want (replace ListName with the name of the list). Some listservs require your full name, but many don't. You don't have to provide your e-mail address; the listserv computer will take it from the message header automatically generated by your e-mail program. To avoid confusing the listserv computer, turn off your signature file, if you use one.

The receiving computer checks its listserv mailbox frequently. It will take your request and add you to the subscriber roll for the specified mailing list. Save the welcome file that the listserv program automatically e-mails you after you subscribe; it contains useful commands and other instructions that may prove handy as you become more familiar with the list.

Unsubscribing from a listserv

Simply start a new message in your e-mail program, and type the following:

Address	listserv@someuniversity.edu Replace someuniversity.edu with the domain name address of the listserv computer.
Subject line	Leave blank
Body of message	unsubscribe ListName FirstName LastName

● ● ● ● ● ● ● ● ● ● ● ● ● ● ● ●

Hooking up your kids with Internet pen pals

One of the most fun, and educational, uses of the Internet for kids is exchanging e-mail with pen pals around the world. Many schools are already incorporating Internet pen pals into classroom activities, and its fairly easy for parents to find pen pals for their kids outside of school. Here are some places to start:

AskERIC

The AskERIC Project at Syracuse University maintains a mailing list describing pen-pal opportunities for kids in kindergarten through grade 12. To get on the list, send an e-mail to:

Address	LISTSERV@SUVM.SYR.EDU
Body of message	Subscribe K12Pals FirstName LastName Replace FirstName LastName with your first and last names.

Most of the kids participating in this project are from the United States. The AskERIC gopher site offers more details on the listserv.

gopher://ericir.syr.edu:70/00/Listservs/K12Pals/K12Pals

EKIDS

EKIDS, an Australian listserv mailing list, covers a variety of kid-related topics, including pen-pal requests. To subscribe, send an e-mail to:

Address	majordomo@citybeach.wa.edu.au
Body of message	subscribe EKIDS

For more information, see the EKIDS home page on the World-Wide Web.

http://www.citybeach.wa.edu.au/ekids.html

KIDLINK

KIDLINK, an international network with participants from 66 countries, offers a variety of online programs for kids ages 10 to 15 (no exceptions). It includes a keypal program for individual kids as well as schools. To participate, kids must first register with KIDLINK. For more information, see the KIDLINK home page on the World-Wide Web:

http://kidlink.ccit.duq.edu:70/0/kidlink-general.html

KIDZMAIL

For another pen-pal list, try KIDZMAIL at the University of Arizona. To subscribe, send e-mail to:

Address	LISTSERV@ASUVM.INRE.ASU.EDU
Body of message	subscribe kidzmail FirstName LastName Replace FirstName LastName with your first and last names.

In response to this message, you'll receive information on participating in the discussion group. You'll generally have to request the most recent log; for example, the March 1995 log was 9503.

Address	LISTSERV@ASUVM.INRE.ASU.EDU
Body of message	GET KIDZMAIL LOG9503 Replace LOG9503 with the most recent log.

You'll then receive a list of the most recent postings to the list. To post your own message, send an e-mail to:

Address	KIDZMAIL@ASUVM.INRE.ASU.EDU
Body of message	Your message

Usenet brings Guam and mainland a little closer

The best way to learn about the rest of the world is to visit it. But sometimes you have to find another way. That's what the grand-mother of 6-year-old RD Gibson, who lives in Agana, Guam, did.

"I asked my grandson if he would like to have e-mail pen pals as I did and he was ecstatic!" recalls Rosemarie Underwood. So she an-swered a teacher's pen-pal request in a Usenet newsgroup, and RD began corresponding with a group of first-graders at a public school in Amherst, Mass.

"Although I have lots of interesting CD-ROM programs for RD, they don't come anywhere near what he learns from his interaction with his friends, especially when pictures and Valentine's Day cards are exchanged," Rosemarie says. "I personally feel that my grandson is a more informed child because of the Internet and all it has to of-fer."

The children began by asking RD about the island he lives on. But their questions bothered RD. "They made him wonder why he knew about life in the States while these children of his own age didn't know about his island, which is a territory of the United States," Rose-marie says.

"Patiently, we answered the questions. Yes, his school has a cafete-ria; yes, we celebrated Christmas but that we did so without a snowman; and so on, until the children began to ask personal ques-tions, such as how many (pets) each had, what their favorite hob-bies were. RD gets to tell the children what life here is really like, and the children on the other side tell him about making snowmen and playing in the snow."

In early 1995, RD lost his pen pals in Amherst after their school dropped its Usenet connection. But his grandmother helped him find new e-mail friends. "He's quite happy to know that at least once a week, a child writes inquiring about him."

Rosemarie hopes more schools will use the Internet to open up the world to their students. She believes teachers and parents need to participate in the experience, too, to help the children better un-derstand what they learn in these valuable exchanges. "Usenet is important to have available for the use of all grades," she says.

Chapter 10

Usenet discussion forums

● ● ● ● ● ● ● ● ● ● ● ● ● ● ●

This chapter will show you

✔ How you can join discussions on Usenet groups.

✔ Specific forums for parents

● ● ● ● ● ● ● ● ● ● ● ● ● ● ●

Another way of getting to the "global meeting place" on the Internet is through Usenet, the Users Network. Each day, more than 100,000 users post messages to Usenet newsgroups. Usenet is a worldwide bulletin-board system with more than 10,000 separate newsgroups—covering everything from early-childhood education to bonsai gardening.

While Usenet messages are often referred to as *news* or *articles,* and the programs you use to read them are called *newsreaders,* most of the postings you'll find on forums will be people's ideas, opinions, and questions.

Forums offer something for everyone

Usenet forums can be great fun for kids, especially shy ones who are intimidated about sharing their opinions in front of a group. When you "speak" on a Usenet group, you're judged only by your words and ideas. However, parents should browse each Usenet forum carefully before setting their kids free on it. Most forums are unmoderated, and just about anything goes. Some contain rough language or sexually explicit materials, and you run some risk of encountering rude or obnoxious people in almost any forum.

As a general rule, the more focused a Usenet group is, the better its quality. For example, the political forum *alt.politics.usa.misc* generates hundreds of postings each day, many of which are simply angry responses to previous messages. By contrast, the *misc.kids* forum — which addresses a full range of issues related to kids — attracts a smaller group of people, all of whom seem sincerely interested in sharing and learning. On this forum, people don't always agree, but differing opinions are more than tolerated.

What you need for Usenet

To read and post messages to Usenet newsgroups, you'll need:

- ✔ **Access to a news server,** which is generally provided by your Internet service provider as part of the regular charge.

- ✔ **A newsreader program,** such as AIR News in Internet in a Box.

How Usenet works

There's no central repository for Usenet newsgroups. Instead, there are thousands of Usenet servers around the world (generally the servers of Internet service providers), which host the same forums and share messages as they're posted.

Let's say you post a new message on the *alt.kids* forum. Your message first goes to your Usenet server. Within a few minutes, the server passes the message along to another Usenet server, which

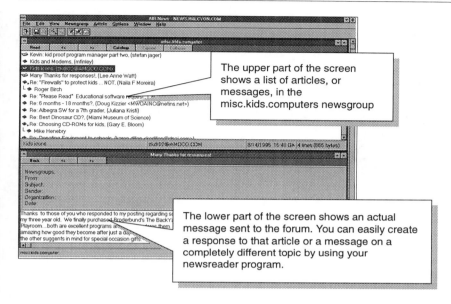

The upper part of the screen shows a list of articles, or messages, in the misc.kids.computers newsgroup

The lower part of the screen shows an actual message sent to the forum. You can easily create a response to that article or a message on a completely different topic by using your newsreader program.

The components of a Usenet article

then passes it to another server down the line. Within 12 hours, your message should appear on every Usenet server in the world. Generally speaking, you're not likely to see many responses to your posting until the next day.

Some Usenet forums are local and not carried worldwide — for example, some service providers have newsgroups for their users only, and certain countries or localities have Usenet groups of regional interest. Unfortunately, you probably won't be able to get in touch with these forums if your service provider doesn't carry them.

Identifying a newsgroup

The first part of a Usenet newsgroup's name indicates the group's category—the general subject-matter area under which it falls. For example, *misc.kids* is in the "miscellaneous" category because it doesn't exactly fit anywhere else.

Here are some of the categories you're most likely to see:

Usenet category	Description
alt	Alternative groups. Covers a wide range of topics including sports and computer programs, but also includes some sexually explicit discussion groups. Some providers do not include these groups.
aus	Australian discussion groups
bionet	Biology
bit	Bitnet-related. Many of the listserv discussions are available.
biz	Business related. Includes discussions from accounting software to jobs offered.
can	Canada. Various discussions groups related to Canada.
clari	Clarinet. A commercial news service that offers reports from the UPI news service through Usenet.
comp	Computer related. Great way to find out information about computers. There is a group from just about every computer system and software program on the market.
de	German-related
eunet	Great way to find information about European groups.
fj	Japanese-related
fr	French groups
geometry	Geometry related. Includes a pre-college geometry problem of the week posted by Swarthmore College.
info	Information on the Internet
k12	School-related. Several groups of children, teachers and librarians.
misc	Miscellaneous groups
news	News about the Internet itself
nlnet	Netherlands discussion groups
no	Norway-related
nz	New Zealand-related
rec	Recreation related with lots of groups dealing with sports, hobbies, travel, pets, music, games, food and crafts.

Usenet category	Description
sci	Science-related
soc	Social issues
talk	The Internet version of talk radio (can be weird).

FAQ lists

Many Usenet newsgroups create extensive FAQ (frequently asked questions) lists, which can make good background reading if you're new to a subject. Thomas Fine of Ohio State University's Department of Computer and Information Science maintains a Web page with a list of Usenet FAQs:

http://www.cis.ohio-state.edu/hypertext/faq/usenet/

Usenet forums for parents

Among the 10,000 Usenet newsgroups, here are some of the forums we think parents will find particularly useful:

Forum name	Topic of discussion
alt.adoption	Adoption issues
alt.animals.badgers	Badgers
alt.animals.dolphins	Dolphins
alt.animals.foxes	Foxes
alt.animals.lampreys	Lampreys
alt.animals.raccoons	Raccoons
alt.bbs.internet	alt.bbs.internet
alt.books.anne-rice	Anne Rice's books
alt.books.beatgeneration	Beat Generation writers
alt.books.isaac-asimov	Isaac Asimov's books
alt.books.kurt-vonnegut	Kurt Vonnegut's books
alt.books.reviews	Literature
alt.books.stephen-king	Stephen King's books
alt.books.technical	Technical books
alt.books.tom-clancy	Tom Clancy's books
alt.child-support	Child support

Forum name	Topic of discussion
alt.cooking-chat	Cooking discussions and recipes ranging from sea urchin to chocolate chip cookies
alt.current-events.russia	Russian events, mostly discussed in English
alt.education.disabled	Education issues concerning the disabled
alt.feminism	Feminist issues
alt.feminism.individualism	Feminism and individualism
alt.history-living	For history buffs
alt.history.what-if	Historical events that might have happened
alt.internet.services	Services available on the Internet, including discussions about Internet providers
alt.journalism	For journalists and journalism students
alt.mythology	Mythology
alt.newbies	For newcomers to the Internet
alt.parenting.solutions	Parenting issues and problems
alt.parents-teens	For parents and teens to discussr problems and solutions
alt.pets.hamsters	Hamsters
alt.pets.rabbits	Rabbits
alt.quotations	The origin of famous quotes
alt.rec.camping	Camping
alt.sci.physics.new-theories	New physics theories
alt.support.arthritis	Arthritis
alt.support.diabetes.kids	Kids with diabetes
alt.support.learning-disab	Learning disabilities
alt.support.single-parents	Single parenting
alt.war.civil.usa	American Civil War
alt.war.vietnam	Vietnam War
bionet.biology.tropical	Tropical biology
bionet.plants	Botany
bit.listserv.bosnet	Bosnia news from a variety of sources
bit.listserv.history	History
bit.listserv.japan	Issues related to Japan
can.schoolnet.chat.students.jr	Canadian chat group (a good place to find pen pals in Canada)
misc.education.home-school.misc	For sharing information, asking questions, and discussing schooling children at home.

Forum name	Topic of discussion
misc.kids.computers	For discussions and questions related to kids and computers
rec.arts.books.childrens	Children's books.
rec.roller-coaster	Rollercoasters
sci.geo.meteorology	Weather
sci.planetary	Planetary science

Part 4

Internet resources

The following annotated index leads to resources found on the Internet that we believe will help your family, at home and at school. We've compiled this list from our own expeditions on the Internet and from suggestions passed on to us by parents, teachers and others.

Most of the resources are available through the World-Wide Web, the most graphical and easiest-to-use means of reaching the information on the Internet. To get to the Web, you need a browsing program, like Mosaic in a Box, which is on the diskette packaged with this book. Once you're on the Web, instead of retyping the addresses we give in the following section, just come to our home page:

http://www.halcyon.com/ResPress/

There you'll find this resource list ready for you online. To go to any of these resources, all you'll have to do is click on the name with your mouse. For more details please see page 103.

A launch pad

This isn't meant to be an exhaustive list of educational or entertainment resources on the Internet. Rather, we hope this collection will launch you on your own electronic voyage of discovery. Many of the resources mentioned here are well-known to experienced Net surfers, but many are more obscure. We believe both types will be valuable to you and your kids.

We've also included resource lists compiled by other people and organizations — starting points — that can lead you to many exciting places on the Internet, often in particular subject areas. You may find yourself adding these to your browser's bookmarks or even turning one of them into your default home page.

Some resources are designed primarily for trained educators, but we think that you may be able to apply some of what they offer in using the Internet more effectively with your kids. Some items have no direct connection to education — for example, information about community and social services, software, games and hobbies — but may help you in your wide-ranging duties as "parent."

If you need help

Besides those resources that you can access through the World-Wide Web, we also include materials you can get at through your e-mail and newsreader programs, namely mailing lists (or list-servs), e-mail addresses, and newsgroups. At first, some of these can be tricky to use, but they'll become second-nature with practice. Review *Chapters 9* and *10* if you have any questions.

There's usually a good reason why you get an error message when you're looking for a resource. We explain the most common types of error messages in *Chapter 6,* so if you have any problems, take a look there.

If all else fails, contact us (*rbpress@halcyon.com*). We'd like to help, if we can. And we'd like to hear about *your* Internet expeditions.

Resource index

Art

African Art
Museum exhibits and explains works of art

This online catalog is based on an exhibition of African art at the University of Virginia's Bayly Art Museum. It combines images and explanatory text discussing the aesthetics and meaning of the displays.

Useful for art; international studies.
URL: http://www.lib.virginia.edu/dic/exhib/93.ray.aa/African.html

ArchiGopher, University of Michigan
Architecture and the fine arts

ArchiGopher, based at the University of Michigan, offers images and writings about architecture and other fine arts. You'll find pictures of Hellenic and Byzantine architecture, an artist's conception of lunar buildings, images of Andrea Palladio's architecture and Wassily Kandinsky's paintings, and other materials you may not find elsewhere.

Useful for architecture; art; images.
URL: gopher://libra.arch.umich.edu
E-mail: wjabi@libra.arch.umich.edu

Art History, Australian National University
View antique prints and sculptures

The Australian National University offers more than 2,800 images of prints primarily from the 15th through 19th centuries, in addition to 2,500 images of architectural sculpture.

Useful for art; images.
URL: http://rubens.anu.edu.au/

Art Quiz, Minneapolis Institute of Arts
Test teaches about artists and their work

An art quiz for parents and kids helps you understand what you've just seen at the online gallery of the Minneapolis Institute of Arts. The test centers on a selected piece of art online and the accompanying text that describes the painting, artist and period. Ten multiple-choice questions and a bonus brain teaser reinforce the ideas surrounding the work, encouraging visitors to think about it in new ways.

Useful for activities and projects; art.
URL: http://www.mtn.org/MIA/germ00_quiz_intro.html

Art-ROM Museum Web
Images and information about exhibitions

Museum Web is a growing host site for information on historic sites, botanical gardens, zoological gardens, planetariums and other types of museums world-wide. It gives profiles of each place along with calendars of events, hours of operation, areas of research expertise, and images of the treasures and attractions they have to offer. You can learn more about such museums as the Arizona Museum for Youth, Bruce Museum, Chinqua-Penn Plantation, Coyote Point Museum for Environmental Education, The Octagon, Tucson Museum of Art, University of Wyoming Art Museum, and Brooklyn Botanic Garden. The site is maintained by Art-ROM Ltd., a marketing and publishing company that specializes in the museum market.

Useful for art; museums on the Web; travel and recreation.
URL: http://www.primenet.com/art-rom/museumweb/

ArtsEdge
Examples and ideas for integrating the Internet into art education

ArtsEdge, supported by the John F. Kennedy Center for the Performing Arts and various government grants, is a collection of resources that can be used in K-12 art education. Its online newsletter offers examples and ideas about how the Internet can be integrated into the art curriculum. This Web site links to the Information Gallery, a gopher filled with arts and education research and resources. ArtsEdge is maintained by Janice Abrahams of the Clearinghouse for Networked Information Discovery and Retrieval.

Useful for art; education.
URL: http://edweb.cnidr.org/janice_k12/artsedge/artsedge.html

ArtServe
Images and history of art around the world

Based at the Australian National University, this Web server offers thousands of images of art and architecture — both thumbnails and full pictures — as well as a few texts related to art history. The image archives include prints from 15th- to 19th-century Europe; classical, medieval, and Renaissance architecture and sculpture; and miscellaneous works from other periods and regions.

Useful for art; images.
URL: http://rubens.anu.edu.au/
E-mail: gremarth@fac.anu.edu.au

Chelyabinsk Art Page
Art of the South Ural region of Russia

This Web site is operated by a Technical University in Chelyabinsk, the largest city in the South Ural region of Russia. Click to *Arts and Music* for a profile of arts and entertainment in that city, which includes a profile on the *Children's Jazz Studio.*

Useful for art; international studies.
URL: http://www.urc.ac.ru/

Clip Art on the Internet
Links to image banks for projects of all kinds

If you're looking for an image of some kind to enhance a project or decorate a World-Wide Web page, start here. This page, provided by the University of Wyoming, links to diverse and extensive collections of images available to the public on the Internet, such as those at the Louvre museum.

Useful for art; images.
URL: http://www.uwyo.edu/cte/Internet.html

Education Resource Center
Digital art and teacher packets

The Education Resource Center at the Dallas Museum of Art offers a collection of digital images available through the gopher of the University of North Texas. You can view and dowload (in GIF format) images of sculptures, jewelry, and other art objects from Central and South America. The center is currently working on a series of Electronic Teaching Packets, which will contain downloadable sets of digital images and electronic texts. You can e-mail questions about the museum or art in general to the museum's staff.

Useful for art; images.
URL: http://www.unt.edu/dfw/dma/www/erc.htm
E-mail: dma@gopher.unt.edu

FineArt Forum Directory
Art and technology resources

The FineArt Forum, based at Mississippi State University, is a directory of online resources for artists. This directory is meant to serve as a resource and jump-off point for people interested in art and in the possible relationships between art and technology. Items on this list can be accessed via the World-Wide Web, but are not necessarily Web pages; you can find descriptions and addresses for art-related electronic periodicals and other documents, library catalogs, databases, software archives, bulletin boards, and mailing lists, as well as links to online exhibitions and information.

Useful for art; museums on the Web.
URL: http://www.msstate.edu/Fineart_Online/art-resources.html

Krannert Art Museum
Browse art images or take a tour

This art museum at the University of Illinois at Urbana-Champaign offers images of many of its more than 8,000 art objects. It also offers virtual visitors an electronic tour of its halls.

Useful for art; images; museums on the Web.
URL: http://www.ncsa.uiuc.edu/General/UIUC/KrannertArtMuseum/KrannertArtHome.html

Michael C. Carlos Museum
Images of art from prehistoric cultures

The Michael C. Carlos Museum, located at Emory University, provides a selection of art images with a focus on prehistoric cultures. You can tour on-screen galleries devoted to the art (largely sculptures and carvings) of the Ancient Americas, Ancient Egypt, Ancient Near East, Asia, Greece and Rome, and Sub-Saharan Africa. The site also offers annotated prints and drawings covering the periods from the Renaissance through the 20th century. Inline images are in GIF format, and many of these link to larger images in JPEG format.

Useful for art; international studies.
URL: http://www.cc.emory.edu/CARLOS/carlos.html

Ohio State University at Newark Art Gallery
Tour the gallery, enjoy the exhibits

The Art Gallery of the Ohio State University at Newark offers a collection of images via the World-Wide Web. The site includes an exhibit of the works of artist Roy Lichtenstein (with further exhibits to come), a short movie showing the interior of the gallery, and links to other arts resources on the Web.

Useful for art; images.
URL: http://www.cgrg.ohio-state.edu/mkruse/osu.html

Photography and Instructional Graphics
Image archives and clip-art sources

This Web page, from the University of Alabama, is a jump-off point for resources in photography and the graphic arts. It includes direct links to several image archives and a list of clip-art resources on the Internet.

Useful for art; images.
URL: http://www.dopig.uab.edu/

Pixel Pushers
Digital art and photography on display

This Web page is an online version of Pixel Pushers, a traveling exhibition of digital art and photography (based in Canada and emphasizing Canadian artists). You can view thumbnails of art works, then optionally download full-color images in JPEG format. The server also offers artist biographies and a "guest book" with comments from viewers.

Useful for art; images.
URL: http://www.wimsey.com/Pixel_Pushers/

Selected Pictures, QuickTime Movies and Sounds
Audio files and images

This information bank contains a grab bag of downloadable graphic images, QuickTime movies, and sound files from around the world. You'll find paintings by Van Gogh and other artists, biological images from Harvard University, nature and science pictures from the Smithsonian Institution, Space Shuttle images, a white shark exhibit, pictures from Africa and Mexico, and other images. The sound files include guitar sounds, German musical samples, and various sound effects.

Useful for art; images; music.
URL: gopher://informns.k12.mn.us:70/11/best-k12/images

University Laboratory High School
Student art plus resources for art instruction

Visual Art is an experimental Web site at the University Laboratory High School at the University of Illinois. Its contents, based on courses taught by art teacher Karen Hellyer, feature original art by students and online resources for art instruction. Of special interest is Artspace, an electronic gallery with thumbnail images (linked to larger originals) of computer graphics, photography, acrylics, drawings, and mixed-media art by the school's students and faculty members.

Useful for art; images; schools on the Web.
URL: http://superdec.uni.uiuc.edu/departments/finearts/art/docfiles/arthome.html

Visionary Creation of the Imagination
What will they think up next?

This online gallery — one of the most creative on the Web — contains surrealistic art, including oil paintings and pencil drawings.

Useful for art; images.
URL: http://wwwis.cs.utwente.nl:8080/speelman/

WebLouvre
If you can't visit Paris in person, visit it virtually

This virtual exhibition of artworks from Paris' Louvre museum opened in March 1994 on the World-Wide Web. You can take a short tour of Paris, look at more than 150 of the museum's famous paintings as well as a Medieval art exhibit, and learn more about the Louvre and other museums in Paris.

Useful for art; travel and recreation.
URL: http://mistral.enst.fr/~pioch/louvre/

Commercial

Consumer Information Center
Publications on parenting and learning activities

The Consumer Information Center, part of the U.S. General Services Administration, offers a number of online booklets with helpful information on parenting and learning activities. Some examples: pamphlets with creative ideas to help children develop their artistic skills in theater, writing, music, dance, and the visual arts; a guide that explains how to tell the difference between learning problems and disabilities; and a resource book with worksheets and checklists to help parents and kids plan for college financially and academically. Some texts are available online in their entirety; for others, ordering information is provided. You can order the *CIC Catalog* online as well.

Useful for activities and projects; art; health and social services; parenting; scholarship and college information.
URL: http://www.gsa.gov/staff/pa/cic/cic.htm
E-mail: catalog.pueblo@gsa.gov

Consumer Products Safety Commission
News on hazardous products, recalls

The U.S. Consumer Products Safety Commission (CPSC) offers a variety of online information for consumers. You'll find guidelines on reporting hazardous products, press releases describing hazardous products and recalls from 1990 to the present, and important CPSC announcements.

Useful for consumer information.
URL: gopher://cpsc.gov

EDGAR Dissemination Service
Information on public companies, patents

The Internet EDGAR Dissemination project, designed as a testbed for the informational possibilities of the Internet, provides access to materials filed electronically with the U.S. Securities and Exchange Commission (SEC) by publicly traded companies. The index includes 10-K and dozens of other reports for the current year. At this site, you can also find materials from the U.S. Patent and Trademark Office, the Federal Reserve Board, and the General Services Administration.

Useful for commercial; investments.
URL: http://www.town.hall.org/
E-mail: mail@town.hall.org
To subscribe: majordomo@town.hall.org
Message body: subscribe edgar-daily [your e-mail address]

FinanceNet
Economic data, currency conversion, and financial news

FinanceNet links to financial resources around the World-Wide Web. It includes government economic data (federal, state, local, and international), a currency converter, information on accounting and internal auditing, financial news, and the like. FinanceNet represents the information clearinghouse of the Joint Financial Management Improvement Program, a sponsored organization of the U.S. General Accounting Office.

Useful for investments.
URL: http://www.financenet.gov/wwwlib.htm

Foreign Exchange Rates
Latest currency figures

The Federal Reserve Bank of New York provides its 10 a.m. Eastern time exchange rates for major foreign currencies: the British pound, Canadian dollar,

French franc, German mark, Swiss franc, Japanese yen, Dutch guilder, Belgian franc, Italian lira, Swedish krone, Norwegian krone, and Danish krone.

Useful for consumer information; investments.
URL: gopher://una.hh.lib.umich.edu:70/00/ebb/monetary/tenfx.frb

Insurance Information Institute
Articles on filing claims, home safety, and more

The gopher of the Insurance Information Institute provides a free collection of articles for insurance consumers. Topics covered include filing claims, home safety issues, lowering insurance premiums, and the like. You'll also find information about insurance-related books you can buy.

Useful for consumer information.
URL: gopher://infx.infor.com:4200

Internal Revenue Service (IRS)
Income tax forms and filing information

If you're looking for information about filing your income tax return or need a particular form, you may find it at the Web site set up by the IRS. Using special viewing software (available over the Internet), you can even print out and submit some of these forms to the agency. Answers to many commonly asked questions about filing income tax returns are provided here in hypertext files. If you need further help in filing your return, the site lists phone numbers for IRS offices and other organizations nationwide that provide assistance to the general public, disabled people, senior citizens, and businesses.

Useful for consumer information.
URL: http://www.ustreas.gov/treasury/bureaus/irs/irs.html

Security APL Financial Services
One stop for financial market information

Investment firm Security APL Inc. provides stock market quotes and general market information. You can get the latest quote for a particular stock (updated every 15 minutes), check the current Dow Jones Industrial Average, keep an eye on activity at some of the world's major stock markets and indexes (updated every 3 minutes), monitor the ticker, or view graphs of market activity for the day or over the past 25 years. Quotes are provided by North American Quotations Inc., a Canadian company.

Useful for investments.
URL: http://www.secapl.com/cgi-bin/qs

Small Business Administration (SBA)
For established, aspiring entrepreneurs

If you're interested in starting, financing, or expanding a business, take a look here. The SBA provides contacts and full-text training aids that may be useful to the entrepreneur. You can learn how to write a business plan and find forms for some of the programs the SBA offers to help startups and existing businesses.

Useful for commercial.
URL: http://www.sbaonline.sba.gov

Stocks and Commodities
Links to stock, commodity, economic information

Looking for daily petroleum prices, stock market quotes, even information about national incomes? Here's an extensive set of links to services and information on stocks and commodities, as well as economic news. Some information is delayed and certain services are still experimental, but all appear to be free of charge and available on the Internet. The page is maintained by Federico Brown of Internet Interactive Marketing.

Useful for investments.
URL: http://www.onr.com/stocks.html

Street Cents Online
Consumer and money management advice for teens

Street Cents Online, an offshoot of a weekly Canadian TV program for teenagers, advises young people on managing money and making smart consumer choices. One weekly topic was hair, with such sample topics as how to get the haircut you want at a salon, a look at shampoo ads on TV, and a comparison of hair-coloring products.

Useful for consumer information.
URL: http://www.screen.com/streetcents.html
E-mail: streetcents@screen.com

White Rabbit Toys
Gifts for kids

White Rabbit Toys, a toy store in Ann Arbor, Michigan, specializes in toys that encourage children to create and explore. Its products come from around the world; some examples are Brio from Sweden and Primetime Playthings from the United States. You can order toys from White Rabbit's online catalog, which contains images and descriptions. An online menu even lets you choose the paper you'd like your gift wrapped in.

Useful for consumer information.
URL: http://www.toystore.com/~wrt

Educational issues

Advanced Placement Program
College credit for high-school students

The Advanced Placement (AP) Program, operated by the College Board and Educational Testing Service (ETS), offers a series of examinations that allow high-school students to earn college credit before they matriculate. AP exams — which are generally taken in conjunction with rigorous AP preparation courses — are available in 16 disciplines to students around the world. AP provides background on its programs, test schedules, policies and fees, details on how to subscribe to its discussion lists, and related information.

Useful for scholarshipand college information.
URL: gopher://gopher.ets.org:70/11/ets.tests/collegeb/ap

American Universities
Programs and resources at U.S. institutions

This "home page of home pages" connects you to the Web servers of 145 universities, colleges, and/or departments around the United States, which provide varying amounts of information about their programs and services as well as links to other Internet resources in many disciplines.

Useful for scholarshipand college information.
URL: http://www.clas.ufl.edu/CLAS/american-universities.html

Center for Talented Youth
News about programs for outstanding students

Based at the Johns Hopkins University, the Center for Talented Youth (CTY) offers accelerated academic programs for young people with outstanding ability in writing, mathematics, and other subjects. Offerings include summer programs in a range of subjects for grades 2-12 and writing "tutorials by mail" for grades 6-12. Tuition is generally low, and financial aid is available. The CTY gopher and Web sites give news and updates about the center's programs, talent searches, and other related opportunities. The Web page offers online abstracts of CTY's curriculum and resource materials are available, and you can order the complete documents by mail.

Useful for scholarshipand college information.
URL: http://www.jhu.edu/~gifted

Collection of Links to U.S. Community Colleges
Catalogs, other information

Based at Fayetteville (N.C.) Technical Community College, this gopher site lets you reach the servers of community colleges throughout the United States. Prospective students can learn about course offerings and the admissions process for hundreds of schools.

Useful for scholarshipand college information.
URL: gopher://gopher1.faytech.cc.nc.us:70/11c%3A/ccgofers

College and University Home Pages
Campus information at your fingertips

This Web site provides links to home pages for universities and colleges worldwide. The schools are listed alphabetically as well as by region or state. Entries offer general campus information. Links are also provided to departments within universities or colleges that offer sufficient information about their activities.

Useful for scholarshipand college information.
URL: http://www.mit.edu:8001/people/cdemello/univ.html

College Money Matters
Preparing to pay for that college education

Developed by Signet Bank, this Web site provides information on student loans, answering questions and pointing to sources of financial assistance, from government loans to saving and investing options. *Don't Miss Out* by Robert and Anna Leider is an online guide through the complexities of student financial aid.

Useful for scholarshipand college information.
URL: http://www.infi.net:80/collegemoney/

Consortium for School Networking Discussion List
New resources

COSNDISC is a discussion group sponsored by the Consortium for School Networking (CoSN). It contains announcements of new lists, services, grants, and other developments of interest to educators, as well as calls for help and calls for discussion.

Useful for education; mailing lists (listservs) and newsgroups.
E-mail: cosndisc@list.cren.net
To subscribe: listproc@list.cren.net
Message body: subscribe cosndisc YourFirstName YourLastName

Daily Report Card News Service (RPT CRD)
News about K-12 education

The Daily Report Card News Service is an e-mail bulletin that summarizes news in the world of K-12 education. A service of the Education Commission of the States and the National Education Goals Panel, it is e-mailed to subscribers three times per week. The bulletin includes breaking news, book reviews, reactions, reports on legislative action, and promising practices in education.

Useful for education; mailing lists (listservs) and newsgroups.
URL: gopher://copernicus.bbn.com:70/11/k12/drc
E-mail: RPTCRD@GWUVM.GWU.EDU
To subscribe: listserv@gwuvm.gwu.edu
Message body: Subscribe Rptcrd YourFirstName YourLastName

Early Childhood Education Online (ECEOL-L)
Hints for parents and teachers

Created by a group of early childhood educators, this forum offers a variety of helpful information for parents and teachers. You'll find advice on classroom techniques, along with discussions of such topics as curriculum, discipline, child abuse, and the use of technology in early childhood education. Other resources include bibliographies and reviews of books and articles.

Useful for education; mailing lists (listservs) and newsgroups.
URL: gopher://gopher.cic.net:3005/00/listservs/Early-Childhood-Education
E-mail: ECEOL-L@maine.maine.edu (to participate)

To subscribe: LISTSERV@MAINE.MAINE.EDU
Message body: SUB ECEOL-L YourFirstName YourLastName

EdNet
Issues and resources in education

The EdNet mailing list focuses on issues, projects, news, and resources related to education. The list is supported and maintained by the School of Education at the University of Massachusetts at Amherst.

Useful for education; mailing lists (listservs) and newsgroups.
E-mail: ednet@lists.umass.edu
To subscribe: listserv@lists.umass.edu
Message body: subscribe ednet YourFirstName YourLastName

Education Listservs Archives
Is this the list for you?

Before signing up to receive postings or digests from a lot of different listservs, take a look here. You can read through subscribers' archived messages and information about a variety of education-related discussion groups.

Useful for education; mailing lists (listservs) and newsgroups.
URL: gopher://ericir.syr.edu:70/11/Listservs

Education Program for Gifted Youth (EPGY)
Distance learning for math students

Stanford University's Education Program for Gifted Youth (EPGY) is a special remote educational opportunity for gifted young people (grades 6-9) around the world. Kids can enroll in online courses in higher mathematics, proceeding through the curriculum at their own pace. It's possible for students in their early teens to take calculus and other courses not normally offered in junior high schools (or even in some high schools). The Web page includes background on EPGY and admissions information.

Useful for scholarshipand college information.
URL: http://kanpai.stanford.edu/epgy/pamph/pamph.html
E-mail: alper@epgy.stanford.edu

FEDIX/MOLIS On-Line Information System
Opportunities for minority students

A partnership of 10 federal agencies, led by the U.S. Department of Energy, provides a pair of databases that contain useful information on scholarships and minority opportunities. The Federal Information Exchange (FEDIX) database focuses on minority opportunities and post-graduate research funding available through these agencies. The Minority On-Line Information Service (MOLIS) database details the offerings of nearly 150 minority universities and colleges, including facilities, equipment, course offerings, and scholarships and fellowships.

Useful for scholarshipand college information.
URL: http://web.fie.com/

GiftedNet and Center for Gifted Education
Precollegiate program and forum

The Center for Gifted Education at the College of William and Mary maintains resources and a mailing list on the education of gifted children. You'll find case studies of gifted-education programs, information about research in the field, details about graduate programs in gifted education, information about the center's own program for gifted precollegiate students, and links to related resources.

Useful for scholarship and college information.
URL: gopher://eagle.birds.wm.edu:70/11/SOE/CFGE
E-mail: giftednet-l@listserv.cc.wm.edu
To subscribe: listserver@listserv.cc.wm.edu
Message body: subscribe giftednet-l YourFirstName YourLastName

Global Schoolhouse Project
Interactive projects and mailing lists for students

Funded in part by the National Science Foundation, Global Schoolhouse (GSH) is an experiment in the use of the Internet in K-12 education. GSH sponsors several interactive learning projects — such as e-mail discussions and video conferences linking schools in different cities — each year. Several mailing lists allow teachers to share ideas about integrating GSH projects into classroom activities. On GSH's server, you can learn about current projects and the schools participating in them.

Useful for activities and projects.
URL: http://k12.cnidr.org/gsh/gshwelcome.html

Goals 2000: Educate America Act
Read the legislation for yourself

Want to see where the education system in the United States is supposed to be heading? The U.S. Department of Education provides the full text of the Educate America Act, which was signed into law on March 31, 1994.

Useful for education; law and legal issues.
URL: http://www.ed.gov

International Education and Resource Network (I*EARN)
Online projects

I*EARN allows elementary- and secondary-school students worldwide to collaborate on educational projects using electronic mail, online conferencing, and other telecommunications technologies. The organization focuses on projects that it hopes will make a difference in people's health and welfare, such as electronic newsletters on human rights and the environment, a bilingual study of cultural heroes, and a rain forest preservation project. The network includes over 500 member schools in more than 20 countries, and I*EARN hopes to extend its connections to include service and youth organizations worldwide.

Useful for ecology and the environment.
URL: gopher://gopher.iearn.org:7008/
E-mail: iearn@igc.apc.org

Internet Alaska's K-12 and Homeschool Home Page
School resource pointers

Pointers to online educational resources in Alaska are a highlight of this page from Internet Alaska, an Internet service provider. Maintained by home-schooler Susan Teel, the page offers pointers to Web sites of public and alternative schools in Alaska, as well as to information on the Arctic and related subjects. There's also contact information about home schools in Alaska.

Useful for school resources; schools on the Web.
URL: http://www.alaska.net:80/~steel/

J.K. Lasser's Home Page
A variety of tax information

Presented by the major publisher of personal income tax guides, this server contains tax information alerts and answers to many frequently asked questions about taxes. It links to the Internal Revenue Service's online tax forms and instructions, and offers ordering information for J.K. Lasser's various publications.

Useful for consumer information.
URL: http://www.mcp.com/bookstore/jklasser/jklhome.html

Jon's List of Home Schooling Resources
For those who teach at home

This is a growing list of online and community-based resources for home schoolers, acknowledged by some as the most comprehensive so far on the World-Wide Web. It includes annotations about each resource by Webmaster John Shemitz, as well as instructions as to how to subscribe to mailing lists. Also included are Shemitz' reviews of books, programs, and/or games of interest to parents in general and home-schoolers in particular. Among other links, the Web pages section provides direct access to the home pages of other home schoolers. Another section of links points to documents and online materials offered by government and academic sources.

Useful for school resources.
URL: http://www.armory.com/~jon/hs/HomeSchool.html

Kaplan Educational Center
Get a headstart on college planning

Did you know that East and West Coast college admissions committees prefer SAT results, while those in the Midwest favor the ACT? Kaplan Educational Center, which helps students prepare for the SAT tests, provides tips like this and other information about college entrance exams, such as sample questions and test dates. You can also find suggestions on how to begin planning for college, from choosing a school to securing financial aid.

Useful for scholarshipand college information.
URL: http://www.kaplan.com/etc/precoll/precoll_index.html

Middle School Discussion List (MIDDLE-L)
Targeting needs of adolescents

This discussion group focuses solely on issues in middle-level education and the needs of young adolescents. It is co-owned by the Center for Early Adolescence at the University of North Carolina, Chapel Hill, and the ERIC Clearinghouse on Elementary and Early Childhood Education. Subscribers include teachers, librarians, administrators, and parents.

Useful for mailing lists (listservs) and newsgroups.
URL: gopher://quest.arc.nasa.gov/0/NASAK-12/teacherres/middle/midschool
E-mail: MIDDLE-L@VMD.CSO.UIUC.EDU
To subscribe: listserv@vmd.cso.uiuc.edu
Message body: subscribe middle-l YourFirstName YourLastName

Mind Extension University (ME/U)
Distance education courses for adults

Mind Extension University offers distance education courses to adults who want to earn college credit or pursue a degree from home. This site provides information about ME/U, the programs it provides in conjunction with more than 30 universities nationwide (such as George Washington and California State), and the Education Channel, the cable TV network on which its courses are broadcast.

Useful for adult, continuing and distance education; educational TV and radio.
URL: http://www.meu.edu/

National 4-H Collection of Reviewed Curricula
Detailed activity guides

The server of the U.S. Department of Agriculture provides information about the curriculum of 4-H, an agricultural organization for young people. You can read about the theory behind 4-H educational programs and learn how to receive detailed activity guides.

Useful for agriculture.
URL: gopher://cyfer.esusda.gov:70/11/CYFER-net/jury/curricula

National Center for Education Statistics (NCES)
Information on schooling

The National Center for Education Statistics, a bureau of the U.S. Department of Education, offers a variety of data about K-12 education on the national, state, and local levels. You'll find reports and statistics on dropout rates, school staffing, teacher demographics, household education levels, private schools, and so on.

Useful for education; reference.
URL: gopher://gopher.ed.gov:10000

National Diffusion Network (NDN)
Hands-on science projects

Funded by the U.S. Department of Education, the National Diffusion Network (NDN) publicizes curricula and programs that have proved successful in K-12 education. On this gopher, you can read the complete catalog of NDN programs, which includes materials in every traditional academic subject and many non-traditional ones as well. Some examples: hands-on science projects for elementary students, high-school physics projects that relate concepts to students' lives, and programs for kids with special needs (learning-disabled, gifted, at-risk). The gopher also provides information about adopting an NDN program in a public or private school.

Useful for school resources.
URL: gopher://gopher.ed.gov/1/programs/NDN

National Distance Learning Center (NDLC) Database
Free learning materials

The National Distance Learning Center (NDLC), based at the University of Kentucky's Owensboro Community College and supported by federal funds, operates this free electronic clearinghouse of learning materials. Of particular interest are its listings for distance learning and correspondence courses, supplementary learning materials for K-12 students, and educational materials offered by the National Parks Service. You can enter a subject or audience that interests you and receive a detailed list of matching resources.

Useful for adult, continuing and distance education; education.
URL: gopher://ndlc.occ.uky.edu

Network Nuggets
News and tips on finding network resources

The Network Nuggets mailing list, part of the British Columbia (Canada) Community Learning Network, offers news and suggestions about finding educational resources on the Internet. Updates are e-mailed each day during the school year, and participants are encouraged to reply with their opinions. The listserv is inactive during the summer. Nuggets are archived and may be searched by keyword.

Useful for mailing lists (listservs) and newsgroups.
URL: gopher://cln.etc.bc.ca:70/11/arcs/nugs
E-mail: network_nuggets-l@cln.etc.bc.ca
To subscribe: listserv@cln.etc.bc.ca
Message body: sub network_nuggets-l YourFirstName YourLastName

Northwest Regional Educational Laboratory (NWREL)
For families, schools

The Northwest Regional Educational Laboratory's (NWREL) evolving server provides a means for educators and researchers in the Pacific Northwest to share information about promising practices and resources. offers an evolving source of information on educational issues, networking Much of the content has been developed by NWREL and the national network of Regional Educational Laboratories and Research Centers. For example, there are links to materials and resources dealing with family issues, drug-free schools and communities, education and work, Indian education, and regional services.

Useful for education; health and social services.
URL: http://www.nwrel.org/

NOVAE Group: Teachers Networking for the Future
Bulletin of pointers

The NOVAE Group is a listserv hosted by the University of Idaho. While its content is primarily aimed at educators, it will point anyone looking for sources of educational material on the Internet in the right direction. E-mailed weekly to subscribers, it comes in the form of a bulletin, and is not a forum for discussion.

Useful for mailing lists (listservs) and newsgroups.
URL: gopher://gopher.cic.net:3005/00/listservs/novae
E-mail: c6460101@idptv.idbsu.edu
To subscribe: Majordomo@uidaho.edu
Message body: subscribe novae (Complete E-mail Address)

NSF Young Scholars
Science camps and classes for high-school students

The Oregon Museum of Science & Industry (OMSI) sponsors a Young Scholars Program with funding from the National Science Foundation. Activities include science camps for teams of high-school students and outdoor science classes for elementary students. The OMSI Web page offers information about these programs.

Useful for scholarship and college information.
URL: http://davinci.vancouver.wsu.edu:80/omsi/omsiys.html

Oak Ridge National Laboratory (ORNL)
Classes, other programs for kids

On the educational server of the U.S. Department of Energy's Oak Ridge National Laboratory (ORNL), you'll find information about the Laboratory's educational programs for K-12 students. These include a series of one-day science classes for kids of various grade levels (offered at ORNL's facility in Oak Ridge, Tenn., or at schools in the area) and a summer research program for economically disadvantaged high-school students.

Useful for scholarship and college information.
URL: http://www.ornl.gov/schools.html

Outreach and Technical Assistance Network
Adult education, parenting help

California's state-funded Outreach and Technical Assistance Network (OTAN) offers a variety of materials for adult education. These include curricular resources in such subjects as elementary- and high-school skills, English as a second language, handicapped education, home economics, parent education, older adult education, and workplace literacy. Other materials include articles, legislative information, an events calendar, demo software, information about grants and funding, and links to related servers.

Useful for adult, continuing and distance education.
URL: gopher://gopher.hlpusd.k12.ca.us

PluggedIn
Kids use technology to tell their stories

Plugged In, a non-profit organization in East Palo Alto, Calif., offers technology-related activities to children from low-income families. Its home page describes some of the projects the group is working on with local youngsters, and in some cases shows examples of their work: video documentaries, computer slide shows, and multimedia self-portraits. The page gives information about how other kids can contribute their own artwork to these projects.

Useful for education; health and social services; Internet and computing.
URL: http://www.pluggedin.org/
E-mail: webmaster@pluggedin.org

Publications for Parents/Helping Your Child Series
Pamphlets on kids, school

Publications for Parents contains online versions of the *Helping Your Child Series*, pamphlets published by the Office of Educational Research and Improvement of the U.S. Department of Education. These include suggestions on helping your child to get ready for school, learn to read and write. and do well in various subjects.

Useful for education; parenting.
URL: http://www.ed.gov/pubs/parents/

Quality of Education Listserv (BGEDU-L)
Forum for parents, teachers

This discussion group is a forum for parents, teachers, administrators and students concerned with issues related to the quality of education. Although intended to focus on educational issues in Kentucky (BGEDU supposedly is an abbreviation for Bluegrass Educators), the discussions tend to be much broader. Topics include curricula, grading policies, and cultural diversity. You'll also find news about conferences and programs in the field of education. The archives are searchable by keyword.

Useful for mailing lists (listservs) and newsgroups.
URL: gopher://gopher.cic.net:3005/00/listservs/Quality-in-Education
E-mail: BGEDU-L@UKCC.BITNET
To subscribe: LISTSERV@UKCC.UKY.EDU
Message body: SUB BGEDU-L YourFirstName YourLastName

Queen's University Entrance Scholarships
Aid for college-bound students

Provided here is information about more than one dozen different types of scholarships available to high-school graduates and freshmen at Queen's. This is is just one selection from a larger directory of scholarships, prizes, and awards available at this university in Kingston, Ontario, which is considered to be among Canada's Ivy League.

Useful for scholarshipand college information.
URL: gopher://gopher.queensu.ca

Research for Better Schools (RBS)
Learn how others have succeeded

Research for Better Schools (RBS) is a nonprofit corporation providing educational development services for K-12 schools in the Mid-Atlantic region, with a particular focus on science, mathematics, and technology. The RBS server includes information about successful programs and practices in education, background on RBS, and links to other online educational resources.

Useful for education; science.
URL: gopher://gopher.rbs.org
E-mail: inquiry@rbs.org

Scholarship Foundation of America, Inc.
Opportunities for gifted students

Scholarship Foundation of America is a nonprofit organization that recognizes outstanding performance among high-school and college students. You can learn about the foundation's scholarship criteria, recipients, benefactors and special projects, as well as complete an application form online.

Useful for scholarshipand college information.
URL: http://cen.cenet.com/sfa/sfahome.html

Study Tips: 20 Ways to Get the Most Out of Now
Learning better study habits

Provided by Estrella Mountain Community College Center, these tips were written for college students. But guidance on when and how to study, controlling distractions and what to do when you get stuck should be equally valuable to high-school students.

Useful for education; reference.
URL: http://www.emc.maricopa.edu/Student.Success.Guide/studytips.html

Talent Identification Program (TIP)
Programs for exceptional students

Duke University's Talent Identification Program (TIP) is focused on the educational needs of talented young people in grades 7 to 12. TIP offers several programs for bright students around the world, including a "talent search" for seventh-graders in 16 southeastern states, summer programs on the Duke campus, and mentor programs around the country. On the TIP server, you'll find background information about these programs, a directory of additional programs for gifted students, an informational booklet about selecting and applying to colleges, and supporting materials for TIP participants.

Useful for scholarshipand college information.
URL: gopher://arnold.tip.duke.edu

Teel Homeschool Page
Information, activities teach about Alaska

Maintained by Susan Teel, who is home-schooling her three children, this page offers a range of information, from the family's software reviews, to information and images of Alaska, to activities kids can do at home. For example, there are instructions and diagrams on how to make a polar bear cub puppet; and a wintertime curriculum featuring hands-on activities to learn about Eskimo art and how various animals deal with the coldest season.

Useful for activities and projects.
URL: http://www.alaska.net:80/~mteel/homesch/homeschl.html

U.S. Department of Education (ED)
Statistics, suggestions for parents, teachers

The U.S. Department of Education (ED) offers a variety of information for parents, teachers, and researchers. You can read about ED's programs and goals, or browse and download a variety of publications, including ED's *Helping Your Child* series and an article that suggests actions which parents, schools, and communities can take to improve the educational experience for their children. The site also offers statistics, research results, calendars of events, and links to state departments of education and other educational resources. Users can order and receive documents by subscribing through an electronic mail server to the department's catalog, and search some of ED's databases to find a particular document.

Useful for education; school resources.
URL: http://www.ed.gov/
To subscribe: almanac@inet.ed.gov
Message body: send catalog (do not use a signature block)

Woods Hole Oceanographic Institution Guest Students
Study opportunities

The Woods Hole Oceanographic Institution, the largest independent marine-science research institution in the United States, offers a limited number of volunteer positions in its laboratories for high-school and college students. The Woods Hole server provides more information about these opportunities and its research programs.

Useful for scholarshipand college information.
URL: http://www.whoi.edu/whoi/whoi-ed.html#TrainMin

Year-Round Schooling Issues
Hot topics in education

This annotated bibliography from the British Columbia Teachers' Federation (BCTF) focuses on year-round schooling and its effects on kids, school districts, teachers, and families. You'll learn about studies, position papers, and related information available on what the BCTF considers a "hot topic" in the field of education.

Useful for education.
URL: gopher://sun.bctf.bc.ca:70/00/hot-issues/key-issues/yr-schools/yrrndschl

Entertainment

Calvin and Hobbes Home Page
On the lighter side

Bill Watterson's comic strip characters Calvin and Hobbes have their own following in cyberspace, including this page on the Web from Justin Higuchi, an engineering student at the University of Hawaii. You can view a collection of single- and multipanel color and black-and-white strips, plus link to newsgroups, FTP sites, and other Web pages that feature this duo.

Useful for entertainment; images.
URL: http://www.eng.hawaii.edu/Contribs/justin/Archive/Index.html

Children's Page Wooden Toy Exhibition
Pictures from when Grandpa was a kid

Images of wooden toys built in the past century will interest the young and young at heart who visit the Children's Page from Italy. From this page, you also can connect to some other resources from around the world for kids.

Useful for entertainment; images.
URL: http://www.pd.astro.it/local-cgi-bin/kids.cgi/forms

Crime Scene Evidence File
Who did it?

This home page is a non-linear, interactive story. As more people visit, this whodunnit will continue to grow.
URL: http://www.olemiss.edu/~tatca/crime.html

Cybersight Enigma
Put a puzzle together on your computer screen

Older kids and adults can sort the pieces of a puzzle onscreen to create a complete picture. There are 16 pieces to each puzzle, and by clicking on any single piece, you can see what the finished image should look like. You move the pieces about by clicking on corresponding checkboxes below the puzzle, which was created by Internet Marketing, a developer of online promotional software.

Useful for activities and projects.
URL: http://cybersight.com/cgi-bin/cs/puzzle?image=skysurf&order=random

Disney Parks
If you're planning to visit ...

Anyone planning a trip to a Disneyland, Walt Disney World, Tokyo Disneyland or EuroDisney may want to stop here before seeing a travel agent. This unofficial page—one of several created by Disney fan Doug Krause—provides park maps, operating schedules, Disney "passport" prices and blackout dates, maps, restaurants, even restroom locations. If your plans fall through, you can at least connect to other pages about Disney films and memorabilia from here.

Useful for travel and recreation.
URL: http://www.best.com/~dijon/disney/parks/

Dr. Fun and Other Cartoons
From homegrown to high-profile "funnies"

From Dr. Fun's creations (a daily Internet series drawn by Dave Farley, whose day job is in computing at the University of Chicago library) to computer cartoons and the popular *Dilbert* series, these pages have a laugh for just about everyone. To get the most out of the Dr. Fun pages, you need a graphical Web browser.

Useful for images.
URL: http://alpha.acast.nova.edu/fun/cartoons.html

Electric Postcard
Surprise someone special!

Pick a postcard from the selection on the rack, then jot a few lines on the "back", and e-mail it. Make sure, of course, that the recipient can both receive the e-mail notice that a postcard has arrived and claim it at this Web site. The Electric Postcard was designed and is maintained by Judith Donath of Massachusetts Institute of Technology's Media Lab.

Useful for travel and recreation.
URL: http://postcards.www.media.mit.edu/Postcards/

Froggy Page
A prince of a page

Sandra Loosemore—a computer scientist at Yale University who prefers the alias Dr. Frog—shares her lifelong fascination with frogs and froggy things with everyone in cyberspace. If it's on the Internet and focuses on frogs, then there's probably a link to it from this home page: images, clip art, sounds, fables, songs, information about "Famous Frogs", scientific research on amphibians, even how to make an origami frog.

Useful for biology.
URL: http://www.cs.yale.edu/HTML/YALE/CS/HyPlans/loosemore-sandra/froggy.html

Games Domain
Board games, card games, role-playing games, computer games

This U.K.-based server offers materials about all sorts of games—board games, card games, role-playing games, and computer games. You can reach games-related home pages, and the frequently asked questions and answers of dozens of newsgroups, download computer games, find tips on playing some of the more popular computer games, read gaming periodicals, and link to the home pages of commercial games publishers.

Useful for entertainment; travel and recreation.
URL: http://wcl-rs.bham.ac.uk/GamesDomain

Global Show-n-Tell
Kids show off projects and possessions

Show-'n'-tell is no longer confined to the classroom. It's online, too. Through a page of links to other online sites, Global Show-n-Tell lets kids around the world show off their prized projects and possessions. Submissions include drawings, paintings, photos and stories by children from age 5 to 15. The exhibition is free, and is sponsored by Telenaut Communications and ManyMedia.

Useful for activities and projects; images.
URL: http://emma.manymedia.com:80/show-n-tell/
E-mail: show-n-tell@manymedia.com

Interactive WWW Games List
From Tic Tac Toe to puzzles

This collection of interactive games ranges from *Tic Tac Toe* and *Hangman* to brain teasers and puzzles for users with different levels of expertise. Some were developed by the list's compiler Marcel van der Laan, an electrical engineering student at Delft University of Technology in The Netherlands. Links take you to other lists of games on the Internet as well.

Useful for activities and projects.
URL: http://einstein.et.tudelft.nl/~mvdlaan/texts/www_games.html

LEGO Information
Projects and games to play at home

Stumped for something to do with your youngster on a rainy day? Try this page of pictures of LEGO projects you might try at home as well as games you can play with LEGO sets. Kids are encouraged to submit pictures of their own LEGO creations. This site is not connected with the manufacturer of LEGO toys.

Useful for activities and projects; entertainment.
URL: http://legowww.homepages.com/

Mr. Potato Head
Change his face with a click of the mouse

Little ones—and maybe some big ones, too—will enjoy this. By clicking on a series of buttons on your screen, you can gradually build different versions of Mr.

Potato Head. There are several options for each feature—ears, nose, mouth, feet and so on—so you can create a different image each time.

Useful for activities and projects.
URL: http://winnie.acsu.buffalo.edu/cgi-bin/potatoe

rec.puzzles Archive
Answers clear up some mysterious questions

This Usenet newsgroup archive contains files of questions and answers about puzzles in a variety of subjects. Here's where you can find out how telephone area codes are assigned to different regions, and about some unusual coincidences in history.

Useful for activities and projects.
URL: http://archives.math.utk.edu/

Theodore's Tugboat Online Activity Center
For the youngest "Internauts"

Theodore Tugboat is a Canadian children's TV series about a "cheerful tugboat and his many floating friends". In the activity center, provided by the show's producer Cochran Entertainment Inc., little ones can read an illustrated interactive story, download pages for coloring, or send an e-mail request for a postcard of Theodore. From here you can also link to other sites for children, researched and rated by Cochran's Net Navigator Berit Erickson. His finds are also available through the show's electronic-mailing list.

Useful for activities and projects; educational TV and radio; mailing lists (listservs) and newsgroups.
URL: http://www.cochran.com/tt.html
E-mail: theodore@cochran.com

Family life

Bringing Up Baby
Short articles address often worrisome questions

Bringing Up Baby is a collection of short articles on topics ranging from sibling conflict to guns as toys. It is taken from a weekly child-rearing question-and-answer column written by Martha Erickson, director of the Children, Youth, and Family Consortium at the University of Minnesota.

Useful for health and social services; parenting.
URL: gopher://tinman.mes.umn.edu.:80/11/Resources/Children/ShortArticles/BringingUpBaby

City University INROADS
Pursue a degree online

City University's Information Resource and Online Academic Degree System (INROADS) enables students to select, enroll in, and complete courses via the Internet. The university, located in Renton, Wash., offers its Master's in Business

Administration program online, and plans to add a graduate program in teaching and an undergraduate program in computer science.
URL: http://www.cityu.edu/inroads/welcome.html

Conclusion Brochures from Access ERIC
Answers to parents' common questions

Access ERIC, at the U.S. Department of Education's Office of Educational Research and Improvement, has answers to many common questions and concerns raised by parents about their children's education. These concise online articles are based on professional research, and cover topics ranging from what should kids be learning in kindergarten to why many of them don't like math. The articles provide practical ideas and tips on how parents can support the learning process and help their kids become better students.

Useful for education; parenting.
URL: gopher://gopher.ed.gov:70/11/programs/ERIC/ACCESS

Family World (formerly Family Times Online)
Calendars of events, articles

The Family World Web page is a cooperative effort of 30 parenting publications from around the world. It features the combined activity calendars of all participating publications, which may help parents to find family-oriented events in a city they plan to visit. In addition, Family World features articles of interest to everyone in the family, such as: how to cope with chicken pox; how to prevent unintentional poisoning; an explanation of the Entertainment Software Rating System; new medical CD-ROM reviews; how to help your child deal with stress and divorce; and tips on cooking and cycling. From this site, you can reach a variety of other parenting resources on the Internet.

Useful for consumer information; health and social services; parenting; travel and recreation.
URL: http://www.family.com/

FatherNet
Discussion focuses on men's roles in children's lives

FatherNet, a mailing list with a gopher archive, focuses on relationships between men and children. The gopher includes the proceedings of the 1994 conference Family Reunion III: The Role of Men in Children's Lives, as well as related documents addressing social and economic factors affecting men's roles in the lives of children. On the mailing list, you'll find continuing discussion of these issues.

Useful for health and social services; parenting.
URL: gopher://tinman.mes.umn.edu.:80/11/FatherNet
E-mail: cyfstaff@maroon.tc.umn.edu
To subscribe: father@tinman.mes.umn.edu
Message body: Any message
Enter in subject line: (lower case) directory title of discussion topic

Information about Older Children (8-14)
Answers on homework, responsibility

Presented by the National Parent Information Network, this collection of articles addresses questions faced by parents of children ages 8 through 14. Topics include the importance of homework, discipline, teaching kids citizenship and responsibility, and answering questions about sex and drugs.

Useful for education; health and social services; parenting.
URL: gopher://gopher.prairienet.org:70/11/education/eric/npin/
esp.for.parents/older

Information about Teens (14-20)
Parents' concerns about older teens addressed

This collection of articles, provided by the National Parent Information Network, addresses the concerns of parents of teenagers ages 14 through 20. The folder included articles on preventing drug use by teenagers, divorce, and choosing a community college.

Useful for education; health and social services; parenting; scholarshipand college information.
URL: gopher://gopher.prairienet.org:70/11/education/eric/npin/
esp.for.parents/teens

Information about Young Children (birth-8)
Articles on diet, preschool, TV

The National Parent Information Network offers this collection of articles addressing common concerns for parents of infants and young children through age 8. Among the topics, you'll find selections on diet, choosing a preschool, separation anxiety, discipline, self-esteem, adopted children, divorce, assessing child development, and monitoring TV viewing.

Useful for education; health and social services; parenting.
URL: gopher://gopher.prairienet.org:70/11/education/eric/npin/esp.for.parents/early

MetroLine Freebies List
Home safety tips, booklists and other literature at no cost

The MetroLine Freebies List, from the Minnesota MetroNet BBS, is a bibliography of free literature, much of which will be of interest to parents, kids, and K-12 educators. Some examples are home safety tips, materials for the handicapped, book lists for teenagers, and information about resources for minorities.

Useful for health and social services.
URL: gopher://vega.lib.ncsu.edu:70/0ftp%3asunsite.unc.edu%40/pub/docs/about-the-net/libsoft/freebies.txt

National Parent Information Network (NPIN)
Advice in childhood development

The National Parent Information Network (NPIN) is a developing network for parents. Ultimately, its developers hope to offer links to a wide range of resources that provide advice in such areas as childhood development, education, health, and family life (some of which this guide points to directly elsewhere). At press time, NPIN connected to such resources as Parent News, Parents AskERIC (and other ERIC resources), and information from the National Urban League and National PTA. NPIN is a pilot project of the federally funded Education Resources Information Center (ERIC), which offers an extensive body of resources related to education.

Useful for education; health and social services.
URL: http://www.prairienet.org/htmls/eric/npin/npinhome.html

Parenting Pages: Answers & Actions on Child Raising
Tips for trying times

Parenting Pages contains more than 50 concise articles to help parents through difficult patches in child-rearing, as well as pointers to books and videos on parenting issues. Provided by the Help the Children organization, they are written by social workers, psychologists, teachers and other professionals who work with children. Topics range from negotiating food battles and baby-proofing your home to parent-teacher conferences and bedtime problems.

Useful for health and social services; parenting.
URL: http://www.cursci.com:80/parenting/

Parents AskERIC
Specialized service answers questions about kids and education

Parents AskERIC, a service of the Educational Resources Information Center (ERIC) Clearinghouse on Elementary and Early Childhood Education, offers information specifically for parents. You can access a wide range of literature relating to childhood development and education, and subscribe to several mailing lists that discuss topics relevant to early childhood and middle-school education. The AskERIC staff at the University of Illinois, Urbana-Champaign, will also answer your questions via e-mail, usually within 48 hours. You can query them about the education, care, and development of children from birth to early adolescence.

Useful for education; health and social services; mailing lists (listservs) and newsgroups; online "tutors".
URL: http://www.prairienet.org/htmls/eric/npin/paskeric.html
E-mail: askeric@ericir.syr.edu

Parents Helping Parents
Resources for children with special needs

Health and education information to help kids with special needs is the focus of this Web site. You can search an online human services resource directory from Parents Helping Parents, a nonprofit group. A collection of files and direct links also lead to sources of other disability information on the Internet, including newsgroups, gophers and Web pages.

Useful for disabilities; health and social services.
URL: http://www.portal.com/~cbntmkr/php.html

ParentsPlace
Products and services for kids

ParentsPlace is a resource center for parents on the Web. It offers an online mall with links to retailers who specialize in products for children (such as diapers and strollers); annotations and excerpts of books on parenting and kids; "chat rooms" through which parents can communicate with each other; and a classified section in which child-related products and services are advertised.
URL: http://www.parentsplace.com/

Resources for Parent Educators
Information about parents' involvement in schools

This folder on the National Parent Information Network server contains information about organizations and programs for parents involved in their kids' education. You'll also find articles here about such topics as parents' involvement in schools, and initiatives by various states to improve communications between schools and homes.

Useful for school resources.
URL: http://www.prairienet.org/htmls/eric/npin/resources.html

U.S. Postal Service
Prices and procedures for moving the mail

If you need complete 1995 postal rate tables, tips on making sure your mail moves with you to a new address, or the history of the Post Office, look no farther. This Web site contains the full text of press releases and booklets about Post Office products and services, and ordering instructions for other Post Office information useful to consumers and businesses.

Useful for consumer information.
URL: http://www.usps.gov/

Food

CheeseNet
Sink your teeth into this!

This Web site devoted to cheese includes background articles on the history of cheese-making as well as descriptions of the wide variety of cheeses.

Useful for food.
URL: http://www.efn.org/~kpw/cheesenet.html

Health and social services

Administration for Children & Families (ACE)
Fact sheets on aid programs

On its Administration for Children and Families server, the U.S. Department of Health and Human Services provides information about programs for low-income, at-risk, refugee, and other households that may require government assistance. You'll find fact sheets covering medical, educational, employment, and financial aid programs.

Useful for health and social services.
URL: gopher://gopher.acf.dhhs.gov/

Adoptees Mailing List
Moderated forum lets adoptees speak openly to one another

The Adoptees Mailing List is a moderated forum with fairly strict ground rules as to who may participate and what may be discussed. Its administrator, Jeff Hartung, founded the list to allow adoptees to talk more freely among themselves, and as an alternative for those uncomfortable with responding in the more public newsgroup forums. Through the Web page, he also provides information and links to other adoption-related resources on the Internet, such as information on legal issues, genealogy, subscribing to newsgroups and mailing lists, and bibliographies.

Useful for adoption; mailing lists (listservs) and newsgroups.
URL: http://psy.ucsd.edu:80/jhartung/adoptees.html
E-mail: hartung@crl.ucsd.edu
To subscribe: listserv@ucsd.edu
Message body: sub adoptees

AdoptINFO
Studies, reviews and other literature on adoption

AdoptINFO provides research-based information about adoption. This includes a bibliography, literature reviews, an online version of the *National Adoption Information Clearinghouse Publications and Services Catalog*, a study titled *Growing Up Adopted*; and other files and links to adoption resources.

Useful for adoption; health and social services.
URL: gopher://tinman.mes.umn.edu.:80/11/Resources/AdoptINFO

Adoption Information Exchange
Resources for families in Washington state

The Adoption Information Service is an adoption information and referral service that provides information to families in Washington state. Its Exchange List describes resources available in the state.
URL: http://www.halcyon.com/adoption/

AdoptioNetwork
Pointers and links for people interested in adoption

AdoptioNetwork is a page of pointers and Internet links to specific information useful to people interested in adoption, such as birthparents, current and prospective adoptive parents, adoptees, and support-service professionals. Included here are the names and phone numbers of local government and private adoption agencies, attorneys, support groups, Internet newsgroups, national adoption organizations and various publications. The AdoptioNetwork is a volunteer organization formed by adoptive parents in the Washington, D.C., area.

Useful for adoption; health and social services.
URL: http://www.infi.net:80/adopt/

Alternative Learning Strategies for the Physically Handicapped Listserv (ALTLEARN)
Discussions focus on helping disabled students

This discussion group focuses on alternative learning strategies, especially for physically handicapped students. Topics include cooperative education, grading, and technologies for the handicapped.

Useful for mailing lists (listservs) and newsgroups.
URL: gopher://gopher.cic.net/0/cicnet-gophers/k12-gopher/listservs/ALT-Learning-Strategies
E-mail: ALTLEARN@SJUVM.BITNET LIST
To subscribe: LISTSERV@SJUVM.BITNET

Childhood Vaccinations FAQ
Find out about preventive measures

This online document focuses on frequently asked questions (FAQs) about childhood vaccinations, drawing on information found in pediatric textbooks. Specific sections focus on vaccines which are not on the required schedule for children within the United States, such as travel vaccines, vaccines which are not yet approved for use, and vaccines which, in the United States are given only to those with certain risk factors. Entries include a description of the disease, its risk factors, and how common it is, as well as a description of the vaccine, its risk factors and the circumstances under which it is recommended. The FAQ is maintained by Lynn Diana Gazis.

Useful for health and social services.
URL: gopher://sol.csd.unb.ca:70/00/FAQ/misc/news.answers.00182VacP3

Children Youth Family Education Research Network
For at-risk families

The Children, Youth, and Family Education Research Network (CYFERNet) offers information about four national networks focused on improving the prospects of at-risk families. The networks—Child Care, Family Resiliency, Science and Technology, and Collaborations—are headed by university faculty nationwide. CYFERNet provides information about the projects and participants of these four networks, details about 95 federally funded Youth At Risk (YAR) programs nationwide, an events calendar for the networks, and articles on a variety of social issues. It also operates an electronic discussion group on children, youth and family issues. CYFERNet is a joint project of the Cooperative Extension System, the U.S. Department of Agriculture, and the National 4-H Council.

Useful for education; health and social services; mailing lists (listservs) and newsgroups; parenting.
URL: gopher://gopher-cyfernet.mes.umn.edu
E-mail: cyf-l@vm1.spcs.umn.edu
To subscribe: LISTSERV@vm1.spcs.umn.edu
Message body: subscribe cyf-l YourUserid YourName

Children, Youth, and Family Consortium
Policies, programs affecting families

The Children, Youth, and Family Consortium is an organization focused on health, education, and social policy issues affecting children and families in Minnesota. Its Consortium Electronic Clearinghouse (CEC), available via gopher or e-mail, includes articles on social issues, news about upcoming consortium events, and information about Minnesota social programs, much of which families elsewhere will find informative. The consortium also offers an interactive bulletin board, like a mailing list, that allows users to pose questions, offer ideas, and respond to the comments of others.

Useful for education; health and social services; mailing lists (listservs) and newsgroups; parenting.
URL: gopher://tinman.mes.umn.edu.:80/11/IntroHlp/Consortium
E-mail: cyf-l@vm1.spcs.umn.edu
To subscribe: LISTSERV@vm1.spcs.umn.edu
Message body: subscribe cyf-l YourE-mailAddress YourName

Cornucopia of Disability Information (CODI)
Resources from around the world

Based at the State University of New York (SUNY) at Buffalo, the Cornucopia of Disability Information (CODI) server offers resources for local and international audiences alike. It provides medical information about a variety of disabilities, government documents, information about technology for the disabled, sources of legal assistance, employment information, a TDD phone directory, lists of services for the disabled in the Buffalo area, and lists of other Internet resources on disabilities. You can search all CODI resources by keyword.

Useful for disabilities; health and social services.
URL: gopher://val-dor.cc.buffalo.edu

Deaf Education
Resources and strategies for parents and teachers

Based at Kent State University, the Deaf Education gopher focuses on the learning needs of children who are deaf or hard of hearing. It includes resources and instructional strategies for teachers and parents, materials for deaf people, news, a list of addresses and contacts in the field of deaf education, a list of students who want to correspond with the deaf, and links to related servers and mailing lists.

Useful for disabilities; education; mailing lists (listservs) and newsgroups; pen pals.
URL: gopher://gopher.educ.kent.edu:70/11/edgophers/special/deafed

Disability and Rehabilitation Resources
Mailing lists, archives and more

This server at St. John's University offers a wide range of resources on disabilities and rehabilitation, including archives of special education mailing lists, information about repetitive strain injury and chronic fatigue syndrome, and a link to the Parkinson's Disease Information Exchange Network.

Useful for disabilities; health and social services.
URL: gopher://SJUVM.STJOHNS.EDU:70/11/disabled

Disability Resources, Products, Services and Communication
Tips and magazines, with more to come

Still in its infancy, this site hopes to offer a comprehensive listing of and direct links to disability-related resources on the Internet. Currently you can get free disability "tips" and a free copy of a disability magazine. A link to the Disability Mall lets you view images of products and request further information by e-mail about disability services. Disability Resources, Products, Services and Communication is sponsored by Evan Kemp Associates, a company managed by people with disabilities which provides information, products and services to people with disabilities.

Useful for consumer information; disabilities; health and social services.
URL: http://disability.com

E-Clips, Access Foundation
Clippings give information for people with disabilities

E-Clips, from the nonprofit Access Foundation, provides a free online newsletter containing "clippings" with information about products and services for people with disabilities. Information is gleaned from product and service providers as well as users. Readers can contact the source for details about the item (clothing, tools, computer aids, literature and so forth) mentioned in *E-Clips.* A related "newsletter," *Kid-Clips*—for parents, teachers and others working with children who have disabilities—is also available for a nominal fee. In addition, information is available on diskette.

Useful for consumer information; disabilities; health and social services; mailing lists (listservs) and newsgroups.
URL: gopher://SJUVM.STJOHNS.EDU:2070/00/listserv/list%24erv/Access%20E-Clips%20Distribution%20List
To subscribe: danyaon@savvy.com
Message body: YourFirstName YourLastName
Enter in subject line: Subscribe FREE: E-Clips

Facts for Families
Psychiatric disorders in children and teens explained

Facts for Families is a series of 46 information sheets explaining psychiatric disorders affecting children and adolescents. These short, hypertext documents from the American Academy of Child and Adolescent Psychiatry are designed for parents and other family members. The wide range of topics covered include the depressed child, children who won't go to school, stepfamily problems, and family moves.

Useful for health and social services.
URL: http://www.med.umich.edu/aacap/facts.index.html

Fire Safety Tips and News
Handouts on fire prevention

The South County Fire Authority, of San Carlos, Calif., provides electronic handouts on fire prevention information at its home page. While information on "Preventing a Wildland Fire from Destroying Your Home" may not apply to everyone, tips on "What We Can All Do For Fire Safety" may.

Useful for health and social services.
URL: http://www.abag.ca.gov:80/abag/local_gov/city/san_carlos/fire/firedept.html

Healthline
Issues of interest to older students

Through the Healthline server, the University of Montana's Student Health Services offers a variety of information about physical and mental health, focusing on issues of interest to college-age students — sexuality, drugs and alcohol, diet, and the like. Through links, you can also reach health-related Usenet newsgroups, government agency gophers, resources for the disabled, and other materials.

Useful for health and social services.
URL: gopher://selway.umt.edu:700

Internet Adoption Photolisting
Pictures of children, pointers on raising them

This is a photolisting of children available for international adoption as well as a collection of adoption information and links to other sites for adoptive parents. It includes descriptions of books which deal with topics ranging from infertility to raising adopted children to dealing with behavioral problems.
URL: http://www.gems.com/adoption/http://www.gems.com/adoption/

Medical Matrix
Resources to deal with specific health issues

Medical Matrix is a hypertext document that describes — and, in some cases, links to — easily accessible online resources for physicians and health-care workers. Laypeople may find it helpful in locating electronic mailing lists and other Internet resources dealing with specific diseases, health issues and problems, such as cystic fibrosis and long-term care. Compiled by family physician Dr. Gary Malet and education technologist Lee Hancock, the entries are based on Hancock's more comprehensive *Health Sciences Resources List*. Information is categorized by disease and specialty.

Useful for health and social services.
URL: http://kuhttp.cc.ukans.edu/cwis/units/medcntr/Lee/HOMEPAGE.HTML

Medical Resources on the Internet
List leads to documents and discussion groups

This directory, housed on Stanford's Center for Advanced Medical Informatics server, is a good starting point if you're looking for medical information. You can search online medical resources, and find descriptions and addresses for gophers, libraries, mailing lists, electronic journals, online databases, FTP sites, and other Internet sites related to medicine. The information was compiled by Lee Hancock of the University of Kansas Medical Center.

Useful for health and social services.
URL: gopher://camis.stanford.edu/1/bio/Online_Med_Resources

Missing Children Database
Pictures, files and how to report information

This database, maintained by the National Center for Missing and Exploited Children (NCMEC), contains information about and pictures of children who are missing. The page provides a link to the Heidi Search Center files as well as a hotline number for reporting information about missing children. It is provided as a public service by Maxwell Labs.

Useful for health and social services.
URL: http://www.scubed.com:8001/public_service/missing.html

National Institutes of Health (NIH) Information Index
Quick leads

The National Institutes of Health (NIH) Information Index refers you to information about diseases being investigated by NIH or NIH-supported research projects. By querying the database with a keyword, you can find a contact NIH agency and phone number which can provide further information. For example, a search for information about measles turns up contact names and phone numbers for details about measles, German measles and measles encephalitis.

Useful for health and social services.
URL: gopher://gopher.nih.gov/1/clin/nih-infobook

National Network for Child Care
Research on programs and practices

The National Network for Child Care (NNCC), part of the Children, Youth, and Family (CYF) Network, focuses on the discussion and improvement of nonparental child care. Its gopher site includes information on the federal Head Start program, a list of "best practices" for community-supported child-care programs, and various research documents and curricular materials.

Useful for health and social services.
URL: gopher://tinman.mes.umn.edu.:4242/11/ChildCare

National Network for Collaborations
Help for communities trying to help kids

The National Network for Collaboration (NNCO), part of the Children, Youth, and Family (CYF) Network, focuses on creating collaborations—primarily at the community level—that improve the lives of children and families. NNCO staff provide technical assistance for Youth At Risk (YAR) projects and other federal social programs. The NNCO site, still under development, will offer curricula, research, news, and related materials.

Useful for health and social services.
URL: gopher://tinman.mes.umn.edu.:4242/11/Coalitions

National Network for Family Resiliency (NNFR)
Questions welcome

The National Network for Family Resiliency (NNFR), a project of the Children, Youth, and Family (CYF) Network, focuses on helping families to meet various challenges, such as family and community violence, divorce and remarriage, child care, parent education, or grandparenting. It provides a variety of research and curricular materials. If you have a simple question about kids and families, you can e-mail the NNFR's FAMNET mailing list for a direct response, or join the FAMNET mailing list.

Useful for health and social services; mailing lists (listservs) and newsgroups; parenting.
URL: gopher://tinman.mes.umn.edu.:4242/11/Family
E-mail: famnet@esusda.gov
To subscribe: almanac@esusda.gov
Message body: subscribe famnet

Occupational Safety and Health
Information that may help in the home

This independent archive, operated through the Florida Institute of Technology, offers statistics and information about Occupational Safety and Health Administration (OSHA) standards. You'll also find articles about such health and safety issues as indoor air quality, carpal tunnel syndrome, and household waste management.

Useful for consumer information; health and social services.
URL: gopher://ginfo.cs.fit.edu:70/11/OSHA
E-mail: editor@ginfo.cs.fit.edu

PedInfo
Online sources of information about children's health

Short annotations accompany this list of links to online information about children's health, compiled by Dr. Andy Spooner, an instructor in the Department of Pediatrics, Washington University School of Medicine. Topics range from attention deficit disorder to food safety and nutrition, with a special section on parenting resources.

Useful for health and social services.
URL: http://pedinfo.wustl.edu/

SAFE-T-CHILD Online
ID kits, quizzes, and other things to keep kids safe

Information here is based on SAFE-T-CHILD Inc.'s program to help children avoid getting lost, going missing, or being abducted or abused. A short online quiz helps you rate your child's "street smarts," and for a limited time you can get a free child identification kit by completing an online marketing survey. There are also articles on child safety, and ordering information about child-safety books, records and a patented DNA identification kit.

Useful for activities and projects; health and social services.
URL: http://yellodino.safe-t-child.com:2000/

Staying Healthy in Asia, Africa, and Latin America
Advice to travelers

Staying Healthy in Asia, Africa, and Latin America by Dr. Dirk Schroeder, a research associate at Emory University, is an abridged online version of a handbook copublished by Moon Travel Handbooks and Volunteers in Asia. You can do full-text searches of the material, which covers predeparture checklists, signs of dangerous illnesses, how to find medical care abroad and other health advice pertinent to that region. Links to Moon Travel's home page offer you access to a free travel newsletter and information about its other publications.

Useful for health and social services; travel and recreation.
URL: http://www.moon.com:7000/1h/travel.health

U.S. Social Security Administration
Answers on rights and benefits

The U.S. Social Security Administration provides online answers to the public's most frequent questions. Information in both English and Spanish is available about Social Security numbers and cards; benefits for retirement, survivors, children and disabilities; your rights to appeal; Medicare; and other related programs. You can also download or request by e-mail a variety of pamphlets on these topics.

Useful for health and social services.
URL: http://www.ssa.gov/SSA_Home.html/
To subscribe: info@ssa.gov
Message body: send index

Virtual Hospital
Handouts and other information for families

The Virtual Hospital, presented by the University of Iowa College of Medicine, is a multimedia database intended to help physicians quickly answer patients' questions. But there's a lot of valuable information, in plain English, here for the layperson as well, in the way of hypertext handouts from the American Family Physician. Topics include *How to Use Nasal Spray, What Parents Need to Know About Intoeing, How to Protect Your Skin from Sun Damage, Preventing Injuries in Indoor Racquet Sports,* and *Heat-Related Illness: What You Can Do to Prevent It.* The college is building a similar type of database focusing on pediatrics, the Virtual Hospital for Children. Users are advised to double-check information found here with their own health-care providers.

Useful for health and social services.
URL: http://vh.radiology.uiowa.edu

Interdisciplinary

4-H Kindergarten to 3rd Grade Curriculum Manual
Approaches, programs

The server of the U.S. Department of Agriculture includes a folder on the K-3 curriculum offered by 4-H, an agricultural organization for young people. Included is information about 4-H programs and general information about childhood development, learning, and memory. The manual addresses topics ranging from helping kids to develop social interaction and learning skills to citizenship and civic education.

Useful for education.
URL: gopher://cyfer.esusda.gov:70/11/CYFER-net/jury/documents/manual

Academy One
Newsgroups, penpals and online activities for K-12 students

Academy One, operated by the National Public Telecomputing Network, is primarily a system of Usenet newsgroups for K-12 students, their parents, teachers and school administrators. Participants can discuss various topics with one another, find pen pals, and take part in simulated Space Shuttle launches and virtual-worlds projects. The Web site provides information about the program, including a list of online projects, calendar of events, and answers to frequently asked questions about Academy One. You can also request by e-mail a list of affiliate sites through which users can connect to Academy One.

Useful for mailing lists (listservs) and newsgroups.
URL: http://www.nptn.org/cyber.serv/AOneP/
E-mail: info@nptn.org

BBC
Index of ideas for all levels of education

While you may not be able to tune in to the British Broadcasting Corp.'s educational programming, you may find helpful ideas and supplemental material in this index. You can search for information according to age level, subject or use.

Useful for educational TV and radio.
URL: http://www.bbcnc.org.uk/education/bbced/prim.html#Early Learning

Best of the K-12 Internet Resources, InforMNs
Online projects, lesson plans

Some of the best K-12 resources available on the Internet have been pulled together in one place by Internet for Minnesota Schools (InforMNs), a partnership of educational services. You will find links to an assortment of organizations, such as NASA and various school districts, with online educational materials and projects on topics ranging from ecology to government studies. Lesson, images and even sound files can be downloaded. While many of the projects are now over, the information they provide can still be adapted.

Useful for school resources.
URL: gopher://informns.k12.mn.us:70/11/best-k12

Big Sky Miscellaneous Lesson Plans
Debate, self-esteem and other exercises

Montana's Big Sky Telegraph, an educational network, includes this assortment of about 50 "miscellaneous" lesson plans for K-12 on its server. Some examples: self-esteem activities and a "computer Olympics" for elementary students, newspaper studies and conflict management activities for intermediate grades, and debate exercises and parenting lessons for high-school students. The lessons were prepared at summer workshops of the Columbia Education Center, an association of teachers from 14 western states.

Useful for school resources.
URL: gopher://bvsd.k12.co.us:70/11/Educational_Resources/Lesson_Plans/Big%20Sky/misc

CBC Radio
Sound, scripts for science, entertainment, public affairs programs

Even if you can't pick up the signal for the Canadian Broadcasting Corporation (CBC) radio network, you can access some of its most popular science, entertainment and public affairs programming via the Internet. You can receive sound and text files of such programs as *Quirks and Quarks, Basic Black,* and *Sunday Morning.* From *Quirks and Quarks,* for example, you can download stories on ozone depletion, Tourette's Syndrome, the Chernobyl disaster, DNA fingerprinting, computer intelligence, and animal behavior. Sound files are in .AU format, with conversion utilities provided.

Useful for educational TV and radio.
URL: http://debra.dgbt.doc.ca/cbc/cbc.html

Community Learning Network
Lessons, exercises, even a Catch of the Day

The Community Learning Network (CLN) is maintained by the British Columbia (Canada) Ministry of Education as a learning tool for provincial K-12 schools. It offers a wide range of online resources, including lessons and exercises specifically for B.C. teachers and students, along with e-mail and bulletin-board services for members. CLN also offers access to gophers, World-Wide Web pages, and searchable archives of mailing lists. Of note are its Internet Catch of the Day archives, featuring a daily pointer to an educational resource available online.

Useful for school resources.
URL: http://www.etc.bc.ca/home.html

DeweyWeb
Interactive projects for a global classroom

The DeweyWeb is an experimental site at which a group of educators from the University of Michigan are trying to create a "global classroom" for K-12 students worldwide. It presents projects that inform and challenge students to contribute their own ideas and findings. These supervised projects rely on interactive communications (such as e-mail) and simulations. They include simulated expeditions to exotic parts of the world, based on real-life explorations by scientists; a role-playing exercise designed to show students the intricacies of Middle East politics; and a "trip" that teaches students about the geographic, cultural and ecological diversity of Europe and the former Soviet Union.

Useful for international studies.
URL: http://ics.soe.umich.edu

Directory of Scholarly Electronic Conferences
Mailing lists and other forums

The online *Directory of Scholarly Electronic Conferences*, compiled and frequently revised by Diane Kovacs and The Directory Team, describes discussion lists, electronic journals, Usenet newsgroups, and other forums of interest to scholars in a broad range of subjects. Students looking for information on a particular topic — for example, the Bronte sisters in literature — may wish to tap into the appropriate forum. The directory gives Internet addresses for the forums as well as any sites where their archived messages, newsletters and other materials are archived.

Useful for mailing lists (listservs) and newsgroups; reference.
URL: gopher://gopher.usask.ca/1/Computing/Internet Information/Directory of Scholarly Electronic Conferences

Discovery Learning Community
Educational materials complement TV programs

This Web site — a collaboration between television's Discovery Channel and the Learning Channel — offers an online version of Discovery's Educator Guide, filled with program information, schedules, curricular activities and support for Assignment Discovery, TLC Elementary School and other educational programming. The site focuses on a growing number of resources and activities tied to the cultural and historical themes of the documentary *The Promised Land*. These will include a repository of work done by students.

Useful for educational TV and radio.
URL: http://ericir.syr.edu/Discovery/

Diversity University
Classes, collaborative projects, study groups online

Diversity University (DU) is a "virtual" university campus that serves as a host site for a variety of online projects — teaching classes, collaborations, organizing study groups, and so on. The DU Web site provides the documents needed to use the system as well as a connection to the DU MOO. (A MOO is an advanced bulletin-board system that you can use to post messages.) The DU MOO includes a K-12 section. To enter DU, you need a TELNET program. Your World-Wide Web browser can generally start the TELNET program if it's installed on your system.

Useful for activities and projects.
URL: http://pass.wayne.edu/DU.html
E-mail: moo@erau.db.erau.edu

E-Text Archives
Collection is wide-ranging, sometimes controversial

The electronic text archive, at the University of Michigan, offers hundreds of documents online. The archive is open to anyone who wants to place materials there, so the range of documents is wide: fiction and poetry, nonfiction, back copies of periodicals, opinion pieces (and rantings), humor, reference materials, religious and philosophical texts, Greek and Latin classics, book reviews, archived mailing lists, and many other texts. Be advised that some documents are controversial in nature and may be offensive to some people, although pornographic images are prohibited.

Useful for reference.
URL: gopher://etext.archive.umich.edu

Educational TV Listings
Schedules for CNN, Discovery, TLC and PBS

This directory gives schedules and descriptions of educational television programs being shown on CNN, the Discovery Channel, the Learning Channel, and PBS, as well as information on educational videos available from these networks.

Useful for educational TV and radio.
URL: gopher://gaia.sci-ed.fit.edu/11/subj/tv

Electronic Books at Virginia Tech
Works by classic and modern authors

Virginia Tech's Electronic Books gopher provides the full text of more than 130 books, speeches, and other works by great philosophers, political figures, historians, poets, and novelists. You can download texts by such diverse authors as Sophocles, Geoffrey Chaucer, Benjamin Franklin, W.B. Yeats, and John F. Kennedy.

Useful for history; literature.
URL: gopher://gopher.vt.edu:10010/10/25

Empire Internet Schoolhouse
Electronic grab-bag for Internet newcomers

The Empire Internet Schoolhouse is an extensive server offering access to K-12 resources and discussion groups around the Internet. Resources include:p
An Assembly Hallb posting current projects and offering access to online discussion groups.

- Career and Guidance Center for high-school students, offering access to the New York State College admission system and a question-and-answer system for students considering college or work.
- Library and Internet Reference Tools folder containing reference services and information about the Internet.
- Various Academic Wings providing resources by subject.
- School Reform and Technology Planning Center with information on reforming schools and incorporating technology into education.
- Fieldtrips to Other School Systems feature that lets users explore the resources of other school systems via TELNET.
- The New York State Education and Research Network (NYSERNet) provides the Empire Internet Schoolhouse as an extension of its Bridging the Gap program, which promotes collaboration and partnership in the educational community.

Useful for mailing lists (listservs) and newsgroups.
URL: gopher://nysernet.org:3000

English Server
For serious study of the humanities

Carnegie-Mellon University's English Server is a resource for scholarship in many of the humanities—literature, the arts, feminist studies, and history, to name a few. You'll find research and criticism, full-text literature (novels, stories, plays, poetry, and nonfiction), links to library servers, and other important online services for scholars.

Useful for literature.
URL: http://english-server.hss.cmu.edu/
E-mail: postmaster@english-server.hss.cmu.edu

Fieldtrips Mailing List (Fieldtrips-L)
Share the adventure

The Fieldtrips discussion list encourages students to share their knowledge and observations with others around the world. While it is designed for class fieldtrips, the information also will interest individual students who monitor the list. Prior to a trip, a class announces where it is going, allowing others on the list who may want to become virtual "partners" to respond with questions and observations. After the trip, the class posts a summary of what the students saw and learned. This gives subscribers a chance to learn about something or somewhere they might not be able to visit in person. The list is sponsored by the Global Schoolnet Foundation.

Useful for activities and projects; mailing lists (listservs) and newsgroups.
URL: gopher://gopher.cic.net:3005/00/listservs/fieldtrips
To subscribe: majordomo@acme.fred.org
Message body: subscribe fieldtrips-l

Global Campus
Project aims to offer wide range of instructional materials

This collaborative project, led by California State University and California Polytechnic, aims to provide instructional images, video, audio and text files from institutions worldwide. The project has begun by focusing on the subject areas of art history, American Indian history, and marine and cellular biology.

Useful for school resources.
URL: http://www.csulb.edu/gc/

Great Lakes Information Network (GLIN)
For projects in science and social studies

The Great Lakes Information Network (GLIN) is a binational data and information service covering the Great Lakes region of the United States and Canada — including the states of Illinois, Indiana, Michigan, Minnesota, New York, Ohio, Pennsylvania, and Wisconsin, and the provinces of Ontario and Quebec. Students will find fact sheets, calendars, newsletters, directories, and other resources that may be useful for projects in science, history, geography, civics, and related subjects. Materials are provided by a variety of federal, state, and provincial agencies as well as universities and private organizations.

Useful for geography; international studies.
URL: http://www.great-lakes.net:2200/0/glinhome.html
E-mail: cratza@glc.org
To subscribe: GLIN-Majordomo@great-lakes.net
Message body: subscribe glin-announce

Grolier's Encyclopedia
Immediate and up-to-date

The complete *Grolier's Encyclopedia* is available online. To access it, you'll need a TELNET client. Go to the Grolier's Home Page on the Web, then click the hotlink to access the Grolier's Encyclopedia. Your TELNET program should start and connect you to the University of Maryland server. This resource can be busy and hard to access.
URL: http://gagme.wwa.com/~boba/grolier.html (requires TELNET client)

Hot Topics, Reed Interactive
Background to bring you up to speed on current affairs

Hot Topics, updated about twice a month, provides images, explanations and links to on- and offline resources about current affairs issues worldwide, such as woodchipping in Australia, earthquakes in Japan, conflict in the Balkans, and global warming in Antarctica. The site, maintained by Reed Interactive, a division of educational publisher Reed Books Australia, also has a pen pals and projects section for kids.

Useful for pen pals.
URL: http://www.ozemail.com.au/~reed/index.html

Image Server, City University (London)
Graphics of animals, trains and more

Logos, movies, photographs, maps and other images are all available from the Image Server, maintained by London's City University. The images come from around the world and are classified by subject, type and country, such as cars/race/Germany. Younger kids will enjoy the animals collection and the pictures of trains, including one of the book and TV character *Thomas the Tank Engine*.

Useful for images.
URL: http://www.cs.city.ac.uk/archive/image/image.html

Innovative SPI Resources for Educators (INSPIRE)
Focus on school reform

The Innovative SPI Resources for Educators (INSPIRE) gopher, created by the Office of the Superintendent of Public Instruction in Washington state, is designed to help K-12 teachers find useful information on the Internet. It's divided into folders that link to online curricular materials, study projects, discussions of educational reform, and other types of resources. INSPIRE also offers direct links to other educational servers.

Useful for school resources.
URL: gopher://inspire.ospi.wednet.edu

Internet Resources for the K-12 Classroom
Internet tutorials and materials

The Education Program of the National Center for Supercomputing Applications works to show how computers and computer networks can enhance K-12 learning. Among other things, its home page features links, categorized by subject, to informative material located on the Internet suitable for precollege students and teachers, as well as tutorials on using the Internet and World-Wide Web.

Useful for Internet and computing.
URL: http://www.ncsa.uiuc.edu/Edu/

Internet-on-a-Disk
Leads on electronic texts

This periodic newsletter has articles and announcements about free and public-domain electronic texts available on the Internet, and their use in education. These texts also are available on disk (PC or Macintosh format) at a nominal price through the Please Copy This Disk program at this site..

Useful for news sources.
URL: http://www.eff.org/pub/Publications/CuD/E-journals/Internet_on_a_Disk/
E-mail: samizdat@world.std.com (to subscribe)

Irish Web
Maps and political news about Ireland

You can find maps of metropolitan areas and access Web sites in Ireland through an interactive map provided by the University College, Dublin. While many of these offer mainly technical material, some (particularly those at universities) do offer general and tourist-related information about the country. A news service in Ireland also gives bulletins on the local political scene.

Useful for images; international studies; travel and recreation.
URL: http://slarti.ucd.ie/maps/ireland.html

K12Net: The Worldwide Teacher-Student Network
Classrooms come together

K12Net is a loosely organized network of bulletin-board systems (BBSs) based in schools throughout North America, Australia, Europe, and the former Soviet Union. It's found on both the Fidonet network and various Usenet systems. Students, teachers, and parents can exchange ideas and resources using several mailing lists:

* Chat groups for elementary, junior-high, and high-school students.
* Subject-specific discussion groups for teachers (language arts, mathematics, science, special education, and so on).
* Foreign-language discussion groups (French, German, Russian, and Spanish).
* A list for school counselors.
* Various "channel" groups containing news, weather reports, and special reports

Useful for mailing lists (listservs) and newsgroups.
URL: gopher://k12.oit.umass.edu:70/11/umassk12/k12net

K12Pals Mailing List
Find other students to correspond with

The K12Pals mailing list allows elementary and secondary school students to find pen pals with whom they can then privately correspond by e-mail. Pen pals can correspond from home or from a classroom. Requests for pen pals are archived. This mailing list is sponsored by the AskERIC project of the U.S. Department of Education.

Useful for pen pals.
URL: gopher://ericir.syr.edu:70/11/Listservs/K12Pals
E-mail: checkers@ericir.syr.edu
To subscribe: LISTSERV@SUVM.SYR.EDU
Message body: subscribe k12pals YourFirstName YourLastName

KIDLINK / KIDS-96
Mailing lists focus on projects for kids

KIDLINK, a project of Norway's nonprofit KIDLINK Society, is a global network for children ages 10-15, their teachers, and their parents. The current annual edition of the project, beginning in May 1995, is called KIDS-96. KIDLINK actually consists of several mailing lists. A few of these are:

- KIDCAFE: An open forum containing messages written entirely by kids. Users can choose to receive all messages or a daily indexed list. The main KIDCAFE is in English, but Spanish, Portuguese, Japanese, and Nordic versions are also available.
- KIDFORUM: This forum allows exchanges between groups of students (such as classrooms). Discussions focus on specific topics that are announced in advance.
- KIDPROJ: A mailing list for teachers and other adults with news about special KIDLINK projects. Recent projects have included math pen pals, a "writer's corner," and lesson plans on desert ecology and ham radio.
- KIDLEADR: An informal meeting place for teachers, coordinators, parents, and others interested in KIDLINK. Users can exchange ideas, ask questions of each other, and the like.

There's no charge to participate in KIDLINK, but each child must provide some basic information: his or her name and age, plans for the future, and so on — before getting started.

You can learn about current and past projects by using the KIDLINK SEARCHER to sift through the various KIDLINK message archives or documentation files. Send an e-mail message for instructions to SEARCHER@kidlink.org with the word "help" in the subject line.

Useful for pen pals.
URL: http://www.kidlink.org/
E-mail: mark@duquesne.kidlink.org
To subscribe: listserv@vm1.nodak.edu
Message body: subscribe KIDLINK YourFirstName YourLastName

KIDSPHERE (formerly KIDSNET)
Kids and adults exchange ideas

The KIDSPHERE list is a forum for educators, scientists, and other adults who are interested in developing an international computer network for children and teachers. Subscribers can learn about Internet sites suitable for children's use, and post their ideas and experiences.

Useful for mailing lists (listservs) and newsgroups.
E-mail: kidsphere@vms.cis.pitt.edu
To subscribe: kidsphere-request@vms.cis.pitt.edu

KIDZMAIL
A mailing list and source of pen pals for younger children

KIDZMAIL: Kids Exploring Issues and Interests Electronically, based at Arizona State University, is a mailing list for elementary students. It allows kids to find pen pals online and share their ideas about a variety of subjects that interest them, such as school, hobbies and pets.

Useful for pen pals.
E-mail: KIDZMAIL@ASUACAD
To subscribe: LISTSERV@ASUVM.INRE.ASU.EDU
Message body: subscribe kidzmail YourFirstName YourLastName

Kindergarten to Grade 6 Corner
Science projects and pen pals for young students

Young Internet users will enjoy this "corner" on Canada's SchoolNet server, which offers several science-related projects to do at home or at school. Some examples are "Amazing Plant Facts," "Animal Noses," "Chemistry Facts You Don't Want to Know," and "Living on Jupiter". Kids will also find requests for pen pals here.

Useful for pen pals.
URL: http://schoolnet.carleton.ca/

Let's Learn: Educational Fun 'n' Games on the Internet
What to do

For Internet novices, the Let's Learn gopher provides a gentle introduction to the network, its tools and some educational resources. The number of links at this site is not overwhelming, but the material is presented in an easy-to-use and humorous fashion. Designed by the Ontario Institute for Studies in Education, the University of Toronto's teaching arm, it shows educators (and anyone else who's interested) how to do things and where to go once they log on.

Useful for education.
URL: gopher://gopher.oise.on.ca:70/11/resources/IRes4Ed/resources/fun/educational

Library and Information Skills-Building Lesson Plans
Finding what you need

This set of lesson plans focuses on building library and information-seeking skills. Activities teach students how to use library resources to find specific information, how to compare and contrast information, and how to sequence and summarize details.

Useful for school resources.
URL: gopher://ericir.syr.edu:70/11/Lesson/SLMAM/Skills

MariMUSE
Fables, animal information and other resources for young children

The MariMUSE Global Learning Collaboratory at Phoenix (Ariz.) College offers educational materials, mostly for younger kids. It includes text files about animals and their habitats as well as electronic texts of *Aesop's Fables*, *Grimm's Fairy Tales*, and other children's classics. Sections of the server are designed by college students as part of their course work, and other areas point to useful educational resources on the Internet.

Useful for literature.
URL: gopher://pcef.pc.maricopa.edu

MicroMuse at MIT
"Adventures" have an academic twist

MicroMuse, based at the Artificial Intelligence Lab at the Massachusetts Institute of Technology, offers several interactive learning "adventures" for K-12 kids (and college students and adults, too). Some of the MicroMuse adventures include a "logic quest" with a knights-and-knaves theme, tours of Mars and Yellowstone National Park, and adventures incorporating the mythical worlds of Oz and Narnia. As they participate in these adventures, kids develop their reading and writing skills and learn about topics in science, math, and other subjects. Since each adventure is multi-user, with several players interacting at any given time, MicroMuse also helps kids develop social and interpersonal skills. Log in as "guest".

Useful for activities and projects.
URL: telnet://musenet.bbn.com

mlink_news mailing list
Tips and pointers to resources on- and offline

This list provides tips and pointers to sources of print and online information, with a focus on resources of interest to residents of Michigan. The list got its start as a weekly bulletin called *MLink Newsbytes* that was sent to a small circle of librarians and researchers. It is sponsored by the MLink project, a collaboration between the University of Michigan Library and Michigan's public libraries.

Useful for mailing lists (listservs) and newsgroups.
URL: http://mlink.lib.umich.edu
To subscribe: majordomo@mlink.hh.lib.umich.edu
Message body: subscribe mlink_newsbytes [your e-mail address]

PBS Learning Services
Companion materials for educational TV programs

Whether you're simply trying to find program listings or searching for ways to reinforce what your child learns through PBS' instructional TV shows, this is where to look. This Web site provides information about the network's various services that support the use of educational television in K-12 curriculum (as well as preschool and adult learning), plus pointers to curriculum resources, electronic field trips and interactive projects.

Useful for educational TV and radio.
URL: http://www.pbs.org

Pick me!
Pointers to creative and unusual Internet sites

Pick me! is a weekly feature from the News and Observer Publishing Co., of Raleigh, N.C. It discusses an Internet site that's particularly well-done, unusual, or fun. Past "picks" are archived, should you wish to browse.

Useful for reference.
URL: gopher://merlin.nando.net:70/11/pick

Scott Yanoff's Special Internet Connections
Descriptions, links to resources

This catalog of scores of Internet sites—also known as the *Internet Services List*—began life in 1991 as a short list drawn up by Scott Yanoff of the University of Wisconsin-Madison for his personal use. Now widely distributed, it contains pointers to a vast range of information sources on the Internet, with descriptions and direct links.

Useful for reference.
URL: http://www.uwm.edu/Mirror/inet.services.html
E-mail: yanoff@alpha2.csd.uwm.edubbslist@aug3.augsburg.edu

Smithsonian's Education Support
Main point of access to museum

The Smithsonian Institution is planning to centralize its online information and access to its servers through a single home page. In the interim, this site acts as a starting point for accessing that information, and highlights new features and services offered by the museum. From here, for example, you can link to the Center for Earth and Planetary Studies, the National Air and Space Museum, Harvard-Smithsonian Center for Astrophysics, and the Smithsonian's newest member, the National Museum of the American Indian.

Useful for science.
URL: http://www.si.edu/

Smithsonian's Office of Printing & Photographic Services
Pictures of history

The Smithsonian Institution's Office of Printing and Photographic Services offers digital versions of photographs on display at the various Smithsonian museums on the Mall in Washington, D.C., as well as other Smithsonian bureaus, such as the Smithsonian Astrophysical Observatory. You'll find photos of exhibits, historical pictures, animal photos from the National Zoo, satellite pictures, and many other images in GIF and JPEG formats. Most of the photos include explanatory captions.

Useful for images.
URL: ftp://photo1.si.edu/

Student's Corner
Useful connections compiled by a student

Student's Corner was compiled by Robert McKay, a junior high-school student with a FreeNet account. Although it isn't graphically sophisticated, it offers useful and entertaining links for kids and adults alike. There are pointers to an e-mail "smilie" dictionary and the Human Genome Mapping Project, as well as connections to a variety of electronic bulletin boards.

Useful for reference.
URL: http://www.cfn.cs.dal.ca/~aa277/HomePage.html

Summer Home Learning Recipes
Pamphlets offer parents ideas to keep kids busy

The U.S. Department of Education offers *Summer Home Learning Recipes*, a series of four educational pamphlets that parents can use to help their children keep learning during their summer vacation. The series includes:

- Napkin Fractions (grades K-3). Children learn about fractions by labeling and folding napkins.
- The Foreign Touch (grades 4-5). Kids visit ethnic shops and restaurants in their community to learn about other cultures.
- How Much Does It Cost? (grades 6-8). Parents and kids discuss household expenses.
- The Problem-Solving Habit (grades 9-12). Teens learn a six-step approach to assessing and solving problems.

Useful for activities and projects.
URL: http://www.ed.gov/Inet/10. U.S. Department of Education/ OERI Publications/4. ED/OERI Publications — Full Text/ 9. Publications for Parents/10. Summer Home Learning Recipes/

Teaching Ideas and Requests
Index of popular Internet projects

This index is a catch-all for a variety of K-12 educational resources. You can find descriptions and access information for dozens of popular Internet projects, such as the Global Lab, the Internet Hunt, and MicroMuse, as well as other resources in science, language arts, and social studies.

Useful for activities and projects.
URL: gopher://gopher.prs.k12.nj.us:70/11ftp%3AFTP%20Folder%3APublic% 3ATeaching%20Ideas%20and%20Requests%3A

Tryptiks: Travel Guides to Internet Countries
Journey in learning

This Web site contains a set of electronic guides to subjects that are part of the Maricopa Community College District's undergraduate instructional program. Each Tryptik provides hyperlinks to resources in a particular subject—currently biology, English, nursing, psychology, and contemporary social issues. The Tryptik to the Federation of Current Social Issues, for example, provides an alphabetical list of topics, ranging from abortion to the Whitewater investigation, with links to appropriate Internet sites. The goal of the project is to help students learn to use electronic resources in their studies.

Useful for education; Internet and computing.
URL: http://www.emc.maricopa.edu/TrypTiks/TrypTiks.intro.hmtl

Washington Educational Network (WEdNET)
Interactive online projects

The Washington Education Network (WEdNet) links K-12 schools in Washington state, with gopher access for the general public. Several interactive online projects were under development at press time, including studies of Native Americans, dinosaur discussions with paleontologists, teleconferences with state legislators, critical studies of the news media, regional history studies, and student newsmagazines and poetry journals. WEdNet also offers links to other educational resources on the Internet.

Useful for activities and projects.
URL: gopher://gopher.wednet.edu

Whales: A Thematic Web Unit
Activities, projects and oceanography resources

For kids in Kindergarten through Grade 4, this hypertext document offers a set of integrated activities and projects that deal with whale themes in language arts, math, science, social studies and the development of critical thinking skills. For example, there are activities to use with books about whales; students can also study words about whales and try writing a poem. Links are being developed to resources for oceanography, virtual field trips, whale experts and parents on the Internet. Whales is an interactive project designed by the Curry School of Education at the University of Virginia.

Useful for biology.
URL: http://curry.edschool.virginia.edu/~kpj5e/Project.html

Whole Earth 'Lectronic Link's Gopherspace (WELLgopher)
Dip into its links

The WELL is one of the oldest regional computer conferencing systems in the United States, perhaps best known for its conversational forums and "small town" atmosphere. It is operated by the publishers of *The Whole Earth Catalog* and Rosewood Stone, a financial investment company. Its gopher provides a host of links to a broad range of resources on the Internet, as well as information about the WELL's commercial services.

Useful for mailing lists (listservs) and newsgroups.
URL: gopher://gopher.well.sf.ca.us:70/11/The_WELL
E-mail: info@well.sf.ca.us

World School for Adventure Learning
Students link up with wilderness explorers

The World School for Adventure Learning, based in St. Paul, Minn., allows students to follow the expeditions of wilderness explorers. Most recently, students have been following the training exercises of the International Arctic Project, a multinational expedition that plans to cross the Arctic Ocean by canoe and dog sled in the spring of 1995. The World School offers a variety of study materials in print form and online. It sends out updates every day, suggests projects and other activities, poses questions for students, and allows students to communicate with explorers and scholars first-hand. Students study such topics as river ecosystems, bird migration, land reclamation, indigenous cultures, and weather patterns. The gopher contains a section on wildlife news with profiles (written in part by students) of the bald eagle, caribou, gray whale, leatherback turtle, monarch butterfly, Pacific salmon, and other animals.

Useful for international studies.
URL: gopher://ics.soe.umich.edu
E-mail: worldsch@indiana.edu

Young Person's Guide to Hot Web Spots
Places by, for and about kids

The Ontario Science Center offers a section of its server for kids, with links to home pages by, for and about youngsters. Connections take you to libraries, museums, sources of pen pals, kids' networks, and sites with online activities.

Useful for activities and projects.
URL: http://www.osc.on.ca/kids.html

Internet and computing

Apple Computer, Inc.
Hardware and software updates

Apple Computer's home page offers information about the Macintosh computer line and software that works with it.

Useful for software.
URL: http://www.apple.com

Apple Education
Research and reports about technology's effect on education

Designed to show schools how Apple Computer's products can enhance the teaching process, this site may also be helpful to other users. You can read how hardware, software and books can be combined as teaching tools; reports and research by Apple on the effect of technology in education; and various technology news updates from the company.

Useful for education; Internet and computing.
URL: http://www.austin.apple.com:80/education/

ARPANET History
In the beginning there was the ARPAnet

This Web site is for people interested in the history of the Internet. The Advanced Research Projects Agency Network (ARPANET), a military project, was the first large network that tied computers together around the world.

Useful for history; Internet and computing.
URL: http://www.arpa.mil/

BEKS Consortium
Ways to develop intercultural and Internet skills

Developed by educators at four Maryland school "clusters" — Blair, Einstein, Kennedy, and Springbrook — the BEKS Consortium aims to improve learning op-

portunities for students in all four clusters through the use of telecommunications and other high-technology processes. In one project, the seven schools of the Einstein cluster (including one high school, one middle school, and five elementary schools) have established a communications link to the American School in Brasilia, Brazil. Students in both countries learn about one another while gaining proficiency with e-mail and the Internet. The interface was developed in part by high-school students.
URL: http://goober.mbhs.edu/beks/beks.html

Center for Innovative Computer Applications (CICA)
Software central

The Center for Innovative Computer Applications (CICA) is a clearinghouse for shareware and public-domain software for Microsoft Windows, including applications, utilities, drivers, and bitmaps — more than 300 megabytes in all. You can receive all materials free of charge via anonymous FTP. Software for DOS and UNIX is also available.

Useful for software.
URL: ftp://ftp.cica.indiana.edu

Children Accessing Controversial Information (CACI)
For questions and comments

This mailing list discusses children accessing controversial information through computer networks. If you have a question, comment, or simply are curious about kids, the Internet and the issue of free speech, you may want to subscribe to this list.
URL: http://mevard.www.media.mit.edu/people/mevard/caci.html
To subscribe: caci-request@media.mit.edu
Message body: subscribe

Children's Software Reviews
Here's what other parents think

Ever wonder what other parents think of children's software packages? This Web site is a collection of reviews parents have posted on the misc.kids.computer Usenet discussion group. You may post your own reviews to this server.

Useful for consumer information; software.
URL: http://qv3pluto.LeidenUniv.nl/steve/reviews/welcome.htm

Common Knowledge: Pittsburgh
Career planning, educational services

Common Knowledge: Pittsburgh provides wide-area network services to teachers and students in the Pittsburgh, Pa., public school system. It provides pointers to resources in K-12 education and career planning, as well as information about educational and government programs in the Pittsburgh area. The project is a National Science Foundation testbed for K-12 networking.

Useful for school resources.
URL: http://info.pps.pgh.pa.us

CoSN for Parents
Discussions focus on parental involvement, K-12 technology

CoSN for Parents is one of six online discussion groups moderated by the Consortium for School Networking, an organization promoting the use of computer network technology in K-12 education. Parents and others can discuss issues of parental involvement, technology, and more. The only requirement is that you become a paid member of CoSN.

Useful for education; Internet and computing; mailing lists (listservs) and newsgroups.
URL: http://cosn.org/
To subscribe: listproc@cosn.org
Message body: subscribe parents YourFirstName YourLastName

Edutopia
Articles on interactive technology and education

Edutopia is an online newsletter about using interactive multimedia technology to enhance learning. Published semi-annually by the George Lucas Educational Foundation, a charitable organization founded by the innovative filmmaker, it features articles on such topics as how technology assists people with disabilities, teaching and technology; and resources in this field. You can browse the articles at the Web site or send an e-mail request for a free subscription to the newsletter (which can be delivered by electronic or regular mail).

Useful for education; Internet and computing; news sources.
URL: http://www.glef.org
E-mail: edutopia@glef.org

EdWeb, Corporation for Public Broadcasting
"Hyperbook" on education

Andy Carvin's *EdWeb* is a hypertext guide and online tutorial on education, technology, school reform and the Information Superhighway. Designed for teachers and telecommunication enthusiasts, each "chapter" (or link) discusses and/or connects to collections of online educational resources, stories of how technology is used successfully in the classroom, a history of the development of the Internet, and more. The project is sponsored by the Corporation for Public Broadcasting.

Useful for education; Internet and computing; school resources.
URL: http://edweb.cnidr.org

European Schools Project
"Teletrips" let students in different countries study together

The European Schools Project (ESP), based at the University of Amsterdam, links secondary-school students — mainly in Europe, but also in North America and other parts of the world — through "teletrips," which are partnerships among classrooms in different countries that are studying the same topic. The project's goals are to enhance the educational process, raise cultural awareness, improve kids' proficiency in foreign languages, and provide a model for the use of tele-communications in education. ESP maintains a mailing list where you can find out about classrooms looking for partners or post your own teletrip ideas.

Useful for education; Internet and computing; mailing lists (listservs) and news-groups.
E-mail: risc@esp.educ.uva.nl
To subscribe: istproc@esp.educ.uva.nl
Message body: subscribe bbs

Eye on Government
E-mail bulletin examines actions related to the Internet

Eye on Government is a bulletin, not a discussion forum, that praises and ques-tions government actions that have an impact on pubic access to the Internet. Published by the Gopher Jewels Project, most bulletins are written by the pro-ject's manager, David Riggins.

Useful for government studies; Internet and computing; mailing lists (listservs) and newsgroups; news sources.
To subscribe: listproc@einet.net
Message body: subscribe eye-on-government YourName

Gleason Sackman's HotList of K-12 Schools on the Net
Is yours connected?

To grasp just how fast schools around the world are adopting the Internet, visit the HotList of K-12 Schools on the Net, compiled by Gleason Sackman, modera-tor of the net-happenings mailing list. You can find statistics, updated weekly, on the number of schools that have Web, gopher and/or TELNET connections. Fig-ures are organized by state, grade and type of site; There are also statistics for the number of school district, Department of Education and state sites in the United States as well as for schools overseas, showing the type of connection.

Useful for education; Internet and computing; school resources; schools on the Web.
URL: http://toons.cc.ndsu.nodak.edu/~sackmann/k12.html

Global Classroom Youth Congress
Kids have a say in school networking debate

This Web server offers an Internet window on the Global Classroom Youth Con-gress, a "virtual organization" that attempts to bring the voice of youth to the de-bate about global networks and their use in education. The congress is made up of kids from around the world who use a variety of networks.

Useful for Internet and computing; mailing lists (listservs) and newsgroups.
URL: http://www.mit.edu:8001/afs/athena/user/a/w/awillis/www/GCYC/GlobalCR.html
E-mail: GlobalCR@aol.com

Hub
Telecomputing, math and science resources

The Technical Education Research Centers (TERC) Hub server offers educational resources in technology (particularly telecomputing), math, and science. You'll find curricular materials in these subjects, reports on national teaching standards and education reform, public-domain software, a newsletter about TERC network services, and links to related Internet sites.

Useful for Internet and computing; mathematics; science.
URL: gopher://hub.terc.edu/
To subscribe: hub-mail-services@hub.terc.edu
Message body: help

Ideas for Infusion into the Curriculum
Evaluations of the Net as a teaching tool

This server offers summaries and evaluations of Internet sites that may be of value to teachers, trainers, and students. The information was researched and written by graduate students enrolled in Internet telecomputing courses at the University of Nebraska at Omaha and the University of Texas at Austin. Included here are short articles about using the Internet and other telecommunications tools in education and training: using online resources as research tools; connecting a school to the Internet; using telecommunications to teach at-risk students; and new topics for introductory computer science courses.

Useful for education; Internet and computing; school resources.
URL: gopher://SJUVM.STJOHNS.EDU:70/11/educat/nebraska/neb-inf

International Society for Technology in Education (ISTE)
News and ideas

The International Society for Technology in Education (ISTE), a nonprofit organization focusing on improving education through technology, offers a variety of information on its server. You'll find background material on ISTE, selected articles from the organization's 11 journals and newsletters (such as *Computing Teacher*), ideas for incorporating technology into home education, announcements about new educational technologies, and lists of useful books and software. ISTE also sponsors mailing lists that examine such issues as telecommunications and teacher education.

Useful for education.
URL: http://iste-gopher.uoregon.edu/

Internet Computer Index
Freeware, shareware and other online materials

The Internet Computer Index (ICI), a free service of Proper Publishing, offers indexes — with links — to computer-related materials, including freeware and shareware programs, available by gopher or World-Wide Web. ICI is divided into PC, Macintosh, and UNIX sections.

Useful for software.
URL: http://ici.proper.com

Internet Goodies
Pointers to freeware, shareware and documentation online

You need a particular software program but have forgotten where you found it on the Internet. This list may help, offering pointers to freeware and shareware for the Macintosh, Microsoft Windows and other systems, documentation and electronic texts freely available on the Internet. It was compiled — and continues to be maintained — for that very purpose by Marc Baudoin of Ecole Nationale Supirieure de Techniques Avancies in France.

Useful for software.
URL: http://www.ensta.fr/internet/

Internet Hunt
Monthly competition teaches players how to find information

The Internet Hunt, started in 1992 by systems librarian Rick Gates, is a popular competition open to all Internet users. Each month, a team of volunteers posts a set of 10 questions, the answers to which lie somewhere on the Internet. The first person or team to answer every question correctly is declared the winner. Whether you participate or simply follow the posted answers afterward, the Hunt offers enjoyable (and educational) practice in navigating the Internet, particularly for novices. Although the winners of the competition are usually teams from universities or businesses, younger students are also invited to participate. Each question is rated for difficulty, so kids can tackle the easier challenges first.

Useful for activities and projects; Internet and computing.
URL: http://www.hunt.org/
E-mail: webmaster@www.hunt.org

Internet Phone
Using the Net as a phone

This, essentially, is a telephone system that operates over the Internet with no long-distance charges (beyond what you may normally have to pay to connect to your Internet service provider). You need a multimedia PC, that is, a computer that's relatively fast, with speakers, microphones, and high-speed modems (at least 14.4 Kbps). It's far from perfect, but good enough for most families who want to keep costs down, yet still keep in touch. Future versions are expected to include group-conferencing capabilities. Some educational systems may eventually use it for distance education.
URL: http://www.vocaltec.com/

Internet Resources for Use in Education
The findings of educators

Internet Resources for Use in Education is a project of 60 graduate education students at the Ontario Institute for Studies in Education, who in 1993 launched a study of the possible uses of the Internet in education and posted their findings at this site. The server includes a resources section, with pointers to Internet sites that may be useful to educators, and an issues section, which addresses specific topics about the Internet in education (with pointers where appropriate).

Useful for education; Internet and computing.
URL: gopher://gopher.oise.on.ca:70/11/resources/IRes4Ed
E-mail: rmclean@oise.on.ca

InterNIC Directory and Database Services
Answers, tools for getting connected

The Internet Network Information Center (InterNIC) Directory and Database Services is part of the InterNIC Information Services, formed in 1992 and jointly provided and coordinated by General Atomics, AT&T and Network Solutions Inc. with funding from the National Science Foundation. They provide information about how to get connected to the Internet, pointers to network tools and resources, and seminars on a variety of topics.

Useful for Internet and computing; mailing lists (listservs) and newsgroups; reference.
URL: http://www.internic.net/
E-mail: info@internic.net (Reference Desk)
To subscribe: listserv@is.internic.net
Message body: subscribe announce YourFirstName YourLastName

Interpersonal Computing and Technology Listserv
Computers in education

This discussion group focuses on the role of computers and technology in learning. An electronic journal, *IPCT-J*, is also available by e-mail subscription. Published by Georgetown University's Center for Teaching and Technology, it covers issues related to the use of computer technology in the classroom and workplace, among other topics.

Useful for Internet and computing; mailing lists (listservs) and newsgroups.
URL: gopher://gopher.cic.net/0/cicnet-gophers/k12-gopher/listservs/Interpersonal-Computing-Technology
E-mail: GMP@PSUVM.BITNET
To subscribe: listserv@guvm.georgetown.edu
Message body: sub ipct-l YourFirstName YourLastName

Japan Ministry of Posts & Telecommunications
A networking blueprint

How Japan plans to deal with the Information Superhighway is detailed in a White Paper by the Ministry of Posts and Telecommunications, the Japanese government agency responsible for telecommunications.

Useful for government studies; Internet and computing.
URL: http://www.mpt.go.jp/

List of FreeNets
Extensive index leads to networks around the world

Eastern Kentucky University offers a comprehensive list of community networks and FreeNets in the United States, Canada and other countries. The pointers lead to Internet addresses and other background information, as well as direct links to those networks with gophers or home pages. If you can't find a particular network, perhaps it is still in the formative stage, so check the list of known and proposed FreeNets.

Useful for Internet and computing; reference.
URL: gopher://acs.eku.edu:70/11disk%24acs%3A%5B006006.gopherd.gopher_data.tunnels.free%5D

Meta Virtual Environments Page
Explore other online worlds

Based at Georgia Tech University, the Meta Virtual Environments Page contains pointers to virtual-reality resources around the world. You can explore virtual environments, and read articles and other background documents.

Useful for Internet and computing; reference.
URL: http://www.cc.gatech.edu/gvu/people/Masters/Rob.Kooper/Meta.VR.html

MUSEs in Education
An explanation and chance to explore

The National School Network Testbed's server includes a folder explaining Multi-User Simulation Environments (MUSEs) and their use in education. In a typical MUSE, participants interact and construct text "worlds" for one another to explore. The site links to several MUSEs via TELNET, including Massachusett's Institute of Technology's popular MicroMuse.

Useful for activities and projects; education; Internet and computing.
URL: gopher://copernicus.bbn.com:70/11/testbed/muse

National School Network Testbed
Projects aim to link K-12 schools

The National School Network Testbed—under development by Bolt Beranek and Newman (BBN), Inc., with several collaborators and support from the National Science Foundation—is a pilot project aimed at developing a network of K-12 schools across the United States. Testbed projects (some of which are listed elsewhere in this book) include the following:

- Community of Explorers. High-school science teachers collaborating in developing computer simulations.
- MicroMuse. Multi-user, text-based virtual reality for middle-school students.
- Shadows. A network of elementary-school classrooms studying shadows cast by the sun and developing theories about the sun and earth.

Useful for Internet and computing; school resources.
URL: gopher://copernicus.bbn.com:70/11/testbed

National Science Foundation (NSF)
Research from a key Internet player

The National Science Foundation (NSF), a federal agency, plays a central role in the development of online science resources for education. The NSF's home page makes available such information as the results of the research it funds, information on science trends and statistics, and links to many of its educational projects.

Useful for Internet and computing; reference.
URL: http://www.nsf.gov/

National Science Foundation Science and Technology Information System (STIS)
Searchable indexes answer many computing questions

The Science and Technology Information System (STIS) of the National Science Foundation (NSF) gives you access to NSF bulletins, press releases, and other technical documents. You can search the indexes by keyword.

Useful for Internet and computing; news sources.
URL: gopher://stis.nsf.gov/

net-happenings
News and announcements about Internet sites

Provided by InterNIC Information Services, net-happenings is a place to look for new Internet sites and announcements (of conferences, calls for papers, new services, and so on) of interest to the K-12 education community. New updates arrive once or twice per day. net-happenings' databases are WAIS-indexed, letting you search by keyword. The service is available on the World-Wide Web, by e-mail subscription and through Usenet.

Useful for Internet and computing; mailing lists (listservs) and newsgroups.
URL: http://www.internic.net/internic/lists/net-happenings.html
E-mail: guide@is.internic.net
To subscribe: majordomo@is.internic.net
Message body: subscribe net-happenings-digest

NetSurf Internet Training Resources
How to access, use online resources

You don't have to be an Internet trainer to use this page. It contains more than 50 links to information and tips on the different methods of accessing the Internet as well as pointers to online resources. These range from newsgroups and guides to the Internet Hunt, a monthly challenge to find online resources..:

Useful for Internet and computing; reference.
URL: http://www.brandonu.ca/~ennsnr/Resources/

Newbie Newz
Find out what you need to know to get started on the Internet

Newbie Newz is a mailing list designed for Internet novices ("newbies"). Kids, parents, and teachers can read articles and ask questions about using particular protocols or finding resources they need.

Useful for Internet and computing; mailing lists (listservs) and newsgroups.
E-mail: NewbieNewz@IO.COM
To subscribe: NewbieNewz-request@IO.COM
Message body: subscribe NewbieNewz our_email_address

Online World
Guide and newsletter share information on applications, resources

Those new to the Internet can learn how to make the most of Internet applications and resources in *The Online World* resources handbook by Odd de Presno, founder and administrator of KIDLINK, a global network for children. You can register for this online shareware publication here, and read about what's been revised in updated editions, which are posted every two months. A companion product, *The Online World Monitor* newsletter, not only discusses technical subjects but highlights resources offered in different parts of the world; for example, a recent issue focuses on de Presno's trip to Nigeria, giving hypertext links to newsgroups and other online resources about Africa.

Useful for international studies; Internet and computing.
URL: http://login.eunet.no/~presno/index.html

RealAudio
Tune into radio broadcasts as you surf the Net

This software technology from Progressive Networks allows radio stations around the world to broadcast over the Internet. The RealAudio Player works with your Web browser to decode and play audio on demand. Among its earliest supporters are ABC Radio, National Public Radio, the Canadian Broadcasting Corp., and KBS of Korea.
URL: http://www.realaudio.com/

School Internet User Q&A
What teachers, students and parents are asking

This FYI memo — officially titled *Request for Comments (RFC) 1578* — documents the questions most frequently asked about the Internet by K-12 teachers, administrators, and library specialists, as well as parents and students. The memo addresses the role of the Internet in education, implementing an Internet connection, security and ethical issues, collaboration between schools via the Internet, and other topics. The document also suggests readings and points to Internet resources that address the issues discussed. *RFC 1578* was produced by the Internet School Networking division of the Internet Engineering Task Force.

Useful for education; Internet and computing.
URL: gopher://gopher.cic.net:3005/00/fyi/q-a

Scout Report: New Internet Resources
Roundup of what's new in education

The Scout Report, offered by Info Scout Susan Calcari and InterNIC Information Services, is a weekly guide to what it deems the best of recently announced resources on the Internet. The focus is on items of interest in education and research. The report is available through gopher and the Web, with links to all listed resources. You can also sign up to have a copy e-mailed to you each week. This site also has keyword-searchable databases for *The Scout Report* and *net-happenings*, another very useful resource for locating Internet resources..

Useful for mailing lists (listservs) and newsgroups.
URL: http://www.internic.net/infoguide.html
To subscribe: majordomo@dstest.internic.net
Message body: subscribe scout-report

TotWare: Benjamin's Favorites
Free software for toddlers on the Internet

For the youngest computer users, here is an annotated list of links to PC and Macintosh shareware and freeware programs available on the Internet. The list of games and educational programs even comes with a stamp of approval from Benjamin, Webmaster Paul Mende's toddler.

Useful for consumer information; software.
URL: http://www.het.brown.edu/people/mende/totware.html

Virtual Reality in Education Mailing List
Observations, reviews by students

Students, teachers and anyone with an interest in the use of virtual reality in education may want to sign up to this open discussion list. Topics include current and potential uses of virtual reality environments in both traditional and alternative education, the effects of virtual reality environments on the learning process, and the efficacy of using virtual reality as an educational delivery system. The VIRTED list also welcomes reviews of research papers, publications and observations related to educational uses of virtual reality technology.

Useful for education; Internet and computing; mailing lists (listservs) and newsgroups.
URL: gopher://SJUVM.STJOHNS.EDU:2070/11/listserv/list%24nb/virted
To subscribe: LISTSERV@SJUVM.STJOHNS.EDU
Message body: SUB VIRTED YourFirstName YourLastName

Washington University Public Domain Archive
Collection of software, images

The Washington University Public Domain Archive — one of the largest FTP sites in the world — contains a huge collection of freeware, shareware, and graphic images. You'll find software for every type of computer and operating system, as well as images that will be useful in a variety of disciplines, such as mathematics and the life sciences. This archive also mirrors material at other FTP repositories.

Useful for images; software.
URL: http://wuarchive.wustl.edu

Web66: A K12 World Wide Web Project
Using the Web in the classroom

Web66 is a multifaceted project undertaken by the University of Minnesota to teach the K-12 community how to use the World-Wide Web and integrate its resources into the curriculum. The home page provides a Classroom Internet Server Cookbook that gives step-by-step instructions for setting up different types of servers along with hypertext links to all the necessary "ingredients"; and a mailing list through which educators can discuss the use of Web servers in the classroom. Of particular interest is the What's New page, which is modeled after the standard one by the National Center for Supercomputing Applications, but contains announcements of new online education resources and other items of specific interest to students and teachers.

Useful for Internet and computing; mailing lists (listservs) and newsgroups; school resources.
URL: http://web66.coled.umn.edu/
To subscribe: WebMaster@web66.coled.umn.edu
Message body: State: Your request, YourName, YourE-mailAddress

Well Connected Mac
Online resources for Macintosh users

This Web server provides access to a full range of online resources for Macintosh computer users. You can link directly to Mac-related Web pages, find out about mailing lists and other Internet resources for the Mac, get technical specs and pricing information for Apple products, download free software, read articles and reviews, and browse materials from commercial Mac hardware and software vendors.

Useful for software.
URL: http://rever.nmsu.edu/~elharo/faq/Macintosh.html

World Lecture Hall
How to use the Web in teaching

World Lecture Hall, a page on the Web Central of the University of Texas at Austin, offers links to educational materials—course syllabi, assignments, lecture notes, and text and graphics for study—at other Web sites around the world. Aimed at demonstrating how the Web can be used in teaching, the server includes materials in the arts, sciences, and professions, all organized by subject. Although most of the resources collected here are at the college level, many will also interest younger students and their teachers. For example, you'll find anatomical modules of the knee and distal thigh, slides of Renaissance and Baroque architecture, and illustrations and explanations of scenes from Shakespeare plays.

Useful for school resources.
URL: http://wwwhost.cc.utexas.edu/world/instruction/index.html

Ziff Davis Publishing Co.
Major computer magazines available online

Catch up on the latest news about the computer industry in *PC Magazine* and *PC Week*. Recent issues of these two leading trade publications are archived at this Web site by their publisher, the Ziff Davis Publishing Co.

Useful for Internet and computing; news sources.
URL: http://www.ziff.com

Language arts

A.Word.A.Day
Improve your vocabulary

A Word A Day is just one small tool you can use to improve your English vocabulary. This free e-mail service sends out one word and its definition every day, plus a quote drawn from a database of funny, witty or silly lines, some submitted by subscribers. More than 5,000 linguaphiles worldwide subscribe to A.Word.A.Day, which was started by Anu Garg, a computer science graduate of Case Western Reserve University. Other services provided by this server include: Dictionary/by/Mail, Thesaurus/by/Mail, Acronym/by/Mail, Anagram/by/Mail, and Rhyme-n-Reason.

Useful for language arts; reference.
URL: http://www.wordsmith.org/
E-mail: linguaphile@wordsmith.org
To subscribe: wsmith@wordsmith.org
Enter in subject line: subscribe our first name our last name

Acronym/by/Mail
Unravel an acronym without leaving your computer

Acronyms/by/Mail helps you unscramble an acronym, such as *IBM*, without leaving your computer when you send a request by e-mail. It's a free service available on the "wordserver" started by Anu Garg, a computer science graduate of Case Western Reserve University. Other services available from the "wordserver" include: A.Word.A.Day, Dictionary/by/Mail, Thesaurus/by/Mail, Anagram/by/Mail, and Rhyme-n-Reason.

Useful for language arts; reference.
URL: http://www.wordsmith.org/
E-mail: wsmith@wordsmith.org
Enter in subject line: acronym (acronym whose expansion you need to know)

ACRONYMS Dictionary
Quick answers to what words stand for

Acronyms are words, such as *radar* or *scuba,* formed from the first letter or letters of multiple words in an expression. The ACRONYMS Dictionary, compiled by Dave Sill of Martin Marietta Energy Systems, lists nearly 6,000 acronyms along with the words they abbreviate. Some entries also include details about the acronym's meaning or usage.

Useful for language arts; reference.
URL: gopher://info.mcc.ac.uk:70/11/miscellany/acronyms

Anagram/by/Mail
Service helps you sort out the letters

An anagram is a word or phrase made by rearranging the letters of another word or phrase. Anagram/by/Mail is an e-mail service that looks up the word or phrase for which you want to find anagrams. It's a free service available on the "wordserver" started by Anu Garg, a computer science graduate of Case Western Reserve University. Other services available from the "wordserver" include: A.Word.A.Day, Dictionary/by/Mail, Acronym/by/Mail, Thesaurus/by/Mail, and Rhyme-n-Reason.

Useful for language arts; reference.
URL: http://www.wordsmith.org/awad-cgibin/anagram
E-mail: wsmith@wordsmith.org

Banned Books Online
Find out why *Little Red Riding Hood* was censored

Ever wondered why certain books were banned? Now you can find out for yourself. John Ockerbloom of Carnegie-Mellon University has compiled a home page dealing with books that have been censored or suppressed. Titles range from *Ulysses* to *Little Red Riding Hood*, and Ockerbloom describes how and why each book got into trouble, especially with legal and school authorities. Links lead to online editions of each work.

Useful for literature.
URL: http://www.cs.cmu.edu:8001/Web/People/spok/banned-books.html
E-mail: spok@cs.cmu.edu

Big Sky Language Arts Lesson Plans
Reading, writing, grammar skills all covered

The server of Big Sky Telegraph, an educational network based in Montana, contains this folder of lesson plans, classroom activities and games, and other materials for language arts teachers (prekindergarten through grade 12). Lessons address such topics as elementary reading, vocabulary, grammar, comprehension, and creative and expository writing.

Useful for activities and projects; language arts.
URL: gopher://bvsd.k12.co.us:70/11/Educational_Resources/Lesson_Plans/Big%20Sky/language_arts

BookRead Matchmaker Service
Students use e-mail to discuss books

BR_Match, a spinoff of the Western Carolina University (WCU) BookRead project, is a mailing list that allows K-12 teachers and their students to partner up with other classrooms who are reading the same books. Partners can then discuss the books with each other via e-mail or the WCU MicroNet.

Useful for literature; mailing lists (listservs) and newsgroups.
E-mail: BR_Match@wcu.edu
To subscribe: mailserv@wcu.edu
Message body: subscribe BR_Match YourFirstName YourLastName

Canadian Literature Discussion List (CANLIT-L)
Exchange news and views

This bilingual discussion list is a forum for comments, concerns, reviews and questions from anyone interested in Canadian literature, literary publishing, or Canadian children's literature. Topics include writers, trends, literary theory, and the study and teaching of Canadian literature. The list is owned by the Canadian Literature Research Service of the National Library of Canada.

Useful for literature; mailing lists (listservs) and newsgroups.
E-mail: CANLIT-L@NLC-BNC.CA
To subscribe: MAILSERV@NLC-BNC.CA
Message body: SUBSCRIBE CANLIT-L

Children's Literature and Fairy Tales
Find the full texts of fables fast

The New York State Education Department offers a selection of many beloved children's stories and fairy tales. No graphics are included, which may be a drawback in reading to small children, but at least you can find the full texts of *Aesop's Fables*, Kipling's *Jungle Book* and other classics, if you're pressed for time,

Useful for literature.
URL: gopher://unix5.nysed.gov:70/11/K-12%20Resources/
English-Language%20Arts/Children%27s%20Lit%20%26%20Fairy%20Tales

Children's Literature Web Guide
What's new, what's neat

This guide to children's literature resources on the Internet provides an extensive set of links to lists of awards and recommended books, information about authors and fictional characters, electronic copies of children's books, children's literature discussion groups, movie tie-ins, writing by children, and resources for parents and teachers. Keep up-to-date on book awards, festivals, releases from publishers and even obituaries worldwide.

Useful for literature; reference.
URL: http://www.ucalgary.ca/~dkbrown/index.html

Data Text Library of Classic Literature
Hypertext novels online

Data Text Processing, a British firm offering electronic publishing services, provides its growing library of out-of-copyright fiction in hypertext. You can select novels by more than a dozen authors, from Louisa M. Alcott and Joseph Conrad to J. Meade-Falkner and Oscar Wilde.

Useful for literature.
URL: http://www.dircon.co.uk/datatext/library/index.htm

Dictionary/by/Mail
Ask for the definition of a word by e-mail

Dictionary/by/Mail lets you look up the definition of a word using e-mail. It's a free service available on the "wordserver" started by Anu Garg, a computer science graduate of Case Western Reserve University. Send e-mail to wsmith@wordsmith.org with the command "info Dictionary/by/Mail" in the subject line for an explanation of the pronunciation symbols used in the definitions. Other services available from the "wordserver" include: A.Word.A.Day, Thesaurus/by/Mail, Acronym/by/Mail, Anagram/by/Mail, and Rhyme-n-Reason.

Useful for language arts; reference.
URL: http://www.wordsmith.org/
E-mail: wsmith@wordsmith.org
Enter in subject line: define (word you want defined)

EcuaNet
News about Ecuador and other Spanish-speaking countries

EcuaNet, the gopher maintained by the Equatorial Information Corp., offers news and information, in Spanish, about Ecuador and other Latin American countries.

Useful for foreign languages.
URL: gopher://ecua.net.ec

Electronic Reference Tools
Guides to writing

This folder on Syracuse University's AskERIC server offers several reference guides for writing. You can browse or search the *American English Dictionary, Roget's Thesaurus*, and indexes of poetry and rock 'n' roll lyrics.

Useful for language arts; reference.
URL: gopher://ericir.syr.edu/11/Journals/Reference

English-Russian Dictionary
Find the word you need in Russian or in English

This interactive online dictionary translates between English and Russian. Information on obtaining Cyrillic fonts is available on the home page, along with links to other information about Russia, from the Russian software company, Elvis+.

Useful for foreign languages; reference.
URL: http://www.elvis.ru/cgi-bin/mtrans

English-Russian Dictionary & Thesaurus of Computer Terms
Look it up!

The electronic version of *The English-Russian Dictionary and Thesaurus of Computer Terms* — by Russian computer programmers E. Z. Druker, P. Z. Druker, and V. V. Sobotsinsky — translates computer terms between Russian and English. Information on obtaining Cyrillic fonts is included on the server. You can also request the meaning of a term by e-mail.

Useful for foreign languages; Internet and computing; reference.
URL: http://solar.rtd.utk.edu/cgi-bin/slovar
To subscribe: slovar@solar.rtd.utk.edu
Enter in subject line: LOOKUP (word you need defined)

French Connection
For all things French

Designed for students of French, as well as francophiles, the French Connection offers direct links to museums, art galleries, libraries, maps, news bulletins and other items with a French theme. Web pages, gophers and Usenet newsgroup pointers allow you to tap into French art, culture, current affairs, language and Canadiana, in French.

Useful for foreign languages; social studies.
URL: http://ausarts.anu.edu.au/french/french.html

French Language Press Review
Summaries in French of major news events

Students studying French can keep up with major news stories covered by the press in France through summaries in French posted at this site. The information is provided by the French Embassy via Georgetown University.

Useful for foreign languages; news sources.
URL: gopher://burrow.cl.msu.edu:70/11/news/news/general/french_language

Global Student Newswire
Guidelines for aspiring online writers and reporters

Global Student Newswire is an Internet-based wire service for online student newspapers at the high-school and college levels. It allows online campus papers to download and publish reports from student reporters around the world. This Web page provides the information you need to become involved in the project.

Useful for activities and projects; language arts.
URL: http://www.jou.ufl.edu/home.htm
To subscribe: electnws@jou.ufl.edu
Message body: YourFirstName YourLastName YourE-mailAddress
Enter in subject line: GSN: Info request

Gophers in French Around the World
Find documents in French

This gopher at the Universite Pierre et Marie Curie in Paris provides direct links to servers around the world offering resources written in French. Most of the connected sites are universities and government agencies, such as the National Library of Canada, the Pasteur Institute in France, Liege University in Belgium, and the University of Lausanne in Switzerland.

Useful for foreign languages.
URL: gopher://gopher.jussieu.fr:70/11/infoservers/gopher-francophones

Human Languages Page
Lessons, dictionaries, sound bites and more

The Human Languages Page, based at Willamette University, offers an extensive variety of materials for students of languages, from Aboriginal languages to Vietnamese. Its language and literature resources include a series of Spanish lessons, a German-English dictionary, Japanese lessons for travelers, an introduction to the Slovene alphabet, and audio clips of news in Greek. It also offers links to multilingual resources, language labs, vendors of language-learning software, and commercial translation services.

Useful for activities and projects; foreign languages.
URL: http://www.willamette.edu/~tjones/Language-Page.html

International Students Newswire KidNews
Service distributes students' stories

ISN KidNews is a news service for students and teachers around the world. Anyone can electronically submit stories: news, features, profiles, how-to descriptions, reviews, and sports. The stories, with appropriate credit, may be used by anyone. Teachers and students each have their own forums for discussing news gathering, teaching, and computer-related issues, including the nitty-gritty of conducting interviews and publishing a student newspaper. The page was developed by Dr. Peter Owens of the English Department at the University of Massachusetts, Dartmouth, who hopes ISN will eventually publish an electronic newspaper highlighting the most interesting stories it receives.

Useful for activities and projects; language arts.
URL: http://www.umassd.edu/SpecialPrograms/ISN/KidNews.html

Italian Literature
Archive contains fiction and nonfiction works in Italian

This page on Italian literature provides a searchable index of hypertext documents in Italian, ranging from poetry and religious texts to classical and contemporary narratives, such as *Pinocchio* by Carlo Lorenzini, the Italian constitution, Dante's *Divine Comedy* and *Giorni di guerra in Sicilia (War Days in Sicily)* by Grazia Pagliaro. It links to a historical overview of the development of the language and literature of Italy.

Useful for foreign languages.
URL: http://www.crs4.it/HTML/Literature.html

Jeffrey's Japanese-English Dictionary
Look up a word or phrase

This Japanese-English Dictionary on the Web was created by Jeffrey Friedl of Carnegie-Mellon University's Department of Computer Science. If your Web browser isn't capable of displaying Japanese text, you'll have to get some software to do it. The server has details.

Useful for foreign languages.
URL: http://www.cs.cmu.edu:8001/cgi-bin/j-e

KidPub
The place for young writers

This is where kids of all ages can publish their stories, as well as news about their schools and places where they live. Children can also contribute a paragraph to a story being written collaboratively online. Work submitted here ranges from stories by two 6-year-olds about civil rights leader Dr. Martin King Luther Jr. to "The Dinosauria Wars" by a 13-year-old.

Useful for activities and projects; language arts.
URL: http://en-garde.com/kidpub/intro.html

La Red Científica Peruana (Peruvian Scientific Network)
Facts in Spanish

This site, managed by a nonprofit organization in Peru, provides a variety of information about that country — mainly in Spanish, but with English and French materials as well. You'll find information from government agencies, such as statistics, historical articles, and the text of the constitution; images of the country; and news articles from the Peruvian and international press. Links take you to other networks in Peru and around the world.

Useful for foreign languages.
URL: http://www.rcp.net.pe/rcp.html
To subscribe: listasrcp@rcp.net.pe
Message body: add your-email-address noticias

Languages and ESL Resources
Materials and mailing lists

This site offers a mixed bag of materials for teachers and students of foreign languages and English as a second language (ESL). You'll find links to gophers and intercultural mailing lists in French, German, Italian, and Spanish, as well as ESL course outlines.

Useful for adult, continuing and distance education; foreign languages.
URL: gopher://goober.mbhs.edu:70/11/languages

loQtus:The Quotations Web Page
Find out who said what

The loQtus Web page offers thousands of quotations — from "the staunchly literary to the humorous". The site includes quotation archives as well as recent postings.

Useful for language arts; reference.
URL: http://pubweb.ucdavis.edu/Documents/Quotations/homepage.html

Nobel Prize for Literature
Impress the English teacher

Everything you ever wanted to know about the origin and history of this prestigious award plus brief background notes about the latest recipient are available from the Swedish Academy, in both English and Swedish. You will even be able to lay your hands on a list of 20th-century laureates..

Useful for literature.
URL: http://logos.svenska.gu.se/academy.html

One Book List
Add your favorite work to this list

One Book List is a unique project operated by Paul Phillips of InterNIC Information Services. It's a list of people's favorite books — one book per person — with an explanation of what makes each work interesting or enjoyable. Anyone can submit a favorite for inclusion in the list.

Useful for activities and projects; literature.
URL: http://www.primus.com/staff/paulp//one-book.txt
E-mail: paulp@primus.com

Online Writing Lab (OWL)
Tips and tutoring on grammar and composition

The Online Writing Lab at Purdue University provides more than 100 searchable online documents filled with writing tips ranging from the use of grammar, to how to write research papers, resumes, and business letters. High-school students also may find it helpful to e-mail specific questions to the lab's tutors.

Useful for language arts; online "tutors".
URL: http://owl.trc.purdue.edu/
E-mail: owl@sage.cc.purdue.edu
Message body: your question or request
Enter in subject line: owl-request

Patch American High School
Projects explore history of D-Day, fall of the Berlin Wall

Patch American High School, a U.S. Department of Defense Dependents School in Stuttgart, Germany, has tackled a number of ambitious online historical projects. Students and teachers will find a variety of materials relating to D-Day, including a collection of newsreels in QuickTime and MPEG formats, declassified battle plans and maps, famous speeches, and reminiscences of D-Day participants. The latest project — The Berlin Wall Falls: Perspectives from Five Years Down the Road — is a collaboration aiming to link student-produced documents from 30 schools worldwide.

Useful for history; images; international studies; schools on the Web.
URL: http://192.253.114.31/

Project Gutenberg
Download copies of classical and contemporary literature

Project Gutenberg, based at Illinois Benedictine College, has been providing free electronic texts since 1971. You can download hundreds of titles — from *The Adventures of Tom Sawyer* to *Sun Tzu on the Art of War*. Several texts are added each month. Most of the titles are over 75 years old and now in the public domain; however, a few more recent works are offered with the permission of the copyright holder.

Useful for literature.
URL: http://med-amsa.bu.edu/Gutenberg/Welcome.html
E-mail: almanac@oes.orst.edu (for a list of titles offered)
Message body: send gutenberg catalog

Project Libellus
Electronic texts of Latin classics

For those taking Latin in high school, this FTP site, based at the University of Washington, may be a boon. It offers electronic texts of Latin classics in the original. You'll find texts by such authors as Vergil, Caesar, Livy, and Catullus. Future additions may include a Latin-English dictionary and grammar. The site hopes to add classical Greek texts, as well.

Useful for foreign languages.
URL: ftp://ftp.u.washington.edu/pub/user-supported/libellus/texts

Projekt Gutenberg (Germany)
Full texts of German publications

A counterpart to the English Project Gutenberg, this site offers an index of links to the full-text versions of scores of books in German.

Useful for foreign languages.
URL: http://gutenberg.informatik.uni-hamburg.de/gutenb/home.html

Quick & Dirty Japanese
Get going with the basics

This section of Carnegie-Mellon University's English Server is designed for students and anyone else who wants to start speaking Japanese very quickly. It covers only verb conjugations and sentence particles — the basics of the language.

Useful for foreign languages.
URL: gopher://wiretap.spies.com/00/Library/Article/Language/grammar.jap

Radio France International
Lessons and news in French

If you are interested in learning French, Radio France International offers downloadable lessons to get you started. If you already read French, try keeping up-to-date on world affairs with the network's online daily news transcripts in French.

Useful for foreign languages.
URL: http://town.hall.org/travel/france/rfi.html

Ralph Bunche School
Elementary-school students contribute online

Ralph Bunche Elementary School in Harlem, NY, offers its school newspaper on-line. The bulk of the paper is written by students in grades 4-6, but it also includes a section prepared by students at Adam Clayton Powell, Jr., Junior High School (grades 7-9).

Useful for news sources; school resources; schools on the Web.
URL: http://Mac94.ralphbunche.rbs.edu/
E-mail: preese@ralphbunche.rbs.edu

Rhyme-n-Reason.
A new word puzzle every day

Rhyme-n-Reason serves up rhyming-word puzzles by e-mail. A new challenge is created each day and is available free on request from the "wordserver" started by Anu Garg, a computer science graduate of Case Western Reserve University. Other services available from the "wordserver" include: A.Word.A.Day, Dictionary/by/Mail, Acronym/by/Mail, Anagram/by/Mail, and Thesaurus/by/Mail.

Useful for entertainment; language arts; reference.
URL: http://www.wordsmith.org/
E-mail: wsmith@wordsmith.org
Enter in subject line: Rhyme-n-Reason today

schMOOze University
From games to grammar maze for ESL and EFL students

schMOOze University is a site designed for students and teachers of English as a second language (ESL) and English as a foreign language (EFL). It includes language games, a grammar maze, interactive "classrooms," a Usenet feed, and access to gophers. Log in as "CONNECT GUEST".

Useful for adult, continuing and distance education; foreign languages.
URL: telnet://MORGAN.DNSI.COM 8888

Serbian Language Lab
Listen as you learn

This Web page, based at the University of Maryland, teaches the alphabet and simple phrases of the Serbian language. It includes sound files, so you can listen as you learn (with the aid of appropriate software).

Useful for foreign languages.
URL: http://www.umiacs.umd.edu/research/lpv/YU/HTML/jezik.html

Shakespeare on the Internet
Where to find information about the Bard, his plays

Information about William Shakespeare and online versions of his plays are scattered across the Internet. The International Shakespeare Globe Centre, at the University of Cologne, tells you what exactly is out there and where to find it. For instance, it tells you that hypertext versions of the Bard's plays are available through the Massachusetts Institute of Technology, and links you to that collection. It also offers an eclectic range of pointers and links, from discussions on Shakespeare and references to Shakespeare in the *Star Trek* TV series, to movies based on his plays, and other general theatrical information.

Useful for literature.
URL: http://www.rrz.uni-koeln.de/phil-fak/englisch/SHAKESPEARE/engl/indexe.html

Tech Classics Archive
Read the works of the ancient authors

Nearly 200 translated works by 17 classical authors — from Aeschylus and Aristotle to Plotinus and Sophocles — are archived on the server at *The Tech*, the oldest and largest newspaper at the Massachusetts Institute of Technology. The title list is sorted alphabetically by author; titles include single-act plays, single-section books, and multisection books. You can search the archive by keyword, and directly link to sources of other electronic texts and reference works from around the world. The archive was compiled and designed by Dan Stevenson, a physics major and news editor of *The Tech*.

Useful for literature.
URL: http://the-tech.mit.edu:80/Classics/

Thesaurus/by/Mail
Request a synonym from the "wordserver"

Thesaurus/by/Mail can track down synonyms for any word using an online version of *Roget's Thesaurus*, and then send the results to you by e-mail. It's a free service available on the "wordserver" started by Anu Garg, a computer science graduate of Case Western Reserve University. Other services available from the "wordserver" include: A.Word.A.Day, Dictionary/by/Mail, Acronym/by/Mail, Anagram/by/Mail, and Rhyme-n-Reason.

Useful for language arts; reference.
URL: http://www.wordsmith.org/
E-mail: wsmith@lrdc5.lrdc.pitt.edu
Enter in subject line: synonym (word whose synonyms you want to find out)

Time Warner Publications
Up-to-date news on current events and world affairs

The Web server for several Time-Warner publications includes *Time Magazine, Sports Illustrated* and *People*. All or part of the magazines are available electronically before they reach the newsstands. The contents of back issues can be searched and articles retrieved. This server is extremely popular and access can be very slow.

Useful for news sources; social studies.
URL: http://www.timeinc.com/

Travelers' Japanese with Voice
Essentials for visitors

This Web page — presented by Takada Toshihiro of the Information Science Research Lab at Japan's Nippon Telegraph and Telephone Corp. — offers a brief introduction to the Japanese language for travelers. It includes a pronunciation guide and essential expressions for getting around, eating, and shopping. Downloadable sound files are also included, if you have the necessary software to listen to them. You'll also need a World-Wide Web Japanese browser to read the kanji and kana characters.

Useful for foreign languages.
URL: http://www.ntt.jp/japan/japanese/

Trincoll Journal
Join the staff of an online magazine

Aspiring artists and writers are encouraged to submit their work to *The Trincoll Journal*, a student-run multimedia publication at Trinity College. The magazine's home page provides submission guidelines and archives. If you would like a reminder when the latest edition comes out each week, subscribe to the mailing list.

Useful for activities and projects; language arts; news sources.
URL: http://www.trincoll.edu/tj/trincolljournal.html
To subscribe: Journal@mail.trincoll.edu
Enter in subject line: subscribe journal

Universal Survey of Languages
Sound bites and linguistic information

The Universal Survey of Languages is a project aimed at developing a comprehensive online reference point for linguists and laypeople alike, created by users of the Internet with expertise in this field. Currently, you can not only read a brief general description of various languages, but listen to sound clips of each. Eventually, more detailed information on morphological and phonological features, examples of written language, and links to further resources on a particular language are expected to be available here. The survey hopes to cover everything from modern languages, such as Arabic and Armenian, to ancient and invented languages, such as Latin and Esperanto.

Useful for foreign languages; reference.
URL: http://www.teleport.com:80/~napoleon/

University of Chicago Press
The latest publications from academic presses

The University of Chicago Press provides comprehensive online information about its publications, including an online catalog that is searchable by author or subject. The publisher indicates revisions to its works, such as details of changes made to each chapter in the latest edition of *The Chicago Manual of Style*. You can also find information about other online academic publishers and do an extensive search of catalogs of those U.S. university presses now online. UCP plans to create a one-stop electronic catalog for all university presses in the United States.

Useful for language arts; reference.
URL: gopher://press-gopher.uchicago.edu:70/1

University of Chile
Resources in Spanish reflect science and culture

The University of Chile, one of the oldest in Latin America, introduces Spanish-speaking visitors to the culture of that country. This Web site provides a variety of resources to tap into and practice your Spanish: information on the scientific community in Chile, the university and student organizations, conferences, and personal home pages. It also links to Internet sites outside of Chile.

Useful for foreign languages.
URL: http:/tortel.dcc.uchile.cl/index.html

Vietnam War Glossary
An explanation of terms, expressions related to the conflict

This glossary provides definitions for many terms often associated with the Vietnam War. This is part of The Vietnam Veterans Home Page.

Useful for reference.
URL: http://grunt.space.swri.edu/glossary.htm

Vocal Point
Student newspaper contains articles and opinions

Vocal Point is an electronic newspaper created by the K-12 students of the Boulder Valley (Colo.) School District and posted on the World-Wide Web. Each issue focuses on a particular topic—such as censorship and violence—with articles and opinions written by students of all grade levels. The newspaper is heavily illustrated with still pictures and even animations.

Useful for news sources; school resources.
URL: http://bvsd.k12.co.us/cent/Newspaper/Newspaper.html

Waking in Jerusalem
An online illustrated book for younger kids

Waking in Jerusalem by Sharon Katz is the first of several online books planned by Canadian children's book publisher Concertina and InterAccess Technology Corp. Created for kids ages 3 to 7, it tells (in text and illustrations) the story of a little boy who gets up before his parents and watches the city of Jerusalem wake up. Information on ordering hard-copy versions of this and other books is given.

Useful for activities and projects; literature.
URL: http://www.digimark.net/iatech/books

WebIt Mailing List
News and correspondents for students of Italian

The Italian World-Wide Web community has set up the first mailing list in the Italian language for Web users and information providers. WebIt includes news, announcements, archived messages, and an online e-mail form for subscribing.

Useful for foreign languages; mailing lists (listservs) and newsgroups.
URL: http://www.di.unipi.it:80/WebIt/

To subscribe: listserver@unipi.it
Message body: subscribe WEBIT [il vostro nome]

Wiretap Web
Fiction and nonfiction classics online

This electronic library offers the full texts of more than 100 fiction and nonfiction classics — everything from *Aesop's Fables* to *Roget's Thesaurus*. These works include electronic texts released into the public domain by Wiretap itself. You'll also find pointers to various other electronic text projects on the Internet, government documents, and the archives of the newsgroup alt.etext.

Useful for literature.
URL: http://www.spies.com/

Women and Literature
Major authors profiled

Based on the SunSite server at the University of North Carolina, this page offers biographies and portraits of major female literary figures — from Maya Angelou to Virginia Woolf. About 15 authors, from the past and present, are profiled.

Useful for literature.
URL: http://sunsite.unc.edu/cheryb/women/wlit.html

Word Games and Puzzles
Challenge your vocabulary

A good way to expand your vocabulary is by playing with words. This publisher offers several interactive word puzzles and games to help you learn new words. There's also a monthly crossword puzzle to be solved. Syndicate also provides information about the educational software it sells.

Useful for activities and projects; entertainment; language arts.
URL: http://syndicate.com/

Legal issues

Emory Law School Web
Searching for a legal mailing list or law firm?

The Emory Law School Web, still in its formative stages, plans to provide links to legal information scattered across the Internet. It currently provides links to law-related mailing lists, and information about legal firms and lawyers. Information on the server is searchable.

Useful for law and legal issues.
URL: http://www.law.emory.edu/

Law Firms and Individual Lawyers on the Internet
Profiles and answers

Compiled by the Emory University Law Library, these direct links take you to information provided online by attorneys and legal firms from around the world specializing in immigration, family, criminal, and communications law, to name a few areas.

Useful for law and legal issues.
URL: http://www.law.emory.edu/LAW/refdesk/firms.html

Law Lists
E-mail lists, newsgroups may provide the answer you need

In her often updated *Law Lists*, hosted by the University of Chicago, Lyonette Louis-Jacques includes scores of e-mail discussion and distribution lists, electronic journals, newsletters and digest, as well as law-related Usenet newsgroups. Every topic from public policy to animal rights and firearms control appears to be discussed, and those searching for information on a particular legal question may find help here. Instructions on how to subscribe to the lists are given.

Useful for law and legal issues; mailing lists (listservs) and newsgroups.
URL: gopher://lawnext.uchicago.edu:70/00/.internetfiles/lawlists

Legal Domain Network
Scan and search what the experts say about legal issues

Created as a haven for serious discussion of law and legal issues, the Legal Domain Network provides access to many mailing lists in that arena. Although you can't actually post messages on this network unless you have a Usenet reader, you can browse (via gopher or World-Wide Web) discussions taking place among practicing attorneys, law professors and students, and government officials. You can search for information by keyword.

Useful for law and legal issues; mailing lists (listservs) and newsgroups.
URL: gopher://gopher.kentlaw.edu/1/Internet Services/News/lawnet

Legal Info on the Internet
From legal decisions to self-help legal documents

Quadralay, a Texas computer company, is building a set of links to major sources of legal information on the Internet. Its link to Nolo Press' Self-Help Law Center is especially useful for families. Nolo publishes easy-to-use books and software on consumer law subjects such as wills, small claims court, divorce, and debt problems. Families will find descriptions — and online ordering options — for publications dealing with legal issues related to couples, kids, adoption, Social Security and long-term care. Other links available from here include Cornell Law School's Legal Information Institute, the Electronic Frontier Foundation, LegaLink, and the U.S. Supreme Court.

Useful for law and legal issues.
URL: http://www.quadralay.com/www/Other/Legal.html

Mathematics

Ask Dr. Math
Online help for big and little problems

K-12 students who have a math problem or simply want to talk to someone who loves math can contact Dr. Math (actually a group of math students and professors at Swarthmore College). Ask Dr. Math is a project of Swarthmore's Geometry Forum, a program of the National Science Foundation.

Useful for mathematics; online "tutors".
URL: http://forum.swarthmore.edu/
E-mail: dr.math@forum.swarthmore.edu

Ask Prof. Maths
Mathematician accepts queries from K-9 students

Prof. Maths is Professor Tim Kurtz of the Department of Mathematics at St. Bonaventure University, who encourages students in kindergarten through Grade 9 to ask him math questions. Prof. Maths responds directly to each question. He's also open to queries from teachers who want advice on math topics or teaching techniques. Questions and answers are archived periodically and may be retrieved via anonymous FTP.

Useful for mathematics; online "tutors".
URL: ftp://ftp.sbu.edu/pub\prof.maths
E-mail: maths@sbu.edu
Message body: State: Problem, name, grade level, e-mail address
Enter in subject line: Request: K-5 or 6-9 grade levels

Big Sky Mathematics Lesson Plans
Activities and examples included

Part of Montana's Big Sky Telegraph educational network, this server offers a collection of more than 40 K-12 mathematics lesson plans. Each plan includes an objective, overview, activities and procedures, and examples. The lessons were prepared at summer workshops held by the Columbia Education Center, an association of teachers from 14 western states.

Useful for activities and projects; mathematics; school resources.
URL: gopher://bvsd.k12.co.us:70/11/Educational_Resources/
Lesson_Plans/Big%20Sky/math

Claremont High School
Students untangle a math problem

Claremont High School was the first school in California with its own Web server, and continues to experiment with it, providing links to other educational information servers, and home pages for its own students and staff. A subdirectory displays reports, tables and a QuickTime movie of a math and computing project done by the school's "Knot Dudes," which was funded in part by the National Science Foundation and SuperQuest,

Useful for activities and projects; mathematics; schools on the Web.
URL: http://archives.math.utk.edu/

Common Weights and Measures
How to convert between metric and U.S. units

Common Weights and Measures, maintained by the University of California, Berkeley, offers information about mathematical notation, the metric system, and converting between metric and U.S. units. If you need to determine the number of square feet or hectares in an acre, look no further.

Useful for mathematics; reference; science.
URL: http://www.cchem.berkeley.edu/ChemResources/Weights-n-Measures/index.html

CSC Mathematical Topics
Animations and answers from computing experts

The Center for Scientific Computing (CSC), the Finnish national supercomputer center, includes a page of math-related materials, including animations. You may also contact specialists in math at the center.

Useful for images; mathematics; online "tutors".
URL: http://www.csc.fi/math_topics/General.html

Eisenhower National Clearinghouse
Abstracts point to math, science materials

Funded by the U.S. Department of Education and based at Ohio State University, the Eisenhower National Clearinghouse is designed to improve access to resources for K-12 mathematics and science teachers in the United States. It offers a catalog containing abstracts of lesson plans, teaching modules, interactive resources, videotapes, software, and other teaching aids. Some of these items are posted online; others are available through libraries or commercially. The clearinghouse also sponsors a discussion group for teachers and offers links to other educational servers.

Useful for activities and projects; mathematics; school resources.
URL: gopher://enc.org

Fun Math
Puzzles and pictures to learn from

Puzzles, problems and pictures can help students learn and laugh about math. This assortment contains paradoxes, logic puzzles, and images of fractals, crystals, hyberbolics, and knots. They were collected by Kumar Das, George Petrov, Bren Halfwassen, and Douglas Sohn of University Laboratory High School at the University of Illinois

Useful for activities and projects; images; mathematics.
URL: http://www.uni.uiuc.edu/departments/math/glazer/fun_math.html

Gallery of Interactive On-Line Geometry, University of Minnesota Geometry Center
Entertainment for math lovers

This series of interactive games lets math enthusiasts explore the effects of negatively curved space in a pinball-style game, and try out other activities. The page is compiled by the University of Minnesota's Geometry Center, which develops, supports, and promotes computational tools for visualizing geometric structures as part of its research for the National Science Foundation. The interactive software can be downloaded.

Useful for activities and projects; mathematics.
URL: http://www.geom.umn.edu/apps/gallery.html

Geometry Forum
Materials and mentors on math topics

Based at Pennsylvania's Swarthmore College, the Geometry Forum offers materials on geometry and other mathematical topics for a variety of audiences, including K-12 students and teachers. You can browse the resources, download software, and join several newsgroups — including one on precollege geometry and another on geometry puzzles. In the body of your message, indicate the group or groups you wish to join, such as geometry.precollege, geometry.college, geometry.research, geometry.announcements, geometry.forum, geometry.puzzles and geometry.institutes Use dashes instead of dots: geometry-pre-college.

Useful for mailing lists (listservs) and newsgroups; mathematics.
URL: http://forum.swarthmore.edu/
To subscribe: majordomo@forum.swarthmore.edu
Message body: subscribe GroupName

History of Mathematics
Timeline, other files take you from past to present

What did Ahmes or Baudhayana contribute to the study of mathematics? The hyperlinked timeline on this server — maintained by David E. Joyce at Clark University's Department of Mathematics and Computer Science — will tell you. You can also find information about mathematical developments in China, the Arabic sphere, Europe, Greece, India, and Japan. There are also links to more modern fare, such as conference announcements, book lists and other resources on the Internet.

Useful for history; mathematics.
URL: http://aleph0.clarku.edu/~djoyce/mathhist/mathhist.html

Maryland Virtual High School of Math and Science
Skill-building projects

The Maryland Virtual High School of Math and Science, funded in part by the National Science Foundation, is a project that aims to increase high-school students' interest — and proficiency — in math and science. When completed, the Virtual High School will allow students worldwide to work cooperatively on projects in computational science, using modeling software and other high-technology tools. This Web site features several projects, including one based on an overpopulation of squirrels, as well as home pages developed by students enrolled in this magnet program at Montgomery Blair High School.

Useful for activities and projects; mathematics; science.
URL: http://goober.mbhs.edu/~sbuczko/mvhs.html#Resources

Mathematics Archives
Images, animations, software, puzzles and more

The University of Tennessee at Knoxville's Mathematics Archives is an Internet starting point for mathematicians, teachers, and even K-12 students. You can access a tremendous range of math resources, all organized by category. Kids will enjoy the large collection of mathematics art — including fractals, Mandelbrot images, the paintings of M.C. Escher, and other math-related images and animations. Other highlights include public-domain software and shareware for math teachers, reviews of commercial software, math puzzles and other recreational materials, teaching aids, newsgroups, and bibliographies.

Useful for images; mathematics.
URL: http://archives.math.utk.edu/

MathMagic
Challenges teach kids about math and communications

MathMagic is a project that encourages K-12 students to use computers in two distinct ways — to solve math problems and to communicate. Math challenges are posted into four categories (K-3, 4-6, 7-9, and 10-12), a team of students at one location pairs up with a team at another site, and both teams work together to solve the problem. An e-mail list allows teachers to share their observations about the project. When subscribing, substitute K-3, 4-6, 7-9, 10-12 or general for X-Y.

Useful for mailing lists (listservs) and newsgroups; mathematics.
URL: http://forum.swarthmore.edu/mathmagic/
To subscribe: majordomo@forum.swarthmore.edu
Message body: subscribe mathmagic-X-Y-open

MegaMath
Making math intriguing from an early age

Elementary-school students are intrigued by the size of infinity and the fact that the simplest-sounding math problems can challenge even the biggest computers. Through hands-on activities involving graphs, stories, games and other hypertext materials, the MegaMath project tries to show these youngsters that the study of math can be exciting. The project, involving teachers, students and mathematicians, is led by Los Alamos National Laboratory.

Useful for activities and projects; mathematics.
URL: http://www.c3.lanl.gov/mega-math

Mississippi School for Mathematics and Science
Inspiring student stories

On its Web page, the Mississippi School for Mathematics and Science — a public school for gifted 11th- and 12th-graders in Columbus — offers information about its curriculum as well as "resumes" of graduates and current students. These young people explain what they've learned at the school and how they're planning for the future.

Useful for mathematics; scholarshipand college information; schools on the Web.
URL: http://www.msms.doe.k12.ms.us/

T.C. O'Haver's Internet Resources for Mathematics and Science Education
List describes what each resource has to offer

T.C. O'Haver of the University of Michigan's Department of Chemistry and Biochemistry maintains this list of Internet resources for mathematics and science education. The alphabetical listing provides addresses for and descriptions of the resources.

Useful for mathematics; science.
URL: gopher://una.hh.lib.umich.edu:70/00/inetdirsstacks/mathsci%3Aohaver

Music

Composer Biographies
Glimpse the lives of music's masters

Music lover Michael Norrish, a PhD student at Cambridge University, has begun preparing short hypertext biographies of classical composers, complete with thumbnail images. The biography of Johann Sebastian Bach, for example, indicates the works for which he is perhaps best known as well as details about some of his musical idiosyncrasies. The Composers page also links to other online music resources, from classical to jazz, such as a list of composers and suggested pieces for "getting to know them by."

Useful for music; reference.
URL: http://www.cl.cam.ac.uk/users/mn200/music/composers.html

Internet Poetry Archive
Sound clips bring poets' verse to life

Based on the University of North Carolina's SunSite server, the Internet Poetry Archive includes selected poems from noted contemporary poets — such as Seamus Heaney and Czeslaw Milosz — in their original languages and in English translations. The archive includes the text of poems, photos of poets with short biographies, sound clips of poets reading their work, and bibliographies.

Useful for images; literature; music.
URL: http://sunsite.unc.edu/dykki/poetry/home.html

Musi-Cal
Searchable calendar of live music events

Musi-Cal provides easy access to current information about concerts, festivals, gigs and other events featuring live music. You can search by city, musician, type of music and date for an event. The service is provided by Automatrix, Inc., a New York state Internet service provider.

Useful for music; travel and recreation.
URL: http://www.automatrix.com/concerts/

Music Archives at Duke University
Indexes of lyrics, sheet music and images

Duke University's Music Archives offer indexes, which you can search by keyword, to American song lyrics, sheet music, and music images in GIF format. A search using the keywords "O Canada" from the Canadian national anthem, for example, finds a thumbnail and larger image of the Canadian coat of arms in the images database.

Useful for images; music.
URL: gopher://iliad.lib.duke.edu:70/11/DULib_Res/MusicArchives

WWW Virtual Keyboard
You probably won't be confused with Mozart

If your computer is set up for sound, you can try tinkling the keys on this image of a piano keyboard. By clicking on a piano key, you hear the note it represents. The Virtual Keyboard is the brainchild of computer consultant Michael Moncur.

Useful for activities and projects; music.
URL: http://www.xmission.com:80/~mgm/misc/keyboard.html

Youth Music/Youth Culture
From punk rock to pop

Drake University's Jean-Paul Davis and Thomas Swiss compiled the Youth Music/Youth Culture home page as part of their study of music and its effect on culture. Direct links take you to electronic magazines, academic sites for music and culture (such as the study of punk rock's roots), listings organized by type of music, song lyrics, audio clips, and Usenet newsgroups that focus on these topics. You can also connect to home pages created by a range of performers (from Nirvana to Janet Jackson) and their fans

Useful for music; social studies.
URL: http://www.drake.edu/univannounce/thomas/honors123.html

Pen pals

Alaskan Keypals
Find someone to e-mail in Alaska

Kids who want to find an e-mail pen pal may search for a correspondent from Alaska on this list. Courtesy of the Falcon's Nest — the Web site of University Park Elementary School in Fairbanks — the list is divided by grade level, from kindergarten to Grade 6. Adults, particularly educators, can also find pen pals among the teachers and administrators at the school.

Useful for pen pals.
URL: http://www.upk.northstar.k12.ak.us/

EKIDS: Electronic Kids Internet Discussion Server
For kids at home, school

EKIDS is an unmoderated mailing list open to school children from around the world who wish to talk about school, hobbies, sports and anything else that interests them. While parents and teachers may join, they are encouraged not to dominate the discussions. Kids seeking pen pals — or what the list calls "epals" — can also check the list and its hypertext archives, hosted by City Beach Senior High School, Western Australia.

Useful for pen pals.
URL: http://www.citybeach.wa.edu.au/mailarch.html
E-mail: ekids@citybeach.wa.edu.au
To subscribe: majordomo@citybeach.wa.edu.au
Message body: subscribe ekids

KIDS
Letters from kids to other kids

KIDS is a spinoff of the KIDSPHERE mailing list. While KIDSPHERE provides a forum for kids and teachers, KIDS is for postings from children to other youngsters around the world. Both lists are operated by the nonprofit KIDLINK Society.

Useful for mailing lists (listservs) and newsgroups.
E-mail: kids@vms.cis.pitt.edu
To subscribe: kids-request@vms.cis.pitt.edu
Message body: SUBSCRIBE Kids YourFirstName YourLastName

Reference and news sources

Biographical Dictionary
Database gives you the basics on notable figures

From Byron to Iacocca, this reference dictionary contains more than 15,000 entries on notable figures in world history, kept up to date by its creator, Eric Tentarelli. You can search the database by keyword for information not readily available in printed publications, such as to learn who discovered potassium or for a chronological table of world chess champions.

Useful for reference.
URL: http://www.mit.edu:8001/afs/athena/user/g/a/galileo/ Public/WWW/galileo.html

Britannica Online
Service lets subscribers search the encyclopedia

Britannica Online provides an online demonstration and information about accessing the full text of the current *Encyclopaedia Britannica* in electronic form. Subscribers to this service can do various types of searches for information and browse hypertext and images in Britannica's full encyclopædic database, *Merriam-Webster's Collegiate Dictionary (10th Edition)*, and the *Britannica Book of the Year*.

Useful for reference.
URL: http://www.eb.com/

British Library's Online Information Server
British history and literature

The British Library Board has developed a Web site that has a historical and literary flavor. It includes an exhibit on the history and art of map-making as well as a look at poet John Keats.
URL: http://portico.bl.uk/

CARRIE: An Electronic Full-text Library
Full texts available electronically

This full-text electronic library is operated by the University of Kansas. It offers a reference section as well as a link to Rich Rath's Omnivore, a world news service that draws on international news sources from across the Internet.

Useful for library; news sources.
URL: http://history.cc.ukans.edu/carrie/carrie_main.html

Commercial News Services on the Web
Sample, search world's newspapers

This Web page, based at the University of Florida, provides pointers to the online offerings of newspapers from around the world. Most papers provide sample articles from various departments and allow users to search current and back issues. A few include graphics.

Useful for news sources.
URL: http://www.jou.ufl.edu/commres/webjou.htm

Create Your Own Newspaper (CRAYON)
Pick up your custom copy

You can create and receive a customized newspaper, down to the name you choose to give it, online. The CRAYON interface allows you to choose the types of news that you want to read, then pulls it all together on a daily basis from various Internet sources. The finished product is e-mailed to you. CRAYON was created by Jeff Boulter, a computer science engineering student and managing editor of the student newspaper at Bucknell University.

Useful for news sources.
URL: http://sun.bucknell.edu/~boulter/crayon/

Daily News: Free Internet Sources
Where to find it on the Internet

The Daily News doesn't contain the news of the day, but it will tell you where to find it on the Internet. You'll find information about newspapers, broadcasters, and other sources of daily or archived news—divided by region (country, state, city, and so on) or specialty. The server also offers assistance for journalists, e-mail addresses of selected newspapers, and related materials.

Useful for news sources.
URL: http://blick.journ.latech.edu/F-4:5508:news sources

E-Journal of Student Research
Students offer ideas for school projects

Students looking for ideas for school projects may find inspiration in the *E-Journal of Student Research* published by the National Student Research Center (NSRC) at Mandeville (La.) Middle School. You can browse through the current edition or peruse the students' abstracts of language arts, math, science and social science projects in the archives.

Useful for activities and projects; education.
URL: gopher://gopher.terc.edu:70/11/hub/owner/other/NSRC

Educational Resources List and Database
Twin sources for mining the Internet

This pair of mailing lists can help you find new and existing sources of educational information on the Internet. EDRES-L is a moderated forum for announcements and evaluations of online educational resources. EDRES-DB acts as a database for information that appears on EDRES-L. For more information on using EDRES-DB, send an e-mail message to LISTSERV@UNB.CA, with the following command in the body of the message: GET EDRES-DB FAQ

Useful for mailing lists (listservs) and newsgroups.
E-mail: EDRES-L@unb.ca
To subscribe: LISTSERV@UNB.CA
Message body: sub edres-l YourFirstName YourLastName

Electronic Emissary
Experts use e-mail to answer students' questions

Based at the College of Education at the University of Texas at Austin, the Electronic Emissary project places K-12 teachers and their students in contact with subject-matter experts through e-mail. Teachers can ask for a match with a specialist in a particular subject or field, such as astronomy, genetics, meteorology, medieval history, animal behavior, world politics, or virtual reality. If a volunteer expert is available (or becomes available), Electronic Emissary furnishes his or her e-mail address. The Electronic Emissary project is funded by a combination of government agencies, corporate foundations, and charities.

Useful for online "tutors".
URL: ftp://tcet.unt.edu@pub/telecomputing-info/emissary-reports

Electronic Newsstand
Browse or buy current and back copies of popular magazines

The Electronic Newsstand, a service of Online Publishing, lets you browse more than 100 magazines — such as *Business Week, New Yorker, Omni, Classroom Connect, Discover: The World of Science, Saturday Night* and the *Times Literary Supplement.* You can view the table of contents and one or more articles from each magazine's current issue. The newsstand also includes archives of these articles, which you can search by keyword. A few magazines, such as *Maclean's,* even provide special materials for classroom use. Although this server was created to sell magazines (each entry includes subscription information), there's no charge for browsing or for searching back issues.

Useful for news sources.
URL: http://www.enews.com/

Glenview Community Consolidated School District 34
K-8 library catalogs

Illinois' Glenview Community Consolidated School District 34 has apparently achieved a first on the Internet by making the catalogs of seven school libraries, from kindergarten through Grade 8, available online. Users can also browse and search the catalog of the Glenview Public Library, and connect to the ICEBOX, the electronic bulletin-board system of the Illinois Computing Educators, a statewide education group.

Useful for library.
URL: http://www.ncook.k12.il.us/dist34_home_page.html

Internet Multicasting Service
Audio files let you listen to radio programming

The Internet Multicasting Service is a nonprofit "radio station" available on the Internet. It offers two "channels": Internet Talk Radio, focusing on science and technology, and Internet Town Hall, offering public-affairs programming. You can download sound files from either — the service publishes 30-90 minutes of programming per day, and each hour of programming takes up about 30 megabytes. You can play the files on several operating systems using the software provided. You can also subscribe to e-mail announcements of upcoming programs.

Useful for news sources.
URL: http://town.hall.org/radio/index.html
E-mail: info@radio.com
To subscribe: Majordomo@radio.com
Message body: subscribe announce (your e-mail address)

Internet Public Library
Experiment brings real library services to the Web

The Internet Public Library — at the University of Michigan School of Information and Library Studies — is a pilot project aimed at providing an online library open 'round the clock on the Internet. It is testing a reference desk, modeled after that of a traditional library; initially, its librarians are answering questions by e-mail but eventually plan to do so in real time. The IPL also offers an extensive collection of reference materials; a Reading Room with electronic texts; and an Education Division with materials for teaching. The library's Youth Division includes a Story Hour section; Dr. Internet, who helps kids with math and science problems; an entry form for a story contest, an opportunity to ask questions of children's authors (to build fact sheets about them and their work), and an opportunity to discuss children's books. It also plans a bulletin board, where adults may share information about Internet sites for children.

Useful for library; online "tutors".
URL: http://ipl.sils.umich.edu/

Kidopedia
An encyclopedia by and for kids

Kidopedia is a global online encyclopedia being written by and for kids. Some schools have begun writing entries for their own local Kidopedias, from which the best will be chosen for the global encyclopedia. Organizers expect the global Kidopedia to include entries, links to local sites, links to resource people worldwide and a suggestion page. It will be accessible through the Kidopedia home page and, eventually, e-mail.

Useful for mailing lists (listservs) and newsgroups; reference.
URL: http://rdz.stjohns.edu/kidopedia/
E-mail: kidpedia@sjuvm.stjohns.edu
To subscribe: listserv@sjuvm.stjohns.edu

Library Catalogs Accessible on the Internet
Look for a particular publication

Yale University maintains this worldwide list of libraries that have made their catalogs accessible to Internet users.

Useful for library; reference.
URL: gopher://libgopher.yale.edu:70/11/

Library of Congress Home Page
Access to online exhibitions, databases

This is becoming the main entry point to the electronic resources of the Library of Congress. Through this page you currently can link directly to historical collections from the library's *American Memory* exhibition; descriptions of some of its American Special Collections; several of its online exhibits, including the *Gettysburg Address*; Thomas, a database of legislation information on the Internet; Country Studies; the POW/MIA Database from the Federal Research Division; and LC MARVEL and LOCIS, the library's information systems.

Useful for library.
URL: http://lcweb.loc.gov/homepage/lchp.html

Library of Congress LOCIS
Find records on legislation, copyright, more

The Library of Congress Information System (LOCIS) contains over 26 million records located in a variety of databases or files. These include records for materials in more than 400 languages held by the library and other research institutions; summaries, abstracts, chronologies, and detailed status information for bills and resolutions introduced in the U.S. Congress since 1973 (information for the current Congress is up-to-date within 48 hours);.records for materials registered for copyright since January 1978; records describing over 13,000 organizations doing research in science, technology and the social sciences; and records that abstract and cite foreign laws and regulations as well as journal articles on legal topics.

Useful for reference.
URL: http://lcweb.loc.gov/homepage/lchp.html

Library of Congress MARVEL
Online exhibits, extensive catalogs, research tools

The Library of Congress Machine-Assisted Realization of the Virtual Electronic Library (LC MARVEL) is a large-scale project providing access to the library's resources. You can explore the Library of Congress Catalog and other research tools. The LC MARVEL also offers online versions (with both text and GIF image files) of past exhibits at the Library: *1492: An Ongoing Voyage, The African-American Mosaic, Scrolls form the Dead Sea: The Ancient Library of Qumran and Modern Scholarship, Revelations from the Russian Archives,* and *Rome Reborn: The Vatican Library and Renaissance Culture.* The LC Marvel links to Congressional servers and other sites of interest. The library is building a Librarian's Rolodex with answers to frequently asked questions that anyone can tap into—including names and addresses of other major libraries and private researchers; lists of documents, with their call numbers, related to the U.S. budget and the final report on the Iran-Contra affair; how to research Congressional voting records; and even where to look for a copy of the famous newspaper article "Yes, Virginia, there is a Santa Claus."

Useful for library.
URL: gopher://marvel.loc.gov

List of Listservs
Looking for a mailing list?

Profiles of a large number of mailing lists on the Internet are available from this list. While you can't get direct access to the lists and their archives from this Web page, you can find a description of each and how to join it. Mailing lists are grouped by subject, such as biology and chemistry, curricula, and education.

Useful for mailing lists (listservs) and newsgroups.
URL: http://www.clark.net/pub/listserv/listserv.html

Listservs, newsgroups and electronic serials for librarians
A master list

This resource produced by the University of Houston Libraries is primarily intended for librarians, but will be of use to some parents. It lists all library-related listservs as well as instructions for subscribing to the discussion lists.

Useful for library; mailing lists (listservs) and newsgroups.
URL: http://info.lib.uh.edu/liblists/home.htm

Magna Carta
What did the Magna Carta really say?

A lot is said about the *Magna Carta*, but this British Library Board Web site is where you can read a translation of this 1215 document as well as view an image of one of the four surviving copies.
URL: http://portico.bl.uk/access/treasures/magna-carta.html

NCSU Libraries Webbed Information System
Catalogs, indexes, databases

The North Carolina State University (NCSU) Libraries Webbed Information System (formerly Library Without Walls) is modeled after a physical library and offers a wide range of resources:

- Searchable online catalogs, indexes, and databases of the NCSU, University of North Carolina-Chapel Hill, and Duke University libraries, as well as government, newspaper, business and academic sources.
- A "reference desk" offering dictionaries, directories, indexes, Internet guides, and other reference tools.
- *Study carrels*, organized by discipline, offering links to Internet resources.
- Electronic books and journals.
- Public-domain software and utilities.

Useful for reference.
URL: http://dewey.lib.ncsu.edu

Newspaper Services Accessible on the Internet
Worldwide list and links

Maintained by Steve Outing of Planetary News, Inc., this list describes newspapers from around the world that are either currently online (with direct links) or soon plan to be. It indicates their focus, as well as how to access and subscribe to them electronically. The newspapers here include dailies and weeklies, from *The (London) Telegraph* and *The New York Times* to Saskatchewan's *Western Producer* and Rome's *l'Unita*. Many of these, such as *USA Today*, offer free subscriptions to K-12 students.

Useful for news sources.
URL: http://marketplace.com/e-papers.list.www/e-papers.internet.html

On-line Books Page
Browse or search through hundreds of books

The On-line Books Page, maintained by John Ockerbloom, is an index to the full texts of hundreds of books in English available free on the Internet. In addition, it links to hundreds more, in text or hypertext formats, from specialty and foreign-language repositories, as well as information from book catalogs and retailers. You can browse or search by author or title, as well as browse a listing of new books and a listing organized by subject.

Useful for library; literature.
URL: http://www.cs.cmu.edu:8001/Web/books.html

Public Libraries on the Internet
Links to libraries around the globe

This list links to documents and general information at public libraries worldwide. Access to most of the libraries is only available through a TELNET connection. The list is being compiled by the St. Joseph County (Ind.) Public Library.

Useful for library.
URL: http://sjcpl.lib.in.us/homepage/PublicLibraries/PublicLibraryServers.html

Quotations Page
A few words of humor

Computer consultant Michael Moncur collects quotations, mainly of a humorous nature. You can search his database of more than 1,000 quotations using a keyword or author's name, or simply amuse yourself by reading his selected quote of the day. Each time you load the Random Quotations Page, you will be treated to three new entries. The Quotations Page also links to Internet collections of frequently asked questions, commercial software, newsgroups and movie-related archives related to quotations.

Useful for reference.
URL: http://www.xmission.com/~mgm/quotes

School Library Media Network (LM_NET)
Specialists exchange information

The LM_NET discussion list focuses specifically on the needs of school library media specialists. It offers information on new publications (both online and print), services, and activities in the field. Subscribers can share their ideas, ask questions of one another, and explore opportunities to link up with other schools' library media centers. All LM_NET messages are archived at the gopher site.

Useful for school resources.
URL: gopher://ericir.syr.edu:70/11/Listservs/LM_NET
E-mail: LM_NET@suvm.syr.edu
To subscribe: listserv@suvm.syr.edu
Message body: subscribe LM_NET YourFirstName YourLastName

Stanford Netnews Filtering Service
An orderly way to sift through Usenet News

If you've found the daily volume of information about your special interests in the Usenet newsgroups too much to keep up with, the Stanford Netnews Filtering Service probably can help. When you subscribe to the service, you provide profiles of the topics you are interested in following. The service monitors articles in the newsgroups, and periodically sends you any that seem to match your profiles. A practice exercise at this Web site shows you how to sign up and create profiles. This service is part of Stanford University's Electronic Library project, an experiment in large-scale information filtering and dissemination.

Useful for news sources.
URL: http://woodstock.stanford.edu:2000/

Stumpers-List
Tap into professional pool for answers to difficult questions

When you have a research question you simply can't find an answer to, the Stumpers-List mailing list and archive may offer a solution. The list is designed primarily for professional researchers and librarians, who post their questions and receive answers from other subscribers. Questions from "hitchhikers" (people who aren't regular subscribers to the list) are somewhat discouraged. However, anyone can perform a keyword search on the Stumpers monthly archives, available via gopher, for possible answers to their own questions.

Useful for mailing lists (listservs) and newsgroups; reference.
URL: gopher://crf.cuis.edu:70/11gopher_root2%3A%5Bstumpers-l%5D
E-mail: STUMPERS-LIST@CRF.CUIS.EDU
Enter in subject line: Please use this line in questions and answers

Tex-Share Gopher
Academic libraries share online catalogs, databases, texts

Tex-Share is a state-funded project allowing Texas' 52 public academic libraries to share their online catalogs, databases, and electronic-text offerings (such as periodicals and the texts of rare or fragile documents). On the Tex-Share gopher, you can access this rapidly expanding resource — and even copy documents. In the future, Tex-Share may expand to include other public libraries in Texas as well as academic libraries outside the state.

Useful for library.
URL: gopher://gopher.texshare.utexas.edu/

Time Magazine's Daily News Summary
Browse, search the day's events

Time offers a daily roundup of national and international news events. You can also search for more information on each topic in the magazine's database of articles.

Useful for news sources.
URL: http://pathfinder.com/time/daily/time/1995/latest.html

Religion

Ask the Rabbi
Questions and answers about Jewish philosophy

Ask the Rabbi, a service offered by the Office of Information and Communication of Jerusalem's Ohr Somayach, answers questions about Jewish philosophy. Most questions are researched and answered personally by a rabbi at Ohr Somayach, and the most stimulating questions are published in a weekly newsletter, copies of which are archived online.

Useful for online "tutors"; religion.
URL: gopher://jerusalem1.datasrv.co.il:70/11/lists/ask
E-mail: newman@jerusalem1.datasrv.co.il

Lutheran Home Page
Information explains beliefs and activities

Part of Martin Luther's *Small Catechism*, a version of the *Athanasian Creed* and other information about the beliefs and activities of the Lutherans are available at this unofficial Lutheran Home Page, compiled by Matt Bostwick of Ponoma, Calif. Also included are pointers to other Christian and, specifically, Lutheran resources on the Internet.

Useful for reference; religion.
URL: http://www.maths.tcd.ie/hyplan/thomas/lutheran/page.html

Religious Texts
Browse, search the Bible, Quran, other documents

You can examine the text of major documents from several world religions, as well as commentary and study materials at Sun Microsystems' anonymous FTP archive, operated by the University of North Carolina at Chapel Hill. Besides browsing SunSite's religious studies archives, you can electronically search the Bible, Quran, Book of Mormon, various Jainist texts, Tantric studies newsletters, Asian religious resources, even *Aesop's Fables*. The site links to other resources offering background information about such religions as Bahai, Buddhism, Christianity, Islam, Jainism, and Tantrism.

Useful for religion.
URL: gopher://sunsite.unc.edu/1/sunsite.d/religion.d

Schools on the Web

Arbor Heights Elementary School
Third-graders pick their favorite home pages

Third-graders from Seattle's Arbor Heights Elementary regularly travel into cyberspace on exploratory missions. Their changing Top 10 list of direct links reflects their top picks among the resources they discover, from interactive sites where you can play games to a tour of the White House, which includes a sound bite from Socks, the Clintons' cat.

Useful for activities and projects; schools on the Web.
URL: http://www.halcyon.com/arborhts/topten.html

Arleta Elementary School
Graphics and reports from students on the Web

This site shows off the work of elementary-school students in Portland, Ore. Featured are a Pond Project, with graphics and reports from the kids on the damselfly, frog, pond lily and other flora and fauna found in and around ponds; and the Globe Project, with pictures of the kids' papier-mache globes and brief reports on what they felt they had learned about the world while completing this project.

Useful for biology; schools on the Web.
URL: http://buckman.pps.k12.or.us/arleta/arleta.html

Buckman Elementary School
Mixed-age class shows off its projects

A Spanish Counting Book and projects celebrating the civil rights achievements of Dr. Martin Luther King Jr. are just two examples of the work done by students in Room 100, a mixed-age kindergarten, first- and second-grade classroom, in Portland, Oregon. The server shows not only how the students are using the Internet and its tools to display their work, but how they are using it for research and communications.

Useful for foreign languages; history; schools on the Web; social studies.
URL: http://buckman.pps.k12.or.us/

Captain Strong Elementary School
Learn from students about salmon

The Salmon Project was designed by third-grade students at Captain Strong Elementary in Battle Ground, Wash., to help teach other students in the district about Pacific Northwest salmon. Each year the school raises up to 1,000 coho salmon, and the students use images and hypertext to show the life cycle of this and other salmon species. Included is a section on the various hazards faced by the fish, such as those caused by industry, dams and housing development.

Useful for biology; ecology and the environment; schools on the Web.
URL: http://152.157.16.3/doc/salmon/cse.html

Hillside Elementary School
Students use Internet to research and post papers

Hillside Elementary School, in Cottage Grove, Minn., operates a World-Wide Web project for students in grades 3-6. Students post research papers and other writings on the school server, using the Internet itself as their primary resource. The Hillside server's organizers view the project as a way of exploring the possibilities of the Internet in elementary education.

Useful for Internet and computing; school resources; schools on the Web.
URL: http://hillside.coled.umn.edu/

Monta Vista High School
See, and hear, what students are doing on the Internet

This World-Wide Web server, a project primarily of students at Monta Vista High School in Cupertino, Calif., was designed to provide an example of how the Internet could be integrated in K-12 education. Along with information about the school, it provides background details on the construction of the server. Links lead to other online educational resources. There are even sound clips from the school's award-winning marching band.

Useful for Internet and computing; school resources; schools on the Web.
URL: http://www.mvhs.edu/

University Park Elementary School
What's it like to go to school in Alaska?

Falcon's Nest, the Web site at University Park Elementary School, gives visitors, in words and pictures, a clear idea of what life and school are like in Fairbanks, Alaska. If you ever wondered what to do when it's 40 degree below outside, consider some of the suggestions from the second-graders here.

Useful for schools on the Web.
URL: http://www.upk.northstar.k12.ak.us/

Web66 WWW Schools Registry
Which schools have home pages?

Web66—a project of the University of Minnesota to help introduce World-Wide Web technology into K-12 schools—keeps a registry of schools and educational agencies that have Web sites. It provides an onscreen map, on which you can click on a location and view a list of schools that are connected there.

Useful for education; Internet and computing; school resources; schools on the Web.
URL: http://hillside.coled.umn.edu/others.html

Science

1994 IUCN Red List of Threatened Animals
Query the list for specifics

This site contains a database of information about species considered to be threatened worldwide, derived from the *1994 IUCN (World Conservation Union) Red List of Threatened Animals*. A query form allows you to generate a list showing the status of particular animals or particular regions by selecting a specific region; whether the animal is endangered, vulnerable or rare; its species, if known; or class, order or family.

Useful for ecology and the environment.
URL: http://www.wcmc.org.uk/data/database/rl_anml_combo.html

Ask a Geologist (U.S.)
Experts offers pointers on scientific and technical questions

Stumped by a question about earthquakes or some other area of earth science? Try asking the experts through this experimental service of the U.S. Geological Survey, the federal government's principal source of scientific and technical expertise. While they won't answer specific questions ("Is my home in a landslide area?") or endorse commercial products, they probably will be able to point you in the right direction, usually within a couple days of receiving your e-mail request. In time the service hopes to set up a file of answers to frequently asked questions here..

Useful for earth sciences; online "tutors".
URL: http://walrus.wr.usgs.gov/docs/ask-a-ge.html
E-mail: ask-a-geologist@octopus.wr.usgs.gov

Ask a Scientist
Turn to the experts for help

This program, offered through the Newton electronic bulletin-board system, allows teachers and students to question experts in math, science, and computing. Archives of many of the previous questions and answers on topics ranging from acoustics to time travel are available. In addition, you can search the group discussions for information on specific topics. You must register to use the system, but there's no charge. Newton is run by the Argonne National Laboratory, a multipurpose research lab owned and operated by the University of Chicago for the U.S. Department of Energy.

Useful for online "tutors"; science.
URL: http://www.dep.anl.gov/

Ask a Volcanologist
Check the database, or pose your question

From the creators of VolcanoWorld comes this question-and-answer service, intended to fill in any gaps their home page left. Kids (and adults) can query experts from around the world (including some at the Mount St. Helens National Monument and the University of Hawaii) by e-mail. You can also browse through a database of previously asked questions and answers, such as "Why are some lava flows red?", "How is remote sensing used to study volcanoes?" and "What do you need to make a model of a volcano?".

Useful for earthquakes, volcanoes and seismic activity; online "tutors".
URL: http://volcano.und.nodak.edu/vwdocs/ask_a.html

Ask Mr. Science
High-school whizzes answer questions from other kids

This award-winning project encourages K-12 students to e-mail questions related to astronomy, biology, chemistry, geology, or physics to Mr. Science—actually a group of Advanced Placement students at Christianburg (Va.) High School. The students research and formulate a reply within 48 hours.

Useful for online "tutors"; science.
URL: gopher://gopher.cic.net:3005/00/classroom/dr.sci
E-mail: apscichs@radford.vak12ed.edu
Message body: Please ask no more than five questions at a time.

Ask-A-Geologist (Canada)
Experts answer questions about Canada's geology

Not to be confused with a U.S. program of the same name, this question-and-answer service is offered by the Geological Survey of Canada (GSC). E-mail questions, in English or French, on topics related to the geosciences in Canada are answered by GSC experts.

Useful for earth sciences; online "tutors".
URL: http://www.emr.ca/gsc/askageol.html
E-mail: drgrant@gsc.emr.ca
Message body: State: Your name, e-mail and postal addresses
Enter in subject line: Ask-A-Geologist

Barkley Sound Expedition Study Guide
A West Coast safari

A project of the British Columbia (Canada) Community Learning Network, *Safari '94: Barkley Sound Expedition* was originally an interactive exploration of Barkley Sound, a wilderness area on Vancouver Island. Students followed a team of experts—via satellite feed and e-mail—as they explored a sunken ship and photographed wildlife in the ocean and on shore. Video of the expedition is available at the Royal British Columbia Museum in Victoria, B.C., and CLN still offers an online study guide with background information and lesson plans. Future "safaris" may again allow students to view live footage and exchange e-mail questions with explorers.

Useful for activities and projects; ecology and the environment.
URL: http://www.etc.bc.ca/safari/safarihome.html

Bat Conservation International
Austin's most unusual tourist attraction

The largest urban bat colony in the world lives in Austin, Texas, keeping the local population of pests under control. Together with images, some eye-opening facts about this often-maligned animal have been compiled by the nonprofit Bat Conservation International. Some highlights of this home page: Bat Books for Young Readers bibliographies; questions and answers on bat houses (the counterparts to birdhouses); and a history of Austin's population of 1.5 million bats. The server's host, Highland Park Elementary School, also has set up links to lots of online educational resources, including its own home pages and resources..

Useful for ecology and the environment.
URL: http://www.hipark.austin.isd.tenet.edu/bat/main.html

Big Sky Science Lesson Plans
Comprehensive and "mini" activities for K-12 students

On the server of Montana's Big Sky Telegraph, an educational network, you'll find more than 200 science lesson plans (and "mini-lessons") for K-12. Each plan includes an objective, overview, activities and procedures, and examples. The lessons were prepared at summer workshops of the Columbia Education Center, an association of teachers from 14 western states.

Useful for activities and projects; science.
URL: gopher://bvsd.k12.co.us:70/11/Educational_Resources/
Lesson_Plans/Big%20Sky/science

Bill Thoen's Internet Resources in Earth Sciences
List of maps, data, software

Bill Thoen's extensive *Internet Resources for Earth Sciences* shows you where to find maps, data files, software, mailing lists, discussion groups, and other materials of interest. Thoen also explains how to use the Archie Internet search tool to locate earth sciences information on the Internet. This file is periodically updated, and new and updated items are flagged.

Useful for earth sciences.
URL: gopher://liberty.uc.wlu.edu
E-mail: bthoen@csn.org

Biodiversity and Biological Collections
Images and lists of pointers

Cornell University's Biodiversity and Biological Collections gopher offers such resources as a directory of biologists, biodiversity journals and newsletters, and the catalogs of museums, herbariums, and arboretums. A collection of biological images, requiring a JPEG viewer, is also available here.

Useful for biology.
URL: gopher://muse.bio.cornell.edu

Biologist's Guide to Internet Resources
Springboard to databases, newsgroups

This is the full electronic text of *A Biologist's Guide to Internet Resources*, a 30-page list prepared by Una Smith of Yale University. While it does not directly link to them, the guide provides descriptions and online addresses for biology-related databases, directories, bibliographies, newsletters, newsgroups and mailing lists, software archives, search engines, commercial services, and frequently asked questions and answers of interest to biologists and students.

Useful for biology.
URL: gopher://quest.arc.nasa.gov:70/0R0-109372-/Docs/netguide/biology
To subscribe: mail-server@rtfm.mit.edu
Message body: send usenet/news.answers/biology/guide

Biology Image Archive
Photographs from scientists' own albums

The Biology Image Archive contains pictures of plant and animal specimens in compressed JPEG file format, taken from the private collections of scientists from such institutions as Harvard University, New York Botanical Garden, and the Field Museum of Natural History. Most of the images are smaller than 640 x 480 pixels and can be displayed on any VGA or Macintosh screen without cropping. Each image is identified by its scientific name, the place where it was found, the photographer's name and address, and other data. You can use keyword searches to find particular images.

Useful for biology; images.
URL: gopher://muse.bio.cornell.edu:70/11/images

BIOSCI Bionet Biology Resources
Resources supplied by those in the field

Here you'll find several resources related to the study of biology, provided by scientific researchers worldwide who contribute to the BIOSCI network of Usenet newsgroups. You can search for life-sciences articles available in the newsgroupgs, view the tables of contents of journals in biology and related disciplines, and find the addresses of biologists. Links take you to other biology resources from around the world as well as more than 60 e-mail discussion lists.

Useful for biology.
URL: http://www.ch.embnet.org/bio-www/info.html

Blue-Skies
Program, resources help students learn about the weather

Blue-Skies, based at the University of Michigan, offers K-12 students an enjoyable introduction to weather and its workings. Using a free software program, kids can explore interactive U.S. weather maps, simply clicking on a region or city to zoom in for current weather information and National Weather Service forecasts. In using these maps, kids learn how air pressure, temperature, and precipitation interact. Other offerings include international weather maps, Quick-Time movies of recent satellite imagery, information about air pollution and the ozone hole, and images and text about selected weather phenomena (such as hurricanes and tornadoes). The Blue-Skies software operates on Macintosh computers, and a PC version is planned..

Useful for software; weather.
URL: http://groundhog.sprl.umich.edu/
E-mail: blueskies@umich.edu

The Boeing Company
Learn about making airplanes

This Web site, run by the world's largest manufacturer of commercial aircraft, has some useful background information on the company's aircraft.
URL: http://www.boeing.com

Cascades Volcano Observatory
Study natural hazards of the Pacific Northwest

The Cascades Volcano Observatory (CVO) provides information about volcanoes, earthquakes, landslides and other natural hazards. You can find links to images and reports about volcanic eruptions in progress; a growing archive of images of past volcanic activity, such as that at Mount St. Helens; descriptions of CVO programs and publications; and ongoing studies of volcanic emissions and global climate change, among other topics, at the CVO. Also available are links to other volcano-related and geology sites on the Internet. The CVO, part of the U.S. Geological Survey, monitors and warns of natural hazards in the Pacific Northwest.

Useful for earthquakes, volcanoes and seismic activity.
URL: http://vulcan.wr.usgs.gov/home.html
E-mail: webmaster@pwavan.wr.usgs.gov

Charlotte:The Vermont Whale
A puzzling discovery and some pictures

For years researchers have studied the bones of a whale unearthed in rural Vermont, over 150 miles from the nearest ocean, to unravel the history and geology of the area. A University of Vermont project attempted to bring the story of the whale to K-12 students on the Internet, but funding ran out in 1994. Although the Web site is only partly constructed, kids still may be fascinated by the hows and whys of this scientific discovery as well as the images of Charlotte's skeleton.

Useful for biology.
URL: http://www.uvm.edu/whale/whalehome.html

Chemistry Visualization Project (ChemViz)
A better view of scientific concepts

The Chemistry Visualization Project, funded by the National Science Foundation, uses computers and telecommunications to help high-school students visualize difficult concepts of chemistry. You'll need a Macintosh and color monitor to view these files.

Useful for chemistry; images.
URL: gopher://landrew.ncsa.uiuc.edu:70/1ftp%3Aftp.ncsa.uiuc.edu@/Education/ChemViz/

Clementine Lunar Image Browser
Pictures of the moon

This U.S. Navy Web server plans to make over 1 million images of the moon available to the public. The images are searchable by latitude and longtitude or by using an interactive map. The Clementine space project is part of the Navy's Deep Space Program Science Experiment.

Useful for astronomy and space exploration; images.
URL: http://www.nrl.navy.mil/clementine/clib

Conservatoire National des Arts et Métiers / National Conservatory of Arts and Crafts
Practice French as you learn about technology

The National Conservatory of Arts and Crafts in Paris encourages visitors to explore industrial and scientific history through its virtual Museum of Arts and Crafts. Most of the information and links here are in French.

Useful for foreign languages; science.
URL: http://www.cnam.fr/index_english.html

Current Weather Maps/Movies
Up-to-date images from around the world

The Current Weather home page provides maps and movies, with detailed information, for the United States, Atlantic, Europe, Africa, and Antarctica. The images are frequently updated and maintained by Charles Hernich of the Michigan State University UNIX Computer Group.

Useful for images; weather.
URL: http://rs560.cl.msu.edu/weather/

Cyberspace Middle School
Tours, texts and project suggestions for students

Cyberspace Middle School's information and activity pages are designed for students in sixth through ninth grade. It links to virtual tours, lots of images of animals, planets and weather, as well as fact sheets and other literature about astronomy, biology, physics, meteorology and wildlife. Its Science Fair section provides practical suggestions for selecting and completing a science project, plus descriptions of possible projects which students can modify to meet their needs. This home page got its start as part of a science program for middle-school science teachers, funded by the National Science Foundation.

Useful for activities and projects; science.
URL: http://www.scri.fsu.edu/~dennisl/CMS.html

Cygnus Group

Tips on reducing and recycling plastics and other materials

The Cygnus Group helps companies develop and promote waste-preventing strategies, products and packaging. Its environmental education site links to articles and newsletters published by Partners for Environmental Progress (PEP) that encourage people to "use less stuff" by recycling, reducing and reusing materials. It also points to databases and other information on related environmental topics.

Useful for ecology and the environment.
URL: http://www.cygnus-group.com:9011

Daily Planet/Weather World/Weather Machine

For patterns and predictions

The Daily Planet Web server is being used to test and demonstrate Web client/server technology to improve public access to earth sciences data. It is part of a joint project between NASA and the Atmospheric Science Department at the University of Illinois. The department's Weather World Web server and Weather Machine gopher server operate under this umbrella. These two sites will captivate kids (and adults) interested in weather patterns and forecasting:

- *Weather Machine:* This gopher provides directories of weather facts, mostly from the National Weather Service. It includes current weather summaries, forecasts, radar summaries, and some climatological information, all organized geographically. Other offerings include a frequently asked questions and answers about weather, a list of weather newsgroups, phone numbers for road conditions around the United States, and links to related gophers.
- *Weather World:* The Web server emphasizes visual information, with hundreds of current and archived images and 60 MPEG animations. You'll find satellite photos, surface maps, upper air maps and plots, and forecast maps. This server also offers many of the text-based resources available on the gopher.

Useful for weather.
URL: http://www.atmos.uiuc.edu/
E-mail: web-masters@www.atmos.uiuc.edu

Dante Website

Reports and pictures of robots exploring Alaska volcano

This NASA Web page focuses on the Dante explorers, tethered walking robots which have been used to explore volcanoes and other environments hostile to humans. You'll find mission reports and graphic images from the Dante II project, in which scientists remotely explored Mount Spurr, a volcano in Alaska's Aleutian Range in 1994.

Useful for earthquakes, volcanoes and seismic activity.
URL: http://maas-neotek.arc.nasa.gov/dante

Digital Library Project
Search for science, space materials

The University of Michigan, with help from the National Science Foundation and NASA, is developing a major online library. Most information will be related to space and earth sciences. To use the library, go to the *UM Digital Library* and press the search button.

Useful for astronomy and space exploration; earth sciences; library.
URL: http://www.sils.umich.edu:80/UMDL/

Dinosaur Exhibit, Honolulu Community College
Timeline to another age

Honolulu Community College offers this virtual exhibit—including an audio tour—for dinosaur lovers of all ages. It includes images of some of the dinosaur fossils (replicas of originals at the American Museum of Natural History in New York) that are on display at the college, with descriptions and, in some cases, links to images of full-size sculptures. A timeline graphic compares the "age" of the user with that of Triceratops, Stegosaurus and Tyrannosaurus rex. If this whets your appetite for more dinosaur information, you can link to other online sources from here.

Useful for biology.
URL: http://www.hcc.hawaii.edu/dinos/dinos.1.html

Earth Science, Geology & the Environment
Fishing for resources on wetlands?

Based at Texas A&M University, this gopher provides resources on earth science, geology, and the environment, including abstracts on scientific topics ranging from alternative crops and biodiversity to wetlands and wildlife. This site also provides links to other science gophers and bulletin boards.

Useful for ecology and the environment.
URL: http://www.tamu.edu/tamu2/l_subject_3.html

Earth Viewer
Up-to-the-minute map shows where it's day or night

John Walker's *Earth Viewer* is an interactive server that lets you see on a map where it is day or night around the world at the time of your request. You can also choose to look at the earth from a variety of perspectives: from the sun; the moon; the night side of the earth; above any location on the planet specified by latitude, longitude and altitude; or from a satellite in earth orbit. The server can generate images based on a topographical map of the earth, current weather satellite imagery, or a composite image of cloud cover superimposed on a map of the earth. Walker also offers public-domain space simulation software at this site.

Useful for activities and projects; astronomy and space exploration.
URL: http://www.fourmilab.ch/earthview/vplanet.html

Earthquake Lists
Major shakers in world history

The Earthquake Lists, from the U.S. National Earthquake Information Service, offer a variety of interesting information about major earthquakes in world history. You'll find, for instance, lists of the most destructive quakes ever, all quakes of magnitude 7 or greater since 1900, the 10 largest quakes in the United States, and general earthquake facts and statistics.

Useful for earthquakes, volcanoes and seismic activity.
URL: gopher://wealaka.okgeosurvey1.gov

Earthquake Maps
Maps show location of major earthquakes

This Web site at the University of Washington generates maps showing the locations of the most recent earthquakes in the United States and other parts of the world. The data is collected from the U.S. Council of the National Seismic System and the Canadian National Seismograph Network.

Useful for earthquakes, volcanoes and seismic activity.
URL: http://www.geophys.washington.edu/cnss.cat.html

Earthwatch Radio Scripts
Concise information on scientific efforts

Earthwatch Radio is a two-minute program on science and the environment that deals with topics ranging from the cleanup of Ohio's pollution-choked Cuyahoga River to efforts to protect the earth's ozone layer. You can search through the scripts of programs dating back to 1990. Ten programs are produced every two weeks by students and staff at the Sea Grant Institute and the Institute for Environmental Studies of the University of Wisconsin, Madison. More than 150 radio stations in Canada and the United States receive copies of the program.

Useful for ecology and the environment.
URL: gopher://gopher.adp.wisc.edu:70/11/.browse/.METASGIEW

EcoGopher/EcoWeb Project
Access files through this environmental library

EcoGopher and EcoWeb, based at the University of Virginia, offer access to a wide range of environmental information on servers around the world. From here, you can reach library services, university servers, magazines and newsletters, Environmental Protection Agency (EPA) materials, environmental action groups and many other resources. You also can search by keyword through the full texts of these online files.

Useful for ecology and the environment.
URL: http://ecosys.drdr.virginia.edu/EcoWeb.html

EcoMUSE
A mailing list for teachers and students worldwide

EcoMUSE, the Environmental Virtual Community Project, is a mailing list focusing on environmental education, natural science, geography, multiculturalism, and technological issues. Teachers and students — both K-12 and college — can discuss ideas on these subjects with their peers around the world. EcoMUSE also offers a gopher with archived discussions, online documents, and links to related Internet sites.

Useful for ecology and the environment.
URL: gopher://mirna.together.uvm.edu/1/.education/EcoMUSE
E-mail: phansen@lemming.uvm.edu (for free registration)

El Nino
What is an El Nino?

The National Oceanic and Atmospheric Administration (NOAA) provides information explaining the disruptive weather phenomenon known as El Nino. The explanation is easy to understand thanks to colorful real-time graphics, which are based on the readings taken from a network of sensors in the equatorial Pacific Ocean.

Useful for weather.
URL: http://www.pmel.noaa.gov/toga-tao/el-nino-story.html

Electronic Innovators
Program puts kids in touch with volunteer professionals

Electronic Innovators, a program of the Canada SchoolNet system, is designed to put K-12 students in contact with over 400 scientists, engineers, and other volunteer professionals. These "Innovators" are available through three programs:

- *Discussion leaders* monitor some 20 Usenet newsgroups, each relating to a particular age group or subject. Students can post any question they like and get an answer from one or more Innovators.
- *School advisors* are available via e-mail for more personal contact with teachers and students. They assist teachers with curriculum and project development, and act as role models for students.
- *In-class visitors* make personal visits to classrooms.

Useful for online "tutors"; science.
URL: gopher://schoolnet.carleton.ca:419/1/ElecInn.dir
E-mail: tburns@ccs.carleton.ca

Elemental Searches
Students use the Internet to solve chemistry mysteries

Elemental Searches, a lesson plan prepared by high-school chemistry teacher Cece Schwennsen, offers a way for students to interactively learn about chemistry and the Internet at the same time. Following Schwennsen's model, students research a chemical element, using e-mail and bulletin-board resources to contact scientists and learn about new findings.

Useful for chemistry.
URL: gopher://gopher.cic.net/00/cicnet-gophers/k12-gopher/classroom/chem

Endangered and Threatened Species Lists
Animals and plants in jeopardy

This site, available through the Florida Institute of Technology server, contains searchable lists of endangered and threatened plants and animals. You can also search the U.S. Environmental Protection Agency's list of Endangered, Threatened, and Proposed Species for the Pacific Northwest.

Useful for ecology and the environment.
URL: gopher://gaia.sci-ed.fit.edu:70/11/subj/Science/Environmental/end-thr

Energy and Climate Information Exchange (ECIX)
Learn about conservation

The Energy and Climate Information Exchange (ECIX), a project of the EcoNet ecology network, focuses on renewable energy, conservation, and other methods for reducing the use and environmental impact of fossil fuels. You'll find information about biomass, electric vehicles, geothermal energy, global warming, hydroelectric power, solar energy, sustainable development, wind energy, climate change, ozone, and the like. The site also offers a "CO2 Challenge" kit for teachers, environmental newsletters, and other related materials.

Useful for ecology and the environment.
URL: ftp://igc.org
E-mail: ecixfiles@igc.apc.org

EnviroLink Network
Archives contain action alerts, legislation updates, other news

The EnviroLink Network bills itself as the world's largest online environmental information source. It offers archived information such as news releases, action alerts, columns, information about legislation and Supreme Court decisions, and journal issues. You can search the archives by keyword. For serious environmental activists, EnviroLink operates advanced services, such as e-mail and mailing lists, for which you need a password..

Useful for ecology and the environment.
URL: http://envirolink.org/
E-mail: admin@envirolink.org
To subscribe: listproc@envirolink.org (for a list of Envirolink's mailing lists)
Message body: On separate lines, type: HELP and LIST

Environment Canada Weather Maps
Ozone, weather maps are easy to understand

Canada's federal environmental agency creates graphical reports (in GIF format) of both the weather and depth of the ozone layer above Canada and selected areas of the United States, such as Florida, Hawaii and Utah. A weekly map indicates if the ozone layer is thinner or thicker than normal. Daily weather forecasts show high and low temperatures, frontal activity and predicted conditions (snow, fog, sunshine) on an easy-to-read map.

Useful for images; weather.
URL: http://cmits02.dow.on.doe.ca/maps/index.html

Environment in Latin America Network
Discussions on rain forest destruction

The Environment in Latin America Network (ELAN) is a mailing list for people interested in discussing rain forest destruction and other Latin American environmental issues. Subscribers include academic researchers (in the natural and social sciences) as well as activists. Past ELAN discussions are archived on a gopher server.

Useful for ecology and the environment; mailing lists (listservs) and newsgroups.
URL: gopher://csf.colorado.edu
E-mail: ELAN@csf.colorado.edu
To subscribe: listserv@csf.colorado.edu
Message body: Sub ELAN YourFirstName YourLastName

Environmental Education (EE-Link)
Lesson plans on whales are a highlight

EE-Link presents a wide range of resources for educators who want to teach children about environmental issues. For example, it provides extensive information about endangered species, including the full text of the Endangered Species Act, endangered species list, fact sheets and images of threatened and endangered species, and a clickable map of North America on which you can locate endangered species. Online lesson plans on whales are geared toward K-5 students.

Useful for ecology and the environment.
URL: http://www.nceet.snre.umich.edu/
E-mail: eelink@nceet.snre.umich.edu

Environmental Resources Information System
Conservation in Australia

The Environmental Resources Information System (ERIN) is maintained by the Australian Nature Conservation Agency (ANCA). This award-winning site offers a very wide range of environmental information, with an emphasis on Australia. You'll find materials about endangered and extinct species, protected areas, wetlands, climate, bird migration, environmental protection strategies, legislation, international agreements, and the like. You can search the database by keyword. ERIN also includes ANCA library materials, a selection of graphic images (in GIF format), conference reports, and links to several other environmental gophers.

Useful for ecology and the environment.
URL: gopher://kaos.erin.gov.au

EPA Chemical Substance Factsheets
Hazards of household and other chemicals

The Environmental Protection Agency (EPA) Chemical Substance Factsheets provide information about more than 200 household chemicals, including potential health hazards of exposure.

Useful for ecology and the environment.
URL: gopher://ecosys.drdr.virginia.edu/1/library/factsheets/toxics

EPA Environmental Futures Gopher
Collection of materials and contacts

This gopher offers environmental information with an eye to the future. You'll find articles, electronic journals, reports, and other information collected by the U.S. Environmental Protection Agency (EPA). Topics include agriculture, industrial ecology, the Megatrends project, population, and technology. The gopher offers a list of EPA personnel who can provide more information on these subjects. Still under construction, the server was developed by the Future Studies Group within the Office of Strategic Planning and Environmental Data.

Useful for ecology and the environment.
URL: gopher://futures.wic.epa.gov

Exploratorium
Enjoy museum's sights and sounds, and send in a science question

San Francisco's Exploratorium is a museum of "science, art, and human perception." You'll find information about the museum's exhibits and educational programs, scientific images and sounds, software, and a selection of educational publications. The museum's quarterly magazine includes an "Ask Us" column inviting readers to post their own science questions.

Useful for activities and projects; museums on the Web; science.
URL: http://www.exploratorium.edu/

Exploratorium Science Snackbook
Build your own mini-science center at home

Science Snackbook shows you how to build replicas of more than 100 of the hands-on experiments, activities, and demonstrations at San Francisco's Exploratorium museum using common materials. While the entire text and pictures from the book are not available online, some sample "snacks" are. Designed for teachers by teachers, parents and kids from Grade 4 up may enjoy the challenge of building the exhibits at home.

Useful for activities and projects; science.
URL: http://www.exploratorium.edu/papers/Snackbook/Snackbook.html

Field Museum of Natural History
Dinosaurs come alive on virtual tour

Chicago's Field Museum takes virtual visitors on interactive tours of its exhibitions. Children will particularly enjoy the online sampling from *DNA to Dino-*

saurs. Sounds, animations, 3-D images and explanatory text reveal where and when dinosaurs lived, what they ate and how they moved.

Useful for images; museums on the Web; science.
URL: http://rs6000.bvis.uic.edu:80/museum/

FireNet
A forum, images and information about fire behavior and management

Based at the Australian National University, FireNet is an information service for people interested in rural and landscape fires, including professional and volunteer firefighters, educators, and students. You'll find online material about fire behavior, ecological effects, fire prevention, and firefighting. While the focus is on Australian fire issues, there's something here for everyone. A series of color images, for instance, shows step-by-step how a fire consumes a painting of the *Mona Lisa*. To learn more about fire management, you can join the public FireNet forum by e-mail.

Useful for ecology and the environment.
URL: http://life.anu.edu.au:80/landscape_ecology/firenet/firenet.html
E-mail: FireNet@life.anu.edu.au
To subscribe: listserv@life.anu.edu.au
Message body: subscribe firenet YourFirstName YourLastName

FISH-JUNIOR Mailing List
Students can exchange e-mail with marine scientists

FISH-JUNIOR, initially set up by the Swedish University Network (SUNET) in conjunction with the British Columbia (Canada) Ministry of Education, is a discussion list for young people interested in fisheries ecology and other topics in the marine sciences. High-school students can exchange e-mail with marine scientists from around the world. Participants share information on everything from bibliographies and autobiographies to the learning capabilities of octopi.

Useful for biology; mailing lists (listservs) and newsgroups.
URL: gopher://gopher.cic.net:3005/00/listservs/fish-jr
E-mail: FISH-JUNIOR@SEARN.SUNET.SE
To subscribe: LISTSERV@SEARN.SUNET.SE
Message body: SUBSCRIBE FISH-JUNIOR YourName, YourField

Florida EXPLORES!
Images, information about hurricanes and weather in general

Through Florida EXPLORES! (Exploring and Learning the Operations and Resources of Environmental Satellites!), Florida State University provides weather satellite information and images to K-12 teachers and students as well as any interested meteorology buffs. You will also find here information about Florida's climate, and hurricanes and storms in the tropical Atlantic, the Caribbean Sea and the Gulf of Mexico. This page links directly to K-12 resources available on the Florida Information Resource Network (FIRN), such as guides with tips on teaching meteorology, and online booklets for parents who want to help their children with their science studies.

Useful for weather.
URL: http://thunder.met.fsu.edu/explores/explores.html

Franklin Institute Science Museum
Virtual exhibits, movies on science, history

This online museum has several virtual exhibits, including *The Heart: A Virtual Exploration* and *Benjamin Franklin: Glimpses of The Man*. Also featured are several QuickTime movies.

Useful for history; images; museums on the Web; science.
URL: http://sln.fi.edu/

Friends and Partners in Space
Space: The friendly frontier

Looking for information on the Soviet/Russian space program or joint Russian-U.S. space projects? This Web, located at the University of Tennessee Research Services, also include sphotographs and sketches of Soviet space vehicles.

Useful for astronomy and space exploration; images.
URL: http://solar.rtd.utk.edu/~jgreen/fpspace.html

Geological Survey of Canada
Earthquakes in Canada and other geological gems

If you're interested in the geosciences in Canada, this is where to look. This site provides an overview of major earthquake activity in Canada in the 20th century, including a list showing the magnitude and location of the most severe. It also gives descriptions and ordering information about educational materials available from the Geological Survey of Canada, including videos, books, fact sheets and posters about underwater mountain ranges, careers in the earth sciences, minerals and mining, and a variety of scientific projects in which the agency is involved.

Useful for earthquakes, volcanoes and seismic activity.
URL: http://www.emr.ca/

Geology in the Classroom
Ask the experts about earth sciences

This e-mail service is run by the Atlantic Geoscience Center (AGC), a division of the Geological Survey of Canada (GSC). AGC's experts answer questions on the earth sciences, with an emphasis on the geology of eastern Canada and offshore geology. The staff welcomes questions from young people and teachers. With their questions, students should include their name, their teacher's name, school name and address, and preferred e-mail address.

Useful for earth sciences; online "tutors".
URL: gopher://agcgopher.bio.ns.ca/11/agc-english/geology_class
E-mail: agc@agc.bio.ns.ca

Message body: State: Question, name, school, e-mail address

Glaxo Virtual Anatomy Image Browser
Skin and bones, in pictures

If you'd like to look at human cartilage, the spine, ribs, even "just the skin with stuff inside", the Glaxo Virtual Anatomy Browser can probably supply you with a series of animations. The Glaxo Virtual Anatomy Project, a collaboration between Glaxo Inc. and Colorado State University, aims to develop a virtual human anatomy lab for undergraduate anatomy instruction.

Useful for activities and projects; biology; images.
URL: http://www.vis.colostate.edu/cgi-bin/gva/gvaview

Global Entomology Agriculture Research Server
Research on bee behavior

The Carl Hayden Bee Research Center's GEARS server focuses on honey-bee research, but also includes information about other insects. Its Internet Classroom provides a series of articles on such topics as bee behavior and pollination. You can also find details about Africanized honey bees, as well as graphics, photographs, sounds and movies about bees.

Useful for agriculture; biology; images.
URL: http://gears.tucson.ars.ag.gov/

Great White Shark
Photos, not fossils, of a creature with ancient roots

In paleontology, you don't just study fossils; you also study living creatures with histories dating back hundreds of millions of years, like the Great White Shark. The Museum of Paleontology presents an online gallery of images and research based on a study of the Great Whites off the California coast by Douglas Long, a graduate student at the University of California, Berkeley.

Useful for biology.
URL: http://ucmp1.berkeley.edu/Doug/shark.html

GreenDisk Paperless Environmental Journal
Hard-to-find information

GreenDisk offers information on environmental issues scanned from hundreds of sources. You'll find articles on such topics as renewable energy, waste disposal, and endangered species. The journal also publishes research reports, press releases, action alerts, and news summaries from environmental groups and government agencies around the world. According to *GreenDisk*'s publishers, much of this information is unavailable or hard to find in libraries.

Useful for ecology and the environment.
URL: ftp://info.umd.edu@infoM/ReadingRoom/Environment/GreenDisk

Guide to NASA Online Resources
An entrance to NASA's information banks

The Guide to NASA Online Resources showcases NASA and NASA-related scientific, educational and government resources. It includes NASA databases and archives, research announcements, a Space Shuttle launch schedule, pointers to image databases, software archives, and links to other NASA information servers.

Useful for astronomy and space exploration.
URL: http://naic.nasa.gov/naic/guide/

Hands-on Science Centers Worldwide
Educational activities on- and off-line

Mark Maimone's page of Hands-on Science Centers Worldwide— at the School of Computer Science, Carnegie Mellon University —lists museums in Asia, North and South America, Australia and Europe that emphasize interactive science education. It offers direct links to many of them, providing information about the respective museum's operating hours, current exhibitions, and, in some cases, online activities.

Useful for activities and projects; science; travel and recreation.
URL: http://www.cs.cmu.edu:8001/afs/cs/usr/mwm/www/sci.html

Herpetology Web Page
Facts and photos on amphibians and reptiles

On her Herpetology Web Page, Liza Daily brings together images, fact sheets, a range of articles and more obscure information about her favorite animals: reptiles and amphibians. You can look at, learn how to care for, and get a chuckle from information about iguanas, snakes, turtles, crocodiles, and their relatives and friends. Besides the hypertext documents at this home page, this site links to other herpetology-related information, from journals to reports from Usenet newsgroups.

Useful for biology.
URL: http://acs2.bu.edu:3000/Mosaic.Liza/herps/index.html

Highland Park Elementary School
Some student research

Interested in research in botany —by a group of younger students? The *Trees of the World Project* is just one of many you'll find here, all done by students at Highland Park Elementary in Austin, Texas.

Useful for biology; schools on the Web.
URL: http://www.hipark.austin.isd.tenet.edu/home/main.html

History of the Light Microscope
A close look at the microscope

The History of the Light Microscope, a hypertext version of a research paper by Thomas E. Jones of Duke University, details the emergence of this scientific instrument, as well as the lens, through the 19th century. It includes a variety of images and pointers to other resources covering the modern history of the microscope.

Useful for science; social studies.
URL: http://www.duke.edu/~tj/hist/hist_mic.html

Hubble Space Telescope
Look at space images or propose an experiment

The Space Telescope Science Institute can provide students with images from the Hubble Space Telescope and animations. Because this resource contains color photographs, it can be slow to download. You may also propose research ideas for the Hubble Space Telescope.

Useful for astronomy and space exploration.
URL: http://stsci.edu/top.html

Human Genome Mapping Project (U.K.)
Databases on genetics, molecular biology

Although intended by the United Kingdom's Medical Research Council to be used by researchers involved in human genome mapping, this site may be helpful to those with a keen interest in this worldwide scientific project. The databases here provide vast amounts of information on research in the fields of genetics and molecular biology.

Useful for biology.
URL: gopher://gopher.hgmp.mrc.ac.uk

Human Genome Primer on Molecular Genetics
Online introduction to genetics

The Human Genome Primer on Molecular Genetics is an illustrated online book introducing basic principles of molecular genetics pertaining to the international genome mapping project. Besides explaining DNA, genes and chromosomes, it gives an overview of mapping strategies and how data is interpreted. Published by the U.S. Department of Energy, it's taken from the department's June 1992 report on the project.

Useful for biology.
URL: http://www.ornl.gov/seer/Genome/Primer.1.html

Human Genome Project (U.S.)
Putting the project in perspective

This gopher offers background information and updates on the U.S. Human Genome Project, a federally coordinated effort to characterize all human genetic material. Resources here include an outline of the first five years of the project (1991-95), a monthly newsletter searchable by keyword, and information about other resources in genetics (including useful material for teachers).

Useful for biology.
URL: gopher://merlot.gdb.org

Human Genome Research Center (France)
Abstracts on gene-mapping research

Genethon is a Human Genome Research Center in Paris, and is taking part in the worldwide effort to map all the genes in the human body. It provides access to its public data, such as abstracts of its publications, in French and English. It also links to other searchable sources of information in biology and other subjects.

Useful for biology.
URL: gopher://gopher.genethon.fr/1/

Imaging Radar Home Page
Pictures of Earth from the Space Shuttle

NASA's Jet Propulsion Laboratory has a series of spectacular photographs of the earth taken from various Space Shuttle flights using imaging radars. Images range from shots of Mount Everest to Central African gorilla habitat.

Useful for images; science.
URL: http://southport.jpl.nasa.gov/

Information Center for the Environment (ICE)
Rivers, watersheds highlighted

The Information Center for the Environment (ICE) is a cooperative effort of environment scientists at the University of California-Davis and several other organizations. The Web page includes information about ICE projects, documents on California rivers and watersheds, a link to the U.S. National Park Service server, and related materials.

Useful for ecology and the environment.
URL: http://ice.ucdavis.edu/

Institute for Technology Development/ Space Remote Sensing Center
Images show extent of Midwest floods

Dramatic satellite images of the 1993 floods that swamped the Midwest will interest visitors to this site. The images were processed by the Institute for Technology Development/Space Remote Sensing Center (ITD/SRSC), which develops and commercializes remote sensing and geographic information system technologies for federal agencies such as NASA and the U.S. Department of Agriculture.

Useful for astronomy and space exploration; images.
URL: http://ma.itd.com:8000/welcome.html

INTELLiCast
Television-style weather reports on the Web

WSI Corp., which offers weather forecasting data to professional meteorologists and TV stations, has opened its own Web site. This offers TV-style weather maps.

Useful for images; weather.
URL: http://www.tasc.com:80/icast/

Interactive Frog Dissection on the Web
Tutorial lets students practice online

The Interactive Frog Dissection is an online tutorial, combining text with 60 in-line images and 17 QuickTime movies. Not only does it show a frog's organs and how to dissect them, but by using clickable images, it lets you practice these procedures on your computer screen. A possible substitute for school lab work, it was developed by students in the Instructional Technology Program at the University of Virginia's Curry School of Education.

Useful for activities and projects; biology; images.
URL: http://curry.edschool.virginia.edu/~insttech/frog

Internet Lesson Plans
Science ideas and experiments for K-12 classes

This collection of short, simple lessons for K-12 science students is offered by the Internet project at the University of California, San Diego. Subject areas currently include chemistry, biology, earth science, physical science, and physics. A variety of experiments illustrate gravity, the light spectrum, and other scientific phenomena.

Useful for activities and projects; science.
URL: gopher://ec.sdcs.k12.ca.us:70/11/lessons/UCSD_InternNet_Lessons

JASON Project
Field trips take students around the world and beyond

The JASON Project is a series of interactive "field trips" in which K-12 students spend about two weeks following the adventures and experiments of a team of scientists. Its Web site provides, for example, continually updated footage of a volcanic eruption on one of Jupiter's moons as part of a project studying the solar system. Past expeditions have visited the Sea of Cortez and the Hawaiian volcanoes. The JASON curriculum includes both printed materials (available for a fee) and a free online service in which the JASON scientists provide daily e-mail reports on their expeditions, along with answers to selected student questions. The projects are organized by the JASON Foundation for Education, established in 1989 by Dr. Robert Ballard, who discovered and explored the remains of the Titanic.

Useful for activities and projects; images; science.
URL: http://seawifs.gsfc.nasa.gov/JASON.html

John Muir Exhibit
Learn about one of the fathers of conservation

This online exhibit uses fact sheets, tributes, quotations and other materials to describe the life and legacy of John Muir, conservationist, artist and writer. Of special interest is a study guide for K-12 teachers and students that is being developed by the Sierra Club to demonstrate how John Muir cared for nature through his work. This page, developed by Harold Wood and Harvey Chinn, draws information from the John Muir Education Project of Sierra Club California, the John Muir Memorial Association, the Sierra Club Book Store, and the U.S. National Park Service.

Useful for ecology and the environment.
URL: http://ice.ucdavis.edu/John_Muir/about_the_Exhibit.html

Jupiter-Comet Impact Images
Archive shows many facets of collision

The National Space Science Data Center (NSSDC) has archived nearly 200 images of the July 1994 impact of Comet Shoemaker-Levy 9 with Jupiter, taken by the Hubble Space Telescope and by several other telescopes around the world. This was the first collision of two solar system bodies ever observed.

Useful for astronomy and space exploration; images.
URL: http://nssdc.gsfc.nasa.gov/planetary/comet.html

Lesson Plans in Animal Behavior
Curriculum ideas may be adapted

The Visitor Center at the Minnesota Valley National Wildlife Refuge has prepared several K-12 lesson plans based on animal behavior. They cover such topics as identifying species, adaptations, beaver behavior, nocturnal animals, and wetland ecosystems. Although most of the lessons require students to visit the refuge, they may hold useful ideas for parents and teachers outside the region.

Useful for ecology and the environment.
URL: gopher://informns.k12.mn.us:70/11/mn-k12/mvnwr/lessons

Lunar and Planetary Institute
Articles and images on space exploration

The Lunar and Planetary Institute, a NASA program, offers electronic access to current and back issues of the quarterly *Lunar & Planetary Information Bulletin*, with articles on space exploration. You also can view images of the moon in GIF format.

Useful for astronomy and space exploration.
URL: http://cass.jsc.nasa.gov/aboutlpi.html

Mammoth Saga
Remember the Woolly Rhinoceros?

The Swedish Museum of Natural History presents a virtual exhibit on the Mammoth and other animals from the Ice Age.

Useful for biology; museums on the Web.
URL: http://www.nrm.se/mammweb/mamintro.htm

Maryland Earthcast
One stop for weather, earthquakes, volcanoes, ski conditions

Designed by Professor Owen E. Thompson and David Yanuk of the University of Maryland, this menu system leads to many resources that deal with earth sciences. Information is organized by time and subject. Its Nowcast, Forecast and

Hindcast sections provide current, predicted and historical "glimpses" of environmental conditions, from earthquake and ozone conditions to beach and ski conditions.

Useful for earth sciences; weather.
URL: http://metolab3.umd.edu/EARTHCAST/earthcast.html

Material Data Safety Sheets Searches
Database of chemical compounds

Chemistry students and teachers may find this searchable database of chemical compounds a useful research tool. Presented by the Northwest Fisheries Science Center, it includes thousands of compounds, giving their trade names, chemical family, molecular formula and weight, reactive properties, and other data.

Useful for chemistry.
URL: http://research.nwfsc.noaa.gov/msds.html

Meteorology Resources FAQ
Searchable file suggests where to look for answers

Rather than giving actual answers to frequently asked questions, the Meteorology Resources FAQ lists various texts and organizations that laypersons, students and professionals in meteorology, oceanography and related disciplines can turn to for help. You can search each major section in the FAQ by keyword to find resources more quickly.

Useful for weather.
URL: http://www.cis.ohio-state.edu/hypertext/faq/usenet/weather/resources/faq.html
To subscribe: mail-server@rtfm.mit.edu
Message body: mail-server@rtfm.mit.edu

Michigan Technological University Volcanoes
Comprehensive reports

Michigan Technological University maintains information on a number of volcanoes, and has links to organizations that also study volcanic eruptions. This page is likely to have information, including satellite photographs, on any current eruption.

Useful for earthquakes, volcanoes and seismic activity.
URL: http://www.geo.mtu.edu/volcanoes/

Missouri Botanical Garden
Tour the gardens or tap into a huge online database

The Web page of the Missouri Botanical Garden (MBG) includes a text-and-images tour of the garden, current research about flora around the world, links to other biological Web sites, and access to MBG's taxonomic database. The database includes more than 600,000 records, and is searchable by keyword.

Useful for biology.
URL: http://straylight.tamu.edu/MoBot/welcome.html

Museum of Paleontology
Don't miss the dinosaurs

On its Web server, Berkeley's Museum of Paleontology — the fourth-largest museum in the United States — offers images and hypertext files representing its exhibits of fossil plants, dinosaurs, and mammals. These materials provide an overview of the study of fossils, and explain what fossils reveal about ecology and evolution. The museum offers several interactive displays, including a ride on a geological time machine in which the user clicks on a list of onscreen choices and is "transported" to a museum hall with hypertext documents and images about that period.

Useful for biology; museums on the Web.
URL: http://ucmp1.berkeley.edu/exhibittext/entrance.html

NASA Information Services
Home page of home pages for space agency

This is the root home page for NASA home pages, representing many of the agency's centers. Its *Hot Topics* section provides the latest information on Space Shuttle missions and other NASA news.

Useful for astronomy and space exploration.
URL: http://www.gsfc.nasa.gov/NASA_homepage.html

NASA News
For daily updates on Shuttle missions and other reports

The NASA News site posts press releases and status reports on National Aeronautics and Space Administration activities. Space Shuttle buffs can read daily updates about launches and current missions. You can also subscribe to an e-mail service to receive the information automatically.

Useful for astronomy and space exploration.
URL: http://delcano.mit.edu/
E-mail: nasanews@space.mit.edu
To subscribe: domo@hq.nasa.gov
Message body: subscribe press-release

NASA Spacelink
Making principles of science come alive

The NASA Spacelink database offers current and archived fact sheets, lesson plans, reports on electronic "field trips" and Space Shuttle missions, graphics and other instructional information about NASA projects, provided by NASA's Education Division. Teachers will also find ideas for using NASA projects to demonstrate scientific principles. The information is stored at the Marshall Space Flight Center in Huntsville, Ala.

Useful for astronomy and space exploration.
URL: http://spacelink.msfc.nasa.gov/

NASA's FOSTER On-Line Project
Students go along for the ride

Each summer, NASA's Flight Opportunities for Science Teacher Enrichment (FOSTER) program takes precollege teachers on a training flight aboard the Kuiper Airborne Observatory (KAO). In 1994, NASA allowed other teachers and their students to monitor the flight via gopher and the World-Wide Web. This site now offers details about FOSTER and the KAO flight, and archived diaries of the participants. Also available are downloadable lesson plans, a collection of astronomical images, and other space materials.

Useful for astronomy and space exploration.
URL: gopher://quest.arc.nasa.gov:70/11/projects/FOSTER/

NASA's K-12 Internet Project/Initiative
An interactive site for science projects

The home page for NASA's K-12 Internet Project, or Initiative, promises to be a place where students can go and do things, rather than an index of resources. It is undergoing renovations and eventually will house NASA's interactive projects, which allow students and teachers to effectively use NASA's online information and data sets. This initiative is an offshoot of the federal High Performance Computing and Communications (HPCC) Program, a vehicle for building the National Information Infrastructure, or Information Superhighway.

Useful for activities and projects; astronomy and space exploration.
URL: http://quest.arc.nasa.gov

NASA's Welcome to the Planets
Images of space and space vehicles

Some 200 of the best images from NASA's planetary exploration program are presented here. These captioned images show major planets, small bodies in space and various spacecraft. The online exhibition is drawn from NASA's interactive CD-ROM program *Welcome to the Planets*.

Useful for astronomy and space exploration.
URL: http://stardust.jpl.nasa.gov/planets/

National Environment Scorecard
Keep tabs on your elected representatives

The League of Conservation Voters keeps a scorecard on Congressional voting records on environmental issues. The league's interactive map of the United States, available on the Econet server, lets you click to a state or region and check up on elected representatives from that area. You can also find out who are the legislators and delegations with the highest and lowest scores, and view a summary of voting records listed by state and region. A section on Vote Descriptions provides details on the environmental issues and votes faced by both the Senate and House of Representatives in 1994.

Useful for ecology and the environment.
URL: http://www.econet.apc.org/lcv/scorecard.html

National Hurricane Center
Keep track of some of the biggest storms

The National Hurricane Center keeps watch on tropical cyclones in the Atlantic, Caribbean, Gulf of Mexico, and the Eastern Pacific, researching new systems for more accurately forecasting these storms. During the annual May-November hurricane season, you'll find the most up-to-date information on the subject here. In addition, the center has a number of useful — and interactive — "products" that will interest kids. Besides satellite maps, facts about hurricanes and photographs of the destructive Hurricane Andrew wreaked in 1992, you can find a page with numerous graphics analysing Andrew's wind fields. You also can click on an interactive map to retrieve information about current and past surface observations at sites in the Caribbean and southern United States.

Useful for activities and projects; images; weather.
URL: http://nhc-hp3.nhc.noaa.gov/index.html

National Wildflower Research Center
Wild flowers of North America

This is the Web site for this newly opened 42-acre facility, which is one of the best resources in North America for information and education about native plants and their uses in natural and planned landscapes.

Useful for museums on the Web; nature; science.
URL: http://www.onr.com/wildflower.html

Natural History Museum
Major museum makes its presence felt on the Web

The Natural History Museum in London has several galleries on the Web. including one about the earth..
URL: http://www.nhm.ac.uk/index.html

Natural History Museum of Los Angeles County
Natural history, old and new

This virtual exhibit includes information on DNA finger printing. It also includes several prints from the work of Johann Christian Dan Schreber, who in 1774 wrote a multivolume text on mammals of the world.

Useful for museums on the Web; nature.
URL: http://cwis.usc.edu/lacmnh/default.html

NET VET /The Electronic Zoo
Databases, mailing lists, images of animals

The NETVET Veterinary Resources server provides information for veterinarians, college students, and anyone else (including kids) interested in animals and animal welfare. It features the Electronic Zoo, a list of known animal resources available on the Internet, with pointers to help you access some of them directly. Other items here include databases, information about animal-related legislation, materials from various animal interest groups, archived mailing lists and news-letters, and a collection of images of animals.

Useful for biology.
URL: http://netvet.wustl.edu/

New South Polar Times
Researchers reveal life in Antarctica

Through *The New South Polar Times* staff at the Amundsen-Scott South Pole Sta-tion in Antarctica share descriptions of living and working conditions at the South Pole with school children worldwide. Besides reading current and back copies of this biweekly newsletter, kids can question the scientists there by e-mail. The site also provides: a history of exploration at the South Pole; lessons and suggestions for incorporating the newsletter into classroom studies; and links to other resources about the region.

Useful for ecology and the environment.
URL: http://www.deakin.edu.au/edu/MSEE/GENII/NSPT/NSPThomePage.html
E-mail: courtla1@pen.k12.va.us

New York Botanical Garden
One of the most beautiful places on earth

This home page offers an escape from all the hustle and bustle of the big city. This Web also includes descriptions and pictures of the other gardens in New York City.
URL: http://www.pathfinder.com/@@drbCogAAAAAAQLfG/vg/Gardens/NYBG/index.html

Newton Bulletin Board System
Ask about math, science and computing

Funded partly by U.S. government agencies, NEWTON is a national bulletin board designed for teachers and students of mathematics, science, and computer science. It contains Ask a Scientist, an area where you can leave questions and have them answered by a scientist; this service is archived and searchable by topic. NEWTON's server links to several educational mailing lists, as well as other Internet resources about mathematics, astronomy, and earth and environ-mental science

Useful for ecology and the environment.
URL: http://www.dep.anl.gov/

NOAA
Federal agency provides pointers to oceanographic research

This is the home page of the National Oceanic and Atmospheric Administration (NOAA). It provides an index of links to data on weather, the earth sciences, and oceanography from NOAA Data Center and other organizations.

Useful for earth sciences.
URL: http://www.noaa.gov/

Northern Lights Planetarium
Museum sheds some light on the Aurora Borealis

The Northern Lights Planetarium offers hypertext information (but little in the way of graphics) explaining the hows and whys of the Aurora Borealis. If you live in or are planning to go to Norway, you also can find here visitor information about the museum's special-effects shows dealing with the Northern Lights, other natural phenomena and science.

Useful for astronomy and space exploration.
URL: http://www.uit.no/npt/homepage-npt.en.html

Northwest Consortium for Mathematics and Science Teaching (Northwest CMAST)
Database describes programs, materials for Northwest students

Northwest CMAST offers parents in Alaska, Idaho, Montana, Oregon, and Washington a way to learn about programs and resources that could benefit their children in kindergarten through Grade 12. It provides a database containing an annotated list of Northwest projects, practices, and programs in math, science, technology, and environmental education. The database — searchable by keyword — draws on district, state, and informal educational sources for descriptions of their projects and materials, such as books, magazines, reprints, videocassettes, CD-ROMs, and computer programs.

Useful for ecology and the environment.
URL: gopher://gopher.nwrel.org:70/11/programs/same

Ocean Temperatures Around the World
Great way to plan a beach vacation

Ever wondered how the Pacific and Atlantic oceans differ? Take a look at the latest Sea Surface temperature map at the University of Wisconsin. Some of the satellite images are just about suitable for framing.
URL: gopher://gopher.ssec.wisc.edu/11/mcidas.d/other.d

Oceanic Network Information Center
Marine maps, schedules and vessel layouts

OCEANIC, the information system of the Ocean Information Center of the College of Marine Studies, University of Delaware, provides data on several research programs, including the World Ocean Circulation Experiment (WOCE), a collaborative study of the ocean and its currents. Although the raw data is highly technical, and may not interest the layperson, budding oceanographers should enjoy the project descriptions, marine maps, and searchable schedule of research vessels. At its Web site, OCEANIC provides images, deck layouts, and descriptions of many types of vessels. The server also includes a who's-who directory of oceanographers available on the Internet, many of whom may be willing to answer questions from students and teachers.

Useful for biology; images.
URL: http://www.cms.udel.edu/

Oregon Museum of Science and Industry
See and read about exhibits

The Oregon Museum of Science and Industry's site outlines the exhibits it houses. The museum also offers an online edition of its magazine.

Useful for museums on the Web; science.
URL: http://www.omsi.edu/

Oregon Research Institute
Research on adolescence and family life

On its server, the Oregon Research Institute (ORI) offers detailed information about its research projects in the behavioral sciences. ORI researchers investigate topics in such areas as adolescence and families, education, health, and personality. The ORI gopher also includes excerpts from the institute's newsletter, *ORInsights*.

Useful for health and social services.
URL: gopher://gopher.ori.org

Pacific Northwest Laboratory Education Handbook
Hands-on programs

This gopher provides information about educational programs for young people offered by the Pacific Northwest Laboratory (PNL), a national laboratory operated for the U.S. Department of Energy by Battelle Memorial Institute. PNL's programs include a hands-on Saturday science series for local K-8 students, science activities for local families to enjoy together, and a project to improve math and science education in middle schools in Washington and Oregon.

Useful for scholarship and college information.
URL: gopher://gopher.pnl.gov:2070/0/glance/edprog

PaleoPals
Questions and answers about dinosaurs and the like

Kids and adults alike can submit questions about fossils and the study of prehistoric plants and animals to this interactive service offered by the Museum of Paleontology at the University of California, Berkeley. Likewise — and especially if you're a paleontologist — go ahead and send in your response if you think you have an answer to any of the other questions posted here, such as what you should do if you dig up a dinosaur bone in your backyard.

Useful for biology; online "tutors".
URL: http://ucmp1.berkeley.edu
E-mail: palswww@ucmp1

Periodic Table of the Elements, Los Alamos National Laboratory
Graphical "table" takes you to background chemistry notes

Los Alamos National Lab has created a very graphical and searchable representation of the chemical elements. By clicking on the name of an element in the table, you can read a page of information about is, including its atomic number, symbol, weight, electron configuration and history. This site also links to other periodic tables on the Internet.

Useful for chemistry.
URL: http://www-c8.lanl.gov/map/infosys/html/periodic/periodic.map?169,45

Periodic Table of the Elements, University of California
Boiling point, conductivity and other data

This server at the University of California at Santa Barbara provides information on 104 chemical elements. You'll find each element's number, symbol, weight, melting point, boiling point, density, specific heat, conductivity, and other data. Also included are an ASCII Periodic Table and background information about the table.

Useful for chemistry.
URL: gopher://ucsbuxa.ucsb.edu:3001/11/.Sciences/.Chemistry/.periodic.table

Physics Careers Bulletin Board
Find help in choosing a career

Considering a career in physics? The American Institute of Physics provides answers to many questions students have about this field: What can you do with a physics major? What electives should you take? Do you need to go to grad school? Each month the institute profiles six physicists who have used their physics degrees in different ways. You can read their short biographies, then e-mail a question to any of them. You can also browse through archives of previous questions and answers.

Useful for jobs; physics.
URL: http://www.aip.org/aip/careers/careers.html

Physics Resources Around the World
Servers and services

McGill University has put together extensive lists of physics servers and services available on the Internet. Links and pointers to laboratories, physics departments, and other research sites are indexed by topic and by geographic location. You also can find information on physics conferences, computing, and publications. These may be of greatest interest to professional physicists. But job announcements that include postings for university physics students as well as links to online museum exhibitions and images dealing with this branch of science may interest K-12 users.

Useful for physics.
URL: http://www.physics.mcgill.ca/deptdocs/physics_services.html

Planet Earth Images and Movies
Create your own picture of the globe

Need a map of the earth as seen from anywhere in outerspace? This map server at the Byrd Polar Research Institute can create pictures of the globe after you enter the coordinates. (It may take a few tries to get it right.) If you have the right software, you also can view movies of the earth as it rotates.

Useful for astronomy and space exploration; images.
URL: http://white.nosc.mil/earth_images.html

Plant Science Education Network (PHYTOS)
Ideas for hands-on activities

PHYTOS is an international network for plant science educators from the primary through college level. It offers ideas for hands-on student experiments as well as teacher demonstrations. It contains information on the University of Wisconsin, Madison, Bottle Biology program and its activities for students of all ages, including composting, making Korean kimchi and sauerkraut fermentation chambers, stacking ecohabitats, soil experiments and creating insect environments. Through links, you can also reach other Internet resources in the plant sciences.

Useful for activities and projects; biology.
URL: http://nasc.nott.ac.uk:8100/

Popular Mechanics
No question is too tough

This Web site includes lots of information about technology taken from the pages of *Popular Mechanics*, a longtime favorite of backyard mechanics. The *Time Machine* includes excerpts from issues dating back to 1902. You can also search the archives by keyword for mention of any subject in the past six months. If you have a computer-related question — be it about an Internet browser or resource, a software bug or pulling a computer apart — try one of the magazine's online forums.

Useful for Internet and computing; mailing lists (listservs) and newsgroups; news sources; science.
URL: http://popularmechanics.com/

Primatological Resources for Children and Young Adults
Books, videos and slides about apes, monkeys and other primates

The Wisconsin Regional Primate Research Center server lists resources about nonhuman primates (apes, monkeys, and prosimians) that are tailored to children, young adults, and K-12 teachers. Listed materials include fiction, nonfiction, videos and sets of slides on primate behavior, conservation and taxonomy, many of which may be borrowed from the center.

Useful for biology.
URL: http://www.primate.wisc.edu/

Project Athena
Teaching materials for science, math and technology

Project Athena includes a growing collection of K-12 curriculum modules and information on such topics as observing the weather, viewing storms from space, Space Shuttle missions, Pacific Rim earthquakes and planetary orbit. This is a three-year collaboration to develop science, math and technology educational materials using the resources of the Internet. Funded by NASA, it involves school districts in the metropolitan Seattle area, the Washington education department, and Science Applications International Corp.

Useful for mathematics; science.
URL: http://inspire.ospi.wednet.edu:8001/

Puget Sound Green Gopher/Kids for Puget Sound
Data on Washington

The Puget Sound Green Gopher is sponsored primarily by People for Puget Sound, an organization dedicated to protecting and restoring the Puget Sound region of Washington state. On it you'll find environmental information about that region, including pollution reports, growth management and watershed databases, and a newsletter. Also available are details about Kids for Puget Sound (the junior arm of People for Puget Sound), such as copies of *Kids' Sound,* a newsletter containing poetry, letters, and short articles contributed by kids. The gopher also offers links to other environmental information on the Internet.

Useful for ecology and the environment.
URL: gopher://futureinfo.com

Raptor Center
Sights, sounds and some lesson plans about birds of prey

Ever wondered what you should do you find an injured bird, especially if it needed emergency aid? The Raptor Center, an international medical facility for birds of prey, has this and other answers in its files. You can see images and hear the calls of bald eagles and great horned owls. Eventually, the center plans to offer online information about endangered/threatened birds and the environmental issues which effect them. Meanwhile, the center offers activities and lesson plans to show the interdependence of nature, including an experiment done by a 7th-grader using owl pellets.

Useful for biology.
URL: http://www.raptor.cvm.umn.edu/

Recent Earthquakes with map
See where in the world a quake has happened

This server at Carleton University uses the Xerox map servicer and information from the U.S. Geological Survey to show the location of recent earthquakes.
URL: http://www.civeng.carleton.ca/cgi-bin/quakes

SciEd
A catalog of resources for students and teachers

Alan Cairns, of Bellevue High School in Washington, has taken a stab at cataloging all the useful Web resources for teaching and learning science and math. The page of resources for chemistry, for example, links to tutorials, journals, reviews, images, databases and safety sheets, among other instructional materials. The SciEd home page also contains many links and pointers to material on other subjects, from art and literature to current evens and travel.

Useful for mathematics; science.
URL: http://www.halcyon.com/cairns/science.html
E-mail: acairns@halcyon.com

Science and Math Initiatives Solve Me (SAMISM)
Try solving these puzzlers

The Solve Me section of the Science and Math Initiative (SAMI) database poses math and science "challenges" to students and teachers at all levels. Problems posted at press time related to real-life puzzles, such as coloring maps, and demonstrations of math theory. Solutions, and even new problems, can be e-mailed to the Web site, where they will be posted. SAMI is part of Creating Connections, a project designed to improve math and science education in the rural United States. Eventually, this Web site will link to the national standards for math and science, alternative assessment ideas and rubrics, along with additional information and history about the challenges.

Useful for activities and projects; mathematics; science.
URL: http://www.c3.lanl.gov/~jspeck/SAMISM-home.shtml
E-mail: betasami@bvsd.k12.co.us

Science at Home
Simple experiments the whole family can learn from

Science at Home — the hypertext draft of a publication from Los Alamos National Laboratory — describes hands-on activities to help families learn science, using inexpensive materials that are easy to find around most homes. For example, using items found in kitchen cupboards, you can solve puzzles such as "Does a Waterdrop Have Skin?" and "Who Makes the Best Bubbles?" Using items in the laundry room, you can discover "How to Make a Balance Scale" and how "Opposites Attract in a Shocking Way!"

Useful for activities and projects; science.
URL: http://education.lanl.gov/SE/RESOURCES/Science.at.home/Welcome.html

Science Behind Jurassic Park
Studying ancient dinosaurs with modern technology

How do paleontologists use computers to study dinosaurs? A short article from InfoLane outlines how paleontologist Jack Horner, consultant on Steven Spielberg's *Jurassic Park*, uses computers and CAT scan machines to examine 30 million-year-old dinosaur fossils. It links to a more detailed article, *Dinosaur Eggs and Bones*, describing the techniques.

Useful for biology.
URL: http://infolane.com/infolane/apunix/sci-jur.html

Science Bytes
Read and see what working scientists do

Hypertext articles and images from *Science Bytes* are now available online. Published by the University of Tennessee, the magazine is a pilot project to show children what working scientists at the university do. It also includes project ideas that parents and teachers can work on with kids at the elementary and secondary school levels. An article on dragonflies, for example, contains hyperlinks to the scientists mentioned in it, questions and answers about these insects, and a reading list for finding more information. Other articles discuss such topics as enrichment activities for zoo animals and mapmaking.

Useful for news sources; science.
URL: http://loki.ur.utk.edu/ut2kids/science.html

Science Museum of Minnesota
An adventure back in time

The Science Museum of Minnesota features a Maya adventure that includes several descriptions of Mayan archaeological sites. It also includes an interactive adventure.

Useful for activities and projects; international studies; museums on the Web.
URL: http://www.ties.k12.mn.us:80/~smm/

Science Resources for K-12 Teachers
Class outlines, lesson plans offer ideas

This subdirectory of the NASA Ames Research Center's K-12 server contains class outlines and lesson plans for science teachers in elementary, middle, and high schools. The site is still under development, but its organizers plan to offer materials in the life, physical, and earth/space sciences, as well as several interdisciplinary topics.

Useful for science.
URL: http://quest.arc.nasa.gov
E-mail: feedback@quest.arc.nasa.gov.

Science Tracks
Hands-on activities teach about science and careers

Science Tracks is an electronic book packed with science activities to teach kids, at home or at school, about various aspects of science and science-related careers. Each activity page offers instructions for teaching a hands-on science project. such as building a high-capacity model barge using aluminum foil and toothpicks. A "bibliography" of online movies, audio archives, libraries, interactive puzzles and games provides background and additional science resources. The book was published as part of British Columbia's Sixth Annual Science and Technology Week in 1994.

Useful for activities and projects; science.
URL: http://www.etc.bc.ca/apase/scitech/homepage.htm

Sea World/Busch Gardens Animal Information Database
Facts and fun

From American alligators to Bengal tigers, students can learn about land and sea animals in the Animal Information Data Base, provided by Sea World and Busch Gardens. The Animal Bytes section gives fast facts on physical characteristics, habitat, behavior and other aspects of how certain animals live, plus "fun facts,"

such as a lion's roar can be heard up to five miles away. Sections of the Sea
World Teacher's Guides, for different grade levels, are also available here. Using
hypertext links to the text and images in the animal database, these guides provide ideas for hands-on activities that help children learn about science, math, geography, art and language.

Useful for biology.
URL: http://www.bev.net/education/SeaWorld/homepage.html
E-mail: Sea.World@bev.net

Smithsonian's Center for Earth and Planetary Studies
Planetary images

Supported by NASA, the Smithsonian Institution's Center for Earth and Planetary Studies (CEPS) boasts an extensive collection of imagery of the planets and
their satellites. This includes an extensive collection of Space Shuttle photographs that grows with each mission. Recent photos and archived images — of
the Rabaul Caldera eruption in Papua New Guinea, the Grand Canyon and the
deployment of the Magellan Spacecraft, for example — are all on display.

Useful for images; museums on the Web; science.
URL: http://ceps.nasm.edu:2020/homepage.html

Smithsonian's Museum of Natural History
Botany, zoology, paleontology data

This site offers informational resources, newsletters, and gopher links in the subject areas of botany, zoology, and paleontology. Using one or more keywords,
you can search its Conservation Bibliography, which includes more than 6,400
references to literature on conservation biology drawn from a weekly review of
the new journals and books received by the Smithsonian Institution's Botany
and Natural History libraries and from suggestions submitted by subscribers to
its Biological Conservation Newsletter. The National Zoo in Washington, D.C.,
also posts information about its activities here, including notices of new arrivals,
tips on the best times to visit the animals and schedules of events to be held at
the zoo, such as presentations and animal-book signings.

Useful for biology; museums on the Web.
URL: http://nmnhwww.si.edu/nmnhweb.html

Solar System Live
Model of the solar system lets you pick the settings

John Walker's interactive *Solar System Live* lets you view the entire solar system — or just the inner planets (through the orbit of Mars). Among the parameters you can set in what Walker calls his "interactive orrery for the Web" are
time and date; viewpoint; observing loc ation; and orbital elements to track an as-
teroid or comet. You can also find public domain astronomy and space simulation software at this site.

Useful for activities and projects; astronomy and space exploration.
URL: http://www.fourmilab.ch/solar/solar.html

Space Adventures for Young Scientists
Shedding light on the aurora borealis

This Web site is operated by the Poker Flat Research Range and is part of the University of Alaska at Fairbanks. It is the world's only scientific rocket-launching facility owned by a university. Of special interest is a presentation on the aurora borealis, or Northern Lights.

Useful for astronomy and space exploration.
URL: http://dac3.gi.alaska.edu/

Space Environment Laboratory
What's the weather like in space today?

The National Oceanic and Atmospheric Administration's Space Environment Laboratory conducts research related to the sun and the environment between the earth and the sun, offering some of its data in real-time or near-real-time. Besides images (many in GIF format) of the sun, it provides current forecasts for the "weather" in space. From this page, you can visit other sites that offer information about solar activity, space and related projects.

Useful for astronomy and space exploration.
URL: http://www.sel.noaa.gov/

Space Shots, Washington University
Detailed images from NASA projects

This site, still under construction, offers access to downloadable images in GIF format from NASA space projects. You'll find Viking 1's detailed photos of Mars, taken from both space and the surface, as well as pictures of lunar rovers and Mars landers.

Useful for astronomy and space exploration.
URL: http://wwwcache.hensa.ac.uk/

Space Shuttle Clickable Map
What do those funny things on the Space Shuttle do?

An interactive image of the Space Shuttle has been prepared by a student at Embry-Riddle Aeronautical University, in Daytona Beach, Fla. It explains what the various parts of the Shuttle do, as well as provides background information on the space vehicle.

URL: http://seds.lpl.arizona.edu/ssa/space.shuttle/docs/homepage.html

Space Telescope Electronic Information System
Photos of space, volcanoes

Kids interested in astronomy will enjoy the Space Telescope Electronic Information System (STEIS), which offers space photographs taken by the Endeavour and Magellan spacecraft, by the Hubble telescope, and by satellites orbiting the earth. The gopher features Exploration in Education, a series of "electronic picturebooks" offering full-color photos (with accompanying text) of Venus and Mars, the Shoemaker-Levy comet impact with Jupiter, Hawaiian volcanoes, and other phenomena. Electronic PictureBooks require a Macintosh computer, HyperCard software, and a color monitor. STEIS also links to other astronomy resources on the Internet.

Useful for astronomy and space exploration.
URL: gopher://stsci.edu

SPACESIM
Ideas for "trips" into outer space

SPACESIM is a monthly electronic magazine that contains activities, experiments, and suggestions to help student "astronauts" conduct lab and medical experiments during simulates trips into space. It is part of the Educational Space Simulations Project by Chris Rowan in association with the National Association of Space Simulating Educators. The site offers current and back issues, shareware software for space simulations, and information about the project.

Useful for activities and projects; astronomy and space exploration.
URL: http://chico.rice.edu/armadillo/Simulations/simserver.html

StarMap, Mount Wilson Observatory
Custom maps for stargazing

Amateur and backyard astronomy enthusiasts can now get customized maps of what the sky above should look like, courtesy of California's Mount Wilson Observatory. StarMap, written by Bob Donahue of the Center for Astrophysics, takes information you provide onscreen and produces a printable PostScript map for stargazing. This home page also offers a "virtual tour" of the observatory and information about astronomical research being conducted there.

Useful for activities and projects; astronomy and space exploration.
URL: http://www.mtwilson.edu/

Stars and Galaxies
Learn about the origin, life cycle, behavior of heavenly bodies

From Bradford Technology Limited, Armagh Planetarium and Mayfield Consultants, this site aims to explain the origin and life cycle of stars and galaxies, how their energy is generated and how they behave. Audio clips, movies and satellite images are available here, as well as a variety of pictures of galaxies and other phenomena in the universe that you can observe through a telescope.

Useful for astronomy and space exploration; images.
URL: http://www.eia.brad.ac.uk/btl/sg.html

Student Astronomers at Harvard-Radcliffe
Calendars, reports for stargazers

On their Web page, Student Astronomers at Harvard-Radcliffe (STAHR) provides information about the group's activities as well as general astronomy and starwatching materials. You'll find a calendar of space launches and other major dates, the weekly *Jonathan's Space Report*, and (through links) data on the Loomis-Michael Observatory and other astronomy resources on the Internet.

Useful for astronomy and space exploration.
URL: http://hcs.harvard.edu/~stahr/
E-mail: stahr@husc.harvard.edu

Students for the Exploration & Development of Space
Solar show-and-tell

Students for the Exploration and Development of Space (SEDS) is an international organization of high-school and university students working to promote space study and exploration. *The Nine Planets,* by Bill Arnett, is a multimedia tour of the solar system. It combines text, pictures, sounds and movies. to describe each of the planets and major moons in the solar system. Find out which are the biggest and the brightest, when they were discovered, and how their names were assigned. This server also gives background information about the group and links to other space-related materials.

Useful for astronomy and space exploration.
URL: gopher://seds.lpl.arizona.edu

Top 20 Comet Shoemaker-Levy images.
A "popularity" contest

As its name suggests, this site lists and allows you to view the 20 most popular Comet Shoemaker-Levy images from NASA's Jet Propulsion Laboratory, Send an e-mail message to Webmaster Ron Baalke if you would like to receive a monthly e-mail bulletin alerting you to the results of the latest "popularity contest," as determined by user access statistics at the JPL Comet SL9 Home Page. You also can request that he add you to the Comet P-Shoemaker/Levy 9 Mailing List, which alerts subscribers to news and revisions to the home pages about the comet.

Useful for astronomy and space exploration; images.
URL: http://newproducts.jpl.nasa.gov/sl9/top20.html
E-mail: baalke@kelvin.jpl.nasa.gov

Trash Goes to School: Classroom Resources for Environmental Education
Information about recycling, composting, landfills and more

Trash Goes to School is a set of K-12 educational materials addressing solid-waste management. You'll find background information about solid waste and related issues (such as recycling, composting, and landfills), glossaries, and activity ideas. The gopher is divided into K-3, 4-6, 7-8, and 9-12 sections, and activities cover the full range of subjects — math, science, language arts, social studies, home economics. Trash Goes to School was developed by the Cornell Waste Management Institute.

Useful for ecology and the environment.
URL: gopher://nceet.snre.umich.edu/1/classres

U.S. Army Corps of Engineers
Information on flood water levels

Through a multitude of links to U.S. Army Corps of Engineers sites, you can find information on the current water levels of major rivers in the United States. The Seattle District, for example, provides data (updated hourly) for several river basins, as well as information on the dams and recreation areas that the Corps manages.

Useful for ecology and the environment.
URL: http://www.usace.army.mil/

U.S. Geological Survey
Environmental information, online and in print

The U.S. Geological Survey provides information on earthquakes, volcanoes, water resources, and related environmental issues. You can order — often at little or no charge — maps, a natural hazards poster set, and an earthquake information classroom packet.

Useful for earthquakes, volcanoes and seismic activity; ecology and the environment.
URL: http://www.usgs.gov/

Views of the Solar System
Take a tour of the planets

Views of the Solar System — compiled by Calvin J. Hamilton of Los Alamos National Laboratory — takes you on a tour of the solar system. By clicking on an image, you move to a hypertext document and other images of that solar body, be it the sun, planets, moons, asteroids, comets or meteoroids. You can also learn the meaning of unusual terms, browse through statistics about the planets and satellites, and trace the history of space exploration

Useful for astronomy and space exploration; images.
URL: http://www.c3.lanl.gov/~cjhamil/SolarSystem/homepage.html

Virtual Frog Dissection Kit
Explore frog's anatomy on your screen

Lawrence Berkeley Laboratory offers an interactive frog dissection kit on the World-Wide Web. Students can view several computer-generated images of the frog at different stages of dissection, according to parameters they specify. The dissection kit is available in Spanish, German, Dutch, French and Czech, with versions in Japanese and Portuguese in the works. This interactive program is part of the lab's Whole Frog Project, aimed at enabling high-school biology students to explore the anatomy of a frog by using data from high-resolution Magnetic Resonance Imaging (MRI) scans and mechanical sectioning with 3-D surface and volume rendering software..

Useful for activities and projects; biology; images.
URL: http://george.lbl.gov/ITG.hm.pg.docs/dissect/info.html

Visible Human Project
Digital images show parts of the human body

The National Library of Medicine, as part of its Visible Human Project, has begun collecting digital images of the human body as a teaching and research tool.
It provides a sampling of these at its Web site, the most amazing of which is a
head-to-toe series of Magnetic Resonance Imaging (MRI) scans. The library plans
to create complete, 3-D representations of the male and female human bodies,
showing details of the anatomy.

Useful for biology; images.
URL: http://www.nlm.nih.gov/extramural_research.dir/visible_human.html

VolcanoWorld
Reports, images and field trips for K-12 students

VolcanoWorld, funded by NASA, provides information about volcanoes for
school-age kids. It offers reports and pictures of current and recent eruptions, a
developing virtual field trip to Kilauea volcano, a question-and-answer service,
lesson plans, and links to other volcano resources on the Internet. You can view
color photos of volcanoes from around the world, many of which were taken by
astronauts aboard the Space Shuttle, and you can find out how to order videos,
newsletters, and free booklets about volcanoes. The developers of VolcanoWorld,
who include volcanologists, teachers, artists and others, hope to eventually add
interactive experiments to show how volcanoes work.

Useful for activities and projects; earthquakes, volcanoes and seismic activity.
URL: http://volcano.und.nodak.edu

Weather
Clickable map gives current forecast

The Weather page offers an interactive weather map of the United States. You
just point and click on a location to learn its current and extended forecasts, including temperature, humidity, wind speed, barometric pressure, and actual conditions (fog, snow, and so on). Located on the Massachusetts Institute of
Technology's Student Information Processing Board World-Wide Web, the map
draws its information from the University of Michigan's Weather Underground
project. From here, you can connect to popular online weather sites, such as the
Weather Underground TELNET site and maps, satellite images, forecasts, and
animations from the University of Illinois, Urbana-Champaign..

Useful for weather.
URL: http://www.mit.edu:8001/usa.html

Weather Underground
Temperatures, seasonal and climatic reports

This online weather service provides current worldwide temperatures, as well as
seasonal and climatic information. You'll find current weather observations, long-
range forecasts, ski conditions, earthquake reports, hurricane and severe weather
advisories, marine forecasts, and a national weather summary for the United
States. The service is limited to 100 users at a time.

Useful for weather.
URL: gopher://madlab.sprl.umich.edu:3000

Wild Adventurers
Create a custom map of animals' migratory routes

This interactive site, an offshoot of the Journey North project, allows you to build a map onscreen and view the migratory paths of (and other information about) a variety of wild animals, from gray whales and sandhill cranes to monarch butterflies and sea turtles. Links take you to observations by people across North, Central and South America who have actually spotted these animals.

Useful for activities and projects; ecology and the environment.
URL: http://ics.soe.umich.edu:85/IAPMain

Wolves on the Web
This Web site howls

Start here if you want to know more about wolves. This page includes links to photographs, sound files, and groups interested in the preservation of wolves.
URL: http://wwwnncc.scs.unr.edu/wolves/desertm.html

Yukon Wolf Kill
Does killing wolves kill tourism?

This Web site, by the Yukon division of the Canadian Broadcasting Corp., examines the Yukon wolf kill and tourism boycott issue. It includes background stories as well as a Web survey form.

Useful for biology; news sources.
URL: http://www.wimsey.com/yukon/cbc/survey.htmld/

Search tools

Lycos Catalog of the Internet
Perhaps the smartest spider around

This search tool (called a spider) was developed by Michael L. Mauldin, a research scientist at Carnegie Mellon's Center for Machine Translation in the School of Computer Science. Named for a wandering species of spider, Lycos hunts for information across the Internet, with particular emphasis on the World-Wide Web. Since it came online in July 1994, Lycos has cataloged more than 3 million of the estimated 4 million documents on the Web
URL: http://lycos.cs.cmu.edu/)

Open Text Web Index
New search tool could be the top gun of Web indexers

Open Text Corp. of Canada has developed what may be the fastest and most complete World-Wide Web search tool. The service is currently free, but the company may soon charge for it.
URL: http://www.opentext.com:8080/

WebCrawler
Just place your order

The University of Washington's WebCrawler allows you to search for indexed documents containing a particular word or phrase. Using an onscreen form, you enter the word or words you're looking for, and WebCrawler returns a list of possible resources.
URL: http://webcrawler.cs.washington.edu/WebCrawler/Home.html

World-Wide Web Consortium
Search by subject or country

The World-Wide Web Consortium (W3C), an offshoot of the Center for European Nuclear Research's World-Wide Web project, offers both a subject index of Web servers (mostly academic ones) and a registry of servers by country. For some countries, such as France, the locations of servers are plotted on a map.
URL: http://www.w3.org/hypertext/DataSources/Top.html

World-Wide Web Worm
Search the Web in seconds

This is a very fast search tool with flexible options. Developed at the University of Colorado at Boulder, it only searches the Web.
URL: http://www.cs.colorado.edu/home/mcbryan/WWWW.html

Social studies

ACLU Free Reading Room
Focus on issues surrounding the U.S. Bill of Rights

The Free Reading Room of the American Civil Liberties Union (ACLU) is a collection of materials related to the principles set forth in the Bill of Rights. You'll find the ACLU membership newsletter, *Civil Liberties,* and publications on censorship and other issues. The ACLU hopes to expand its offerings to include news releases, calls to action on legislative issues, and legal briefs submitted by the ACLU in important Supreme Court cases.

Useful for civil liberties.
URL: gopher://aclu.org:6601/1

Albert R. Mann Library
How much is spent on farm production, food consumption?

The U.S. Department of Agriculture (USDA) offers more than 100 sets of agricultural statistics on this server. You'll find data on worldwide textile fiber production, farm production expenses, European Community wheat supply, milk and dairy product sales, food spending in American households, U.S. meat supply and consumption, fertilizer use, and so on—all organized into 11 broad subject categories. You can search for the information you need by keyword.
Most of the files here are in Lotus 1-2-3 (.wk1) format, so you can't read them on-screen. Instead, you transfer files to your own computer (via gopher, TELNET, or FTP) and read them using a spreadsheet package or word processor capable of opening .wk1 files.

Useful for agriculture.
URL: gopher://usda.mannlib.cornell.edu

All About Turkey
Facts, figures and photos

All About Turkey includes facts and figures about the country. Located at Ege University, this server provides a picture archive, tourist information, and details about other Internet servers in or related to Turkey.

Useful for international studies.
URL: http://www.ege.edu.tr/

American Civil War Letters and Information
A look at life during the 1860s

This collection of letters from an Iowa soldier to his family and a friend (later his wife) gives a detailed firsthand account of life during the American Civil War. The soldier's great-grandson, Bill Proudfoot, a librarian, built this Web site to share these family records and some family photos with other interested in this period of history. He also provides a useful set of links and pointers to other Internet sources of information and discussion on the Civil War.

Useful for history.
URL: http://www.ucsc.edu/civil-war-letters/home.html

American Government
From political campaigns to daily administration

This server, based at Northwestern University, offers a wide range of materials about the United States system of government. You'll find resources about the executive, legislative, and judicial branches of the federal government, as well as information about political parties, campaigns, public opinion, political documents, and state governments. The server also offers electronic texts and journals, links to other political servers, and a list of related resources on the Internet.

Useful for government studies.
URL: gopher://casbah.acns.nwu.edu:71/1/net.sources.by.discipline/polisci

American Institute for Contemporary German Studies
News and information

The American Institute for Contemporary German Studies (AICGS), affiliated with the Johns Hopkins University, maintains this server containing a growing library of news and data on Germany, information about AICGS programs, and announcements of conferences and other events.

Useful for international studies.
URL: gopher://jhuniverse.hcf.jhu.edu (Type=1) (Port=10005) (Path=1/.aicgsdoc)

American Memory
Manuscripts, movies and more

Mostly drawn from the special collections of the Library of Congress, the American Memory exhibition offers a glimpse into the culture and history of the United States. Still under construction, this site has direct links to photographic, recorded sound, manuscript and early motion picture collections. Examples include portraits of literary figures, celebrities, and the Civil War; research done between 1936 and 1939 on American ethnic communities; and short films, in AVI format, that were shot between 1897 and 1916, and include scenes of President McKinley, the Pan-American Exposition, New York City, and San Francisco.

Useful for history; images.
URL: http://rs6.loc.gov/amhome.html

ArchNet
Take a "walk" around some historic sites

Through this collection of Internet resources for historic archaelogy, hosted by the University of Connecticut, you can take a walking tour of the Mayflower Hill Project in Waterville, Maine; Plimoth Plantation; and the Grove Street Cemetery in New Haven, Conn. You can also find a bibliography of Connecticut's historical and industrial archaeology, as well as links to related information from other Internet sources, such as newsletters and historical preservation organizations.

Useful for history.
URL: http://spirit.lib.uconn.edu/ArchNet/Topical/Historic/Historic.html

Armadillo
Projects integrate themes of Texas history

Armadillo, a project of the Houston Independent School District and Rice University, offers materials for K-12 teachers who want to integrate Texas state history themes into their classroom activities. Suggested projects cover a variety of subjects, and many incorporate multimedia and the Internet. From the server, you can also reach Rice's K-8 School and K-12 Resources pages.

Useful for history.
URL: gopher://riceinfo.rice.edu:1170/11/

Army Area Handbooks & Background Notes
Summaries for over 150 countries

The gopher of the University of Missouri-St Louis contains the text of the U.S. *Army Area Handbooks* for 10 countries. Each provides a concise introduction to that country's history, economy, culture, and political structure. *Army Area Handbooks* are available for the People's Republic of China, Egypt, Indonesia, Israel, Japan, the Philippines, Singapore, Somalia, South Korea, and the former Yugoslavia. You'll also find the U.S. Department of State *Background Notes* for more than 150 countries. These notes briefly summarize the history, culture, government, economy, and diplomatic situation of each country. In addition, this site contains information about selected international organizations.

Useful for international studies.
URL: gopher://umslvma.umsl.edu/1/LIBRARY/GOVDOCS/

Asia Online
An up-to-date look at daily life in Asia

Asia Online's listings of businesses, investment opportunities, conferences, and conventions shows a cross-section of the booming commercial activity in this region. Archives of *China Business Journal, China News Digest,* and other magazines provide an up-to-date look at daily happenings, culture and art in Asia. The site, operated by Silk Route Ventures, also links to a number of other online information sources in Asia.

Useful for international studies.
URL: http://www.ncb.gov.sg:1080/

Asia Pacific Region Information
Find current information on the region

Thailand's Asian Institute of Technology is building this wide-ranging site covering the nations of the Asia Pacific region. You'll find materials about Brunei, Cambodia, China, Indonesia, Korea, Laos, Malaysia, Myanmar (Burma), the Philippines, Singapore, Thailand, and Vietnam. The server, which links to several others, provides information on such topics as tourist attractions, business practices, currency, criminal justice, human rights, and national economies. The resources are gathered from a variety of sources, both inside and outside the region.

Useful for international studies; social studies; travel and recreation.
URL: gopher://emailhost.ait.ac.th:70/11/AsiaInfo

Augustana College Special Collections
The way it used to be

Augustana College in Illinois has developed an outstanding site for the historical collections that are used in conjunction with elementary and high-school classes taught in that state. The *Elementary Collection* contains historical information and photographs about farm life, Native Americans, and early transportation.

Useful for Aboriginal and Native American studies; agriculture; history; transportation.
URL: http://www.augustana.edu/library/elem.html

Australian World Heritage Areas
Images, information about cultural, historic sites

The World Heritage Committee, part of UNESCO, focuses on preserving areas — both natural and human-made — that it judges to be of cultural or historic importance, such as the Pyramids of Egypt and the Grand Canyon of the United States. At this Web site, you can find general information about the listing process as well as images, maps, and detailed descriptions of World Heritage sites in Australia, such as the Great Barrier Reef, Tasmanian Wilderness and Shark Bay. This information is presented as part of a project by the Australian Department of the Environment and associated agencies, and is managed by the Environmental Resources Information Network Unit.

Useful for science.
URL: http://kaos.erin.gov.au/land/conservation/wha/auswha.html

Big Sky Social Studies Lesson Plans
From the Civil War to criminal court system

The server of Montana's Big Sky Telegraph educational network includes this collection of more than 180 K-12 social studies lesson plans and "mini-lessons" on topics ranging from the Civil War and the Oregon Trail to the criminal justice system and resolving conflict. Each plan includes an objective, overview, activities and procedures, and examples. The lessons were prepared at summer workshops of the Columbia Education Center, an association of teachers from 14 western states.

Useful for activities and projects; social studies.
URL: gopher://bvsd.k12.co.us:70/11/Educational_Resources/Lesson_Plans/Big%20Sky/social_studies

Bosnia
Current information on political and military activity

This gopher provides detailed information from NATO and related organizations on the latest military and political activity in Bosnia. It also links to lesser-known gopher sites providing information on international and strategic affairs, such as Radio Free Europe/Radio Liberty Research Institute (with daily reports on Eastern Europe and the countries of the former Soviet Union), the Stockholm International Peace Research Institute, and the George C. Marshall European Center for Security Studies.

Useful for international studies.
URL: gopher://gopher stc.nato.int

C-SPAN
Historical texts and companion materials to TV programs

The gopher of the C-SPAN cable television network offers the text of historical documents such as the U.S. Constitution and Lincoln's Gettysburg Address. Students will also find companion materials to C-SPAN programming — such as the popular *Close Up* programs, which feature citizens discussing topics with national leaders.

Useful for educational TV and radio; government studies; history.
URL: gopher://c-span.org
E-mail: c-spaneduc@aol.com

California State Legislature
The latest legislation and contact information

On this server, you'll find a full range of information about the current legislative session in California — the text and status of bills, committee information, and details about members of the Assembly and Senate (including phone numbers and e-mail addresses). You can find information about elected representatives for a particular district just by entering a ZIP code. Links take you to servers for the legislatures of other states.

Useful for government studies.
URL: http://www.sen.ca.gov/

Canadian Kids Home Page
Canadiana for kids

Although the focus at this Web site is on things Canadian, there are a lot of interesting and entertaining resources for those from other parts of the world, too. Navigation is simplified by symbols that indicate whether resources are Canadian, contain images or contain sound files. There are pointers and links to activities at the Canadian Council of Science Centres as well as the Canadian TV program *Theodore Tugboat*; book lists (some in hypertext); visitor information at various museums; and even whale-watching and travel tips from the province of New Brunswick. You can also surf to sites for kids and families in other parts of the world.

Useful for international studies.
URL: http://WWW.OnRamp.ca/~lowens/107kids.htm

Canadian Museum of Civilization
Archaeology, history and folk culture on display

By clicking your mouse on an interactive floorplan, you can learn about the programs, services, and facilities at the Canadian Museum of Civilization, its Children's Museum, and its affiliate, the Canadian War Museum. You can view a selection of artifacts representative of archaeology, ethnology, folk culture, and the history of Canada.

Useful for international studies; museums on the Web.
URL: http://www.cmcc.muse.digital.ca/cmcchome.html

CapWeb: A Guide to the U.S. Congress
Data on elected representatives

CapWeb offers an "unauthorized" hypertext guide to the U.S. Congress that is searchable and contains links to related resources. For senators and members of the House of Representatives, it gives full addresses, including e-mail (if they exist); information about state delegations; and committee assignments. Images include inlines of members of Congress and thumbnails that link to larger originals on the C-SPAN server. CapWeb plans to post party rosters, party leadership, and pointers to state government Internet resources. CapWeb is an independent project of PolicyNet, a service of Issue Dynamics, Inc.

Useful for government studies.
URL: http://policy.net/capweb/congress.html

Carter Center
Reports and speeches on fighting hunger, poverty, oppression

The Carter Center in Atlanta, Ga., is a nonprofit, nonpartisan public policy institute founded in 1982 by former President Jimmy Carter and his wife, Rosalynn. The center is dedicated to fighting disease, hunger, poverty, conflict, and oppression through collaborative initiatives in the areas of democratization and development, global health, and urban revitalization. The Web site includes transcripts of speeches and information on how to order the center's many reports.

Useful for government studies; presidential libraries.
URL: http://www.emory.edu/CARTER_CENTER/homepage.htm

Center for International Security and Arms Control
A look at world security

This multidisciplinary research organization is dedicated to the study of issues of international security. A few of the organization's documents are available over the Web.

Useful for government studies; international studies.
URL: http://www-leland.stanford.edu:80/group/CISAC/

Central Intelligence Agency
Research on foreign countries

The U.S. Central Intelligence Agency has published a hypertext edition of its annual *Factbook*. Profiles give concise and current descriptions of the geographic, historical, social, economic and political makeup of each country. Also included are maps (in both JPEG and GIF formats) of each country, showing the locations of major geographic features and cities, as well as reference maps of the entire world and of its different regions. Other useful information found in the book's appendices includes: the United Nations system; weights and measures; and selected international environmental agreements.

Useful for international studies.
URL: http://www.ic.gov/

China News Digest
Archive includes articles on the Beijing Massacre

China News Digest offers an archive of the magazine's articles, as well as related publications. Included is information about the Beijing Massacre of June 4, 1989. You can also link to other online information related to China.

Useful for international studies.
URL: http://www.cnd.org
E-mail: CND-INFO@CND.ORG (for general and subscription information)

CityNet
Stories and more from globetrotters

CityNet provides extensive information about communities around the world, with subject matter ranging from travel and entertainment to local business, government, and community services. Resources are searchable by country, continent or region. The pointers and direct links are to sites developed by private "netizens", Internet access providers, chambers of commerce, government, and tourism bureaus. Some useful connections include maps, language resources and true stories of travelers (taken from the rec.travel.library Usenet newsgroup archives) who've been to these places.

Useful for travel and recreation.
URL: http://www.city.net/

Congressional Quarterly
Features and news about U.S. politics and government

CQ's server gives you access to the data files of *Congressional Quarterly*, "the nation's leading nonpartisan authority on Congress and American politics." You'll find current feature stories and news briefs, an archive of past stories, information about pending legislation, election updates, contact information for members of Congress, and promotional material for *CQ*..

Useful for government studies; news sources.
URL: gopher://gopher.cqalert.com
E-mail: mhenderson@cqalert.com

Crisis in Rwanda
Reports form the front lines

This Web page offers reports, images, and opinions on the Rwandan crisis from various sources—primarily relief organizations and news services.

Useful for international studies.
URL: http://www.intac.com/PubService/rwanda/

Croatia
Information from libraries, museums and other institutions

This experimental gopher, based at the University of Zagreb, Republic of Croatia, provides information about that nation in both English and Croatian. It links to the servers of libraries, museums, art galleries, and other Croatian institutions, providing images, news, descriptions of exhibits, and even a navigational guide to the country's Adriatic coastline.

Useful for international studies.
URL: gopher://diana.zems.etf.hr

Croatian Advertisements Forum
The Croatian bulletin board

Internet users may post messages and advertisements related to Croatia on this unique bulletin board. Students, for example, post messages to the forum looking for information on Croatia.

Useful for Croatia; international studies.
URL: http://tjev.tel.etf.hr/ccloser/

DeLorme Mapping
Maps on current affairs

Want to see where the epicenter of the 1995 earthquake in Kobe, Japan, was? Or where the Chechen conflict in the former Soviet Union has been taking place? The samples on this server allow you to view maps related to recent current events such as these. Delorme specializes in mapping software, databases and printed atlases for the consumer, education, business, and government markets.

Useful for images.
URL: http://www.delorme.com/
E-mail: webmaster@delorme.com

East Asian Studies
Online resources about Asia and the Pacific Basin

Intended for librarians, this page of links from the Committee on East Asian Libraries is useful to anyone seeking information on this region. It offers a standard list of subject headings—such as arts, business, and travel—linked to text and images for each country: Japan, South Korea, North Korea, China, Taiwan, Hong Kong, Macao, the Philippines, Singapore, and Australia, as well as Asia in general.

Useful for international studies.
URL: http://darkwing.uoregon.edu/~felsing/ceal/welcome.html

Economic Democracy Information Network
Political, economic subjects

Based at the University of California at Berkeley, the Economic Democracy Information Network (EDIN) houses a wide range of information of a political and economic nature, focusing on the state of California. You'll find text files addressing such topics as economy and trade, defense conversion, labor issues, race and racism, gender and sexuality, the environment, human rights, education, health care, housing and welfare, and political theory. EDIN also offers links to online news services, magazine archives, government databases, California community gophers, and other Internet resources.

Useful for government studies.
URL: gopher://garnet.berkeley.edu:1250

Electronic Frontier Foundation (EFF)
For information about your online civil rights

The archives of the nonprofit Electronic Frontier Foundation (EFF) provide information about the issues and debates shaping the future of electronic communications, particularly as they relate to civil liberties. These include EFF news releases, recent and proposed legislation, materials for online activists, archives of electronic publications, records of trials and legal cases, information alerts, You can also contact the foundation if you have questions about your online rights or wish to join.

Useful for civil liberties.
URL: http://www.eff.org/
E-mail: ask@eff.org (general questions about EFF, legal, policy or online resources)

FAQ Lists About Countries/Regions
Answers about countries worldwide

If you have a quick question about Hong Kong or Hungary, India or Iran, this list of frequently asked questions (FAQs) may provide an answer. It offers FAQs on a growing number of regions and countries, drawing upon information supplied by readers responding to various soc.culture Usenet groups. Housed on the University of Illinois' National Center for Supercomputing Applications server, many of the FAQs provide hypertext links to other related documents.

Useful for international studies.
URL: http://www.ncsa.uiuc.edu/Edu/Classroom/Social/places.html

Flags
Icons, images and information from around the world

If you want to find out what the flag of a particular country looks like, try this page which links to a database at the Australian National Botanic Gardens. You'll find information, images, and icons of national flags from around the world. It also shows international maritime signal flags and their meanings; motor racing flags; and the Semaphore flag signaling system.

Useful for images; international studies.
URL: http://155.187.10.12/flags/flags.html

Fourth World Documentation Project
About indigenous people worldwide

The Fourth World Documentation Project, organized by the Center for World Indigenous Studies, provides information about the world's indigenous populations. You can read over 300 documents from authors, researchers, and governments in the Americas, Africa, Asia, Europe, Melanesia, and the Pacific.

Useful for Aboriginal and Native American studies; international studies.
URL: http://history.cc.ukans.edu/history/WWW_history_main.html/Regional/North America/NativeNet Information Network/Other Native gopher sites/Native American Gopher Sites/Fourth World Documentation Project

Freedom Shrine: Historical U.S. Documents
Back to the Mayflower Compact

The Freedom Shrine contains the text of more than 20 major documents from U.S. history. You can read the Mayflower Compact, the Declaration of Independence, the Articles of Confederation, the Treaty of Paris, the Constitution and Bill of Rights, the Monroe Doctrine, the Emancipation Proclamation, Martin Luther King, Jr.'s "I Have a Dream" speech, and many others. You can search all documents by keyword.

Useful for history.
URL: gopher://mail.coin.missouri.edu:70/11/reference/history/shrine

French Cave Paintings
Share in this major archaeological find

In late 1994, archaeologists in southern France discovered a vast underground network of caves decorated with paintings and engravings some 20,000 years old. Color images and detailed explanations of how the caves were unearthed and the significance of the artwork in them were brought online within a month of their discovery.

Useful for archeology.
URL: http://www.culture.fr/gvpda-en.htm

Friends and Partners
Meeting place to learn about Russia and the United States

Friends and Partners is a World-Wide Web server established to promote mutual understanding and cooperation among citizens of the United States and Russia (other former Soviet nations may be included later). The founders hope that the project will soon provide a meeting place for students, teachers, businesspeople, scientists, artists, and anyone else interested in sharing information and ideas with their counterparts in the other nation. Besides offering links to information on the Internet about both countries, the Webmasters here are building an interactive "coffee house" where you can post messages and carry on discussions on topics including culture and society, health, travel, politics, and economics.

Useful for international studies.
URL: http://solar.rtd.utk.edu/friends/home.html

Gateway to Antarctica
E-mail discussion and online documents

A Web page operated by the International Centre for Antarctic Information and Research, Gateway to Antarctica offers a variety of information about that continent for scientists and lay people, including kids. Materials here include a biweekly newsletter, information about ozone depletion and other scientific topics, political and historical background, and an e-mail discussion page. You can also find out about educational resources, maps, and posters available from the International Antarctic Visitor Centre. The server links to other Antarctica-related sites on the Internet.

Useful for science.
URL: http://icair.iac.org.nz/
E-mail: ashby@icair.iac.org.nz

GeoGame
Challenges help students learn about other places

GeoGame, a Global SchoolNet project developed by Tom Clauset, offers a quarterly geography challenge for elementary- and middle-school classrooms. Students in each participating class prepare a profile of the city they live in—its latitude, weather, land formations, points of interest, population, and so on—and send it electronically to the GeoGame coordinators, who then scramble all the cities and profiles, and distribute this information to the entrants. Over the next couple of weeks, students use atlases and other geography resources to match cities with their profiles, then submit their answers as a class. Classes that answer the most questions correctly win.

Useful for activities and projects; geography.
URL: gopher://gopher.csos.orst.edu/R0-9457-/gopher-data/community/ k12-netinfo/current/Geogame for middle-upper elementary

GeoWEB
Building an interactive index of geographic information

GeoWEB is being built into a searchable and interactive index to help geographers and the general public find information available on the Internet: tourist information, maps, lists, geographic information system datasets, and more. The GeoWEB mailing list provides a forum to discuss the development of this site, spearheaded by Brandon Plewe, a graduate geography student at the State University of New York, Buffalo, and Chris Stuber of the U.S. Census Bureau.

Useful for mailing lists (listservs) and newsgroups.
URL: http://gopher.census.gov:70/11s/Bureau/GeoWEB
E-mail: geoweb-owner@census.gov
To subscribe: majordomo@census.gov
Message body: subscribe geoweb

Gerald R. Ford Presidential Library & Museum
A day in the life of a president

This Web site is run by the Gerald R. Ford Library. It includes a special Internet presentation that shows a day in the life of a U.S. president complete with photographs and a copy of Ford's April 28, 1975, entry in his diary.

Useful for history; presidential libraries.
URL: http://http2.sils.umich.edu/FordLibrary/

GlobalInformation & Early Warning System
The food outlook worldwide

This server offers information about the availability of food in various parts of the world, as gathered by the United Nations Food and Agricultural Organization. You'll find reports on the world food outlook, the food situation in Africa, world crop shortages, and Sahel crop developments, as well as special reports and alerts.

Useful for agriculture.
URL: gopher://faov02.FAO.ORG:70/11gopher_root%3A%5Bfao.giews%5D

Global Studies Mailing List
Teachers, students discuss cultures and events

GLGB-HS is a mailing list for students and teachers of global studies or world cultures. Discussions focus on cultural issues and events. Monthly archive files are available.

Useful for mailing lists (listservs) and newsgroups.
URL: gopher://gopher.cic.net:3005/00/listservs/Global-Classroom
E-mail: GLBL-HS@ocmvm.onondaga.boces.k12.ny.us
To subscribe: LISTSERV@ocmvm.onondaga.boces.k12.ny.us
Message body: SUBSCRIBE GLBL-HS YourFirstName YourLastName

Guide to Australia
Images and information about the land Down Under

This Web server links to several online resources about Australia. It includes facts and figures, maps, weather information, materials for tourists (including U.S. State Department advice), historical and political background, and so on.

Useful for images; international studies; travel and recreation.
URL: http://www.csu.edu.au/education/australia.html

Historical Text Archive
Extensive collection focues on U.S. but includes other records

This should be a starting point for any history project, especially those concerning the United States. This site, run by Mississippi State University, is one of the oldest historical archives on the Internet. Besides the U.S., it also has documents and material relating to North Africa, Asia, Latin American and Mexico.

Useful for history; international studies; reference.
URL: http://www.msstate.edu/Archives/History/

Images of My War
Memoirs of active service

Images of My War are the memoirs of an Oklahoma City lawyer who served in Vietnam.

Useful for history; Vietnam War.
URL: http://www.ionet.net/~uheller/vnbktoc.html

Information on Sardinia and Italy
Maps, history and travel information

Annotated maps, history and travel information complete with images of Italy and Sardinia are available courtesy of the Center for Advanced Studies, Research and Development in Sardinia. You also can browse through several hypertext documents, including a virtual magazine filled with photos of the island of Sardinia.

Useful for international studies; travel and recreation.
URL: http://www.crs4.it/HTML/ItSardinfo.html

Israel Information Service
Background on the peace process, daily news summaries

The Israel Information Service (IIS), maintained by the Israeli Ministry of Foreign Affairs, offers several Internet services. Some information is available in both Spanish and French.

- *Gopher server:* You'll find facts about Israel, government information, background on the Arab-Israeli peace process, materials on anti-Semitism and the Holocaust, Hebrew-language resources, daily news updates, and a graphics section containing maps and other images in GIF format that can be viewed online or downloaded.
- *Israeline listserv:* This mailing list provides a daily summary of the Israeli press.
- *Israel-Mideast listserv:* This list offers news, policy papers, press surveys, and opinion pieces.
- *E-mail service:* You can send queries on any subject regarding Israel and receive an answer from IIS staff.

Useful for international studies.
URL: gopher://israel-info.gov.il
E-mail: ask@israel-info.gov.il
To subscribe: listserv@vm.tau.ac.il
Message body: Subscribe ListName YourFirstName YourLastName

Japanese Information
Read this before you take a trip

This Web page, located on the Nippon Telegraph and Telephone Corp. server in Japan, offers a variety of information about that country in both Japanese and English. It includes a "what's new in Japan" section, a sound file of the Japanese national anthem, an interactive map, facts and figures, weather information, background on Japanese culture and customs, tourist information, Japanese sports news, government information, and lists of other Internet resources about Japan.

Useful for international studies; travel and recreation.
URL: http://www.ntt.jp/japan/

Jerusalem One Network
Topics range from theology to tourism

The Jerusalem One Network, maintained by the Jewish International Communications Network (JICN) in Jerusalem, Israel, was created to strengthen world-wide Jewish identity through the Internet. Jerusalem One offers two types of resources:

Gopher server: You'll find a library of Jewish texts, Holocaust archives, materials for Jewish university students, newsletters, a software archive, and information about other Jewish resources on the Internet. Many of the gopher indexes are searchable by word.

Mailing lists: Jerusalem One also hosts more than 50 mailing lists addressing such diverse issues as theology, tourism, employment opportunities, and the media.

Useful for international studies; mailing lists (listservs) and newsgroups.
URL: gopher://jerusalem1.datasrv.co.il

Journey North
Culture, environment and wildlife of the Arctic

The Journey North focuses on life in the Arctic: the various cultures, the environment, and wildlife migration. Arctic Bites is a section of excerpts from newspaper articles, poetry, and Inuit writings about issues in the north. Another section of this Web site provides explanations and reports on the training exercises carried out by researchers from the 1994 International Arctic Project in the Canadian Arctic. Yet another area provides students' observations of wildlife migration. This project is an experiment in using the Web to deliver multimedia education to students, and is part of the University of Michigan School of Education's Dewey-Web.

Useful for activities and projects; geography.
URL: http://ics.soe.umich.edu/ed712/IAPIntro.html

Kremlin Online
A virtual visit to one of Moscow's treasures

You can take an online excursion to Moscow's Kremlin from this site, jointly organized by State Museums of the Moscow Kremlin, COMINFO Ltd. and Relcom Corp. Visitors can ether take a packaged tour or click on a menu to go to a particular site, such as the Cathedral of Annunciation, Lenin's Mausoleum, Red Square or the Residence of the President. Several images and a historical description of the site and its art greet you at each stop. Users are discouraged from copying this material, which organizers plan to publish on CD-ROM.

Useful for international studies.
URL: http://www.kiae.su/www/wtr/kremlin/begin.html

Labor Issues
Archives, discussion groups and other materials on workplace issues

The Labor Issues directory, housed on the Electronic Democracy Information Network (EDIN) server, offers a wide range of materials on labor unions and workplace issues. You'll find archived files dealing with unions in the United States and around the world, materials about women and minorities in the workplace, news about labor legislation, electronic labor discussion groups, even an AFL-CIO boycott list. A subdirectory offers e-mail addresses of labor groups, and points to other online resources of interest.

Useful for history.
URL: gopher://garnet.berkeley.edu:1250/11/.labor

LEGI-SLATE
Information about recent U.S. bills and regulations

LEGI-SLATE is a commercial gopher service that offers the texts of thousands of recent documents pertaining to the U.S. Congress and federal regulatory services. Some data is publicly available to all Internet users, such as information about recent bills and regulations. You can search the legislative information by title, status, number, data, sponsor, chamber, and type. Other free information includes bill cosponsors, a bill digest, and committee reports. Certain areas of LEGI-SLATE (such as Federal Register documents from regulatory agencies) require a subscription.

Useful for government studies.
URL: gopher://gopher.legislate.com

Lithuanian World Wide Web Information Service
News from the Baltic states

The Lithuanian World-Wide Web Information Service is an independent organization offering a variety of information about Lithuania and other Baltic states. You can view a map of Lithuania, listen to the national anthem, and read current and archived news. Other materials include U.S. State Department travel and human rights information, a connection to the BALT-L Baltics mailing list, and links to the Vilnius University server and the Estonian and Latvian Home Pages.

Useful for international studies.
URL: http://www.luc.edu/~tbaltru/lt/

MayaQuest Internet Center
Follow a cycling expedition through Central America

Through the MayaQuest Internet Center, K-12 students can follow a team of cyclists led by Minnesotan Dan Buettner on an expedition into the Mayan ruins of Central America in the first half of 1995. Using laptop computers and satellite communications, the team answers students' e-mail questions. The Web site features a daily journal, images from the expedition sites, a Maya languages chart, teacher tools and guides, a scavenger hunt for students, information on how to keep up with the expedition by using MayaQuest mailing lists and newsgroups; and links to anthropological resources (print, software and online). MayaQuest is sponsored by MECC, a producer of educational software; InforMNs (Internet for Minnesota Schools); and TIES, an Internet services provider.

Useful for activities and projects; history; mailing lists (listservs) and newsgroups.
URL: http://mayaquest.mecc.com/MayaQuest.Home.Page.html
To subscribe: majordomo@informns.k12.mn.us
Message body: subscribe maya-news

Middle East Center
From Mauritania to Pakistan and points in between

The Middle East Center at the University of Utah provides pointers to a broad range of Internet resources relating to the Middle East and North Africa. *The Middle East-North Africa Internet Resources Guide*, compiled by the Center's Joseph W. Roberts, is an up-to-date listing of gopher and World-Wide Web servers, TELNET sites, FTP archives, newsgroups and mailing lists, and organizations with online bulletin boards pertaining to issues in that region. It also links to at least a dozen other related servers.

Useful for international studies.
URL: gopher://mideast01.hum.utah.edu:70/1

Midlink Magazine
An online magazine by kids, for kids

Midlink is an electronic magazine for kids ages 10 to 15. You can browse through current and back issues featuring art, poetry, folklore and stories from middle school students around the world. Each issue shows how things are done in their countries, such as how certain holidays, like Christmas and Halloween, are celebrated. Under the guidance of teacher-editors at schools in the United States, *Midlink* is published every two months.,

Useful for international studies.
URL: http://longwood.cs.ucf.edu:80/~MidLink/

MIT White House information
E-mail service focuses on politics, government

The MIT White House information server offers copies of press releases and other documents by e-mail. You can request information in several subject areas: economy, foreign policy, health care, social issues, speeches by the president and administration officials, and transcripts of press conferences. You also can sign up to discussion lists tackling social policy and political philosophy, or complete and later receive the results of online surveys on various topics. By requesting help at the e-mail address, you will receive a detailed guide to the process of signing up for the various services.

Useful for government studies; mailing lists (listservs) and newsgroups.
To subscribe: Publications@research.ai.mit.edu
Enter in subject line: Help

National Archives and Records Administration (NARA) A.R.C.H.I.V.E.S.
A window on the political, military and diplomatic history of the U.S.

The National Archives and Records Administration (NARA) oversees not only the materials in the National Archives building in Washington, D.C., but also several regional archives and nine presidential libraries nationwide. These holdings comprise millions of documents pertaining to the political, military, and diplomatic history of the United States. Through its Archival Records and Collections

324 Internet for Parents

of Historical Information Via Electronic Sources (A.R.C.H.I.V.E.S.) system on the Internet, NARA makes this vast collection available to the general public. A.R.C.H.I.V.E.S. has two services:

- Archived information available via gopher or World-Wide Web. NARA offers a variety of documents online, including text files and some graphic images. Some examples: Congressional and court records, census data from 1790 onward, photos of exhibits, and announcements for NARA staff.
- Information searches. You can inquire about a particular record—of a civil, military, or diplomatic nature, and at least 20 years old—via e-mail. NARA staff will respond by either e-mail or regular post with the cost of receiving a reproduction of that record.

Useful for government studies; history.
URL: http://www.nara.gov/
E-mail: inquire@nara.gov

National Flags from KIDLINK
Symbolic images from around the world

Norway's KIDLINK network offers graphic images of the national flags of countries participating in the network. The flags are available in a self-displaying file for MS-DOS or as GIF files. To receive the flags, send the two-line command below to the listserv.

Useful for images.
URL: http://kidlink.ccit.duq.edu:70/0/kidlink-general.html
To subscribe: LISTSERV@vm1.nodak.edu
Message body: GET KIDLINK CHARTGIFGET KIDLINK FLAGS

National Library of Canada
Online information about Canada and Canadian issues

The National Library of Canada offers a bilingual server focusing on Internet resources related to Canada. From here, you can access other online libraries, government information, and publications addressing Canadian issues. The library also publishes *Network News*, a newsletter with information about the Internet and networking that is designed for librarians but could be of value to the general public as well.

Useful for library.
URL: gopher://gopher.nlc-bnc.ca

National SchoolNet Atlas (Canada)
Where do bears live in Canada?

This online atlas of Canada includes political, econonic, and environmental maps. It also features a teacher's guide.
URL: http://www-nais.ccm.emr.ca/schoolnet/

Native American Internet Resources
Information from tribes, other sources

This Web server offers links to dozens of Internet sites offering materials for or about Native Americans. You can reach servers operated by governments, universities, and Native American tribes and organizations.

Useful for Aboriginal and Native American studies.
URL: http://hanksville.phast.umass.edu/misc/NAresources.html

Native Americans
Rights and resources, plans and policies

This gopher, created by the National Indian Policy Center at George Washington University, offers information about Native American affairs. It includes press releases and reports from task forces and symposia about such topics as Native Americans' cultural rights and resources, economic development, education, and health and human services.

Useful for Aboriginal and Native American studies.
URL: gopher://gwis.circ.gwu.edu.:70/11/Centers%2C%20Institutes%2C%20and%20Research%20at%20GWU/Centers%20and%20Institutes/National%20Indian%20Policy%20Center

Native Peoples Education) Mailing List
Pen pals, forums on education issues

The NAT-EDU mailing list provides a forum for discussion of educational issues regarding the world's Native peoples. Example topics include cultural biases in standardized testing, finding teaching jobs on American Indian reservations, and requests for Aboriginal pen pals.

Useful for Aboriginal and Native American studies; mailing lists (listservs) and newsgroups.
To subscribe: listserv@indycms.iupui.edu
Message body: subscribe nat-edu YourFirstName YourLastName

NativeNet
Documents, mailing lists, other resources about indigenous peoples

NativeNet provides an umbrella site for documents about Native issues arranged by subject, geographical regions, and cultural groups. It also points or links to a set of mailing lists on subjects related to indigenous peoples worldwide (from which the organization derives its name), as well as Usenet newsgroups, Web sites and gophers on Native affairs. Plans are afoot for pages on Native literature, language, journals, organizations, and bibliographies. Information at this site is also available in Spanish.

Useful for Aboriginal and Native American studies.
URL: http://ukanaix.cc.ukans.edu/~marc/native_main.html

Nessie on the Net
Nellie lives! (At least on the Web.)

There is a Loch Ness monster—well, on the Web at any rate. This resource was developed by a group of Scottish businesses, and includes travel and historical material as well as myths and legends about the Loch Ness monster.

Useful for international studies; travel and recreation.
URL: http://www.scotnet.co.uk:80/highland/index.html

Nordic Pages
Start here for general information and specific links

This is a starting point for information on the Nordic countries—Denmark, Finland, Iceland, Norway and Sweden. It provides general information on each country as well as links to various servers.

Useful for international studies.
URL: http://www.algonet.se/~nikos/nordic.html

North Atlantic Treaty Organization (NATO)
Defense and arms control data

Here you'll find the latest information from NATO and related organizations, such as the North Atlantic Assembly and the Assembly of Western European Union. Most of the information is in English, with certain documents in French. NATO documents include speeches, communiques, and press releases on a range of topics from arms control to defense spending.

Useful for international studies.
URL: gopher://gopher.nato.int

NTIS FedWorld
One stop for information on the U.S. government

The National Technical Information Service (NTIS) FedWorld home page is designed as a "one-stop" center for anyone who wants to locate online servers and publications of the U.S. government. It offers links to more than 100 government Internet sites, searchable by subject area. FedWorld also offers abstracts (with search capability) of recent reports from U.S. government agencies, as well as an FTP archive of NTIS publications in such subject areas as business, health, and the environment.

Useful for government studies.
URL: http://www.fedworld.gov

OMRI Daily Digest
Current news on the former Soviet Union and Eastern Bloc

For a fast and free update on what's happening in the former Soviet Union, and East-Central and Southeastern Europe, you can subscribe by e-mail to the *Daily Digest* of the Open Media Research Institute (OMRI). News reports come from OMRI's 30-member staff of analysts, along with selected freelance specialists.

OMRI is a joint venture between the Open Society Institute and the U.S. Board for International Broadcasting.

Useful for news sources.
URL: gopher://bobcat.oxy.edu:70/11/RFE-RL
To subscribe: LISTSERV@UBVM.CC.BUFFALO.EDU
Message body: subscribe OMRI-L YourFirstName YourLastName

Open Government Pilot
Find out what's happening at the helm in Canada

Sponsored by Industry Canada, the Open Government Pilot offers information about different branches of Canada's federal government—the House of Commons, Senate, Supreme Court, and federal departments and agencies. Here's where you can peruse such documents as Canada's Constitution Act 1982 and the North American Free Trade Agreement in both English and French. You can also download a sound file of the Canadian national anthem and reach provincial-government servers.

Useful for government studies; history; international studies.
URL: http://debra.dgbt.doc.ca:80/opengov/

OpenNet
Declassified documents on nuclear testing and other topics

OpenNet is a searchable bibliographic database of more than 250,000 U.S. Department of Energy documents covering human radiation experiments, nuclear testing, radiation releases, fallout and historical records. Periodically updated, it includes references to all documents declassified and made publicly available since October 1, 1994. You also will find here "sanitized" copies of department documents as well as those that were never classified but are of historical significance. To get a copy of a document, you must contact the department directly.

Useful for government studies.
URL: http://www.doe.gov/html/osti/opennet/opennet1.html

Operation Desert Storm Debriefing Book
A blow-by-blow description

Andrew Leyden has published his 400-page book about the 1991 Persian Gulf War on the Web. This site includes a tremendous amount of background material on the conflict, such as profiles on the leaders and a week-by-week breakdown of events.

Useful for Desert Storm; history; international studies.
URL: http://www.nd.edu/~aleyden/contents.html

Perry-Castañeda Library Map Collection
A map for almost every occasion

An extensive collection of electronic maps is available from the University of Texas at Austin map server. It includes maps of cities in the United States and around the world as well as maps of most countries. The maps originate from a variety of government sources including the U.S. Army, CIA and U.S. Geological

Survey. A word of caution: These maps tend to be large graphic images and can be slow to download.

Useful for geography.
URL: http://www.lib.utexas.edu/Libs/PCL/Map_collection/Map_collection.html

Philip Greenspun's Hypertext Books
Collections of photos and commentaries

Philip Greenspun has self-published several books on the Internet about what he does when he isn't studying or teaching at the Massachusetts Institute of Technology: travel. *Travels with Samantha* weaves together 500 full-color JPEG photos with his impressions of the people and places he visited as he journeyed across North America one summer with his notebook computer ("Samantha") and a ton of photo equipment. (This electronic travelogue went on to win the Best of the Web '94 Award for Document Design.) Greenspun's shorter *Berlin and Prague* contains 80 full-color JPEG photos and his descriptions of the history, architecture and ethnic diversity of this corner of Europe

Useful for international studies.
URL: http://www-swiss.ai.mit.edu/samantha/

Philip Greenspun's Photographs
"Snapshots" of biology and geography

When Philip Greenspun isn't doing graduate-level research or teaching computer science at the Massachusetts Institute of Technology, he travels and takes pictures. His collections include stunning color photos of such subjects as New Mexico, Florida's Everglades and butterflies at Butterfly World in Pompano Beach, Fla. Accompanied by Greenspum's observations, these provide students of geography and biology a real "snapshot" of these areas and animals..

Useful for images.
URL: http://www-swiss.ai.mit.edu/philg/

Project Vote Smart
Performance of politicians evaluated

Project Vote Smart is an organization that collects information about political candidates at the federal and gubernatorial levels in the United States. On its server, the project provides biographical data on candidates, performance evaluations by a variety of interest groups (ranging from liberal to conservative), voting records, campaign finance information, and the text of the project's *U.S. Government Owner's Manual* and *Voter's Self-Defense Manual*.

Useful for government studies.
URL: gopher://gopher.neu.edu:1112/

Race and Racism
For bibliographies, even courses, on ethnic and gender studies

This directory, housed on the Electronic Democracy Information Network (EDIN) server, provides a wide array of information on ethnic and gender studies, bibliographies of books, films and videos, course descriptions at colleges and universities offering related programs, discussion groups, policy and legislation. It addresses the interests and concerns of African Americans, Latinos, Asian Americans, Native Americans and indigenous peoples from around the world.

Useful for Aboriginal and Native American studies; history; international studies.
URL: gopher://garnet.berkeley.edu:1250/11/.race

Road Trip USA
Add your impressions to this "work in progress"

The paperback edition of *Road Trip USA*, from Moon Travel Handbooks, may not be available in time for your crosscountry expedition but don't let that stop you. The publisher offers the rough drafts of each route online, and invites readers to comment. You may even win a free copy of a travel book! The guide, being written by a team of travel writers, will describe the secondary highways, such as U.S. 50, that traverse the United States.

Useful for geography; travel and recreation.
URL: http://www.moon.com:7000/1h/rt.usa

Russian & East European Studies Internet Resources
Interactive databases

Based at the University of Pittsburgh, REESweb (formerly Russia - Newly Independent States Home Page) lists — and links to — online resources available for people studying Russia and Eastern Europe. You'll learn where you can find text resources, interactive databases, directories, software, and other materials. Listed resources are divided by discipline — language, culture, government, economics, science, and so on — as well as by type. From here you can access home pages for the various newly independent states of those regions as well as a variety of online exhibitions.

Useful for international studies.
URL: http://www.pitt.edu/~cjp/rees.html

Russian and East European Network Information Center
From past to present

Operated by the Center for Post-Soviet and East European Studies at the University of Texas at Austin, REENIC links to Internet sources of information on and from Russia and Eastern European countries. It offers online databases, newspapers, libraries, Usenet newsgroups and other resources that focus on: Albania, Belarus, Bosnia-Herzegovina, Bulgaria, Commonwealth of Independent States (former USSR), Croatia, Czech Republic, Estonia, Hungary, Latvia, Lithuania, Macedonia, Moldova, Poland, Romania, Russia, Serbia, Slovakia, Slovenia, and Ukraine.

Useful for international studies.
URL: http://reenic.utexas.edu/reenic.html

Sarajevo Alive
Firsthand information from a wartorn city

This Web site in France contains information on the Bosnian War. It also attempts to be a communications line between war-weary residents of Bosnia and the Internet community. You can complete an online form to send messages to Sarajevo residents.

URL: http://www.cnam.fr/sarajevo/

Shamash: The Jewish Networking Project
Holocaust, Persian Gulf War covered

Based on New York's NYSERNet, Shamash: The Jewish Networking Project offers online resources and telecommunications for Jewish organizations around the United States. The Shamash gopher provides information on such topics as the Israeli economy and politics, Holocaust revisionism, and the Persian Gulf War. Other materials include graphics files, Hebrew language fonts, and archived software. Shamash also sponsors dozens of mailing lists addressing issues in Jewish theology and life; about 10 of these are archived on the gopher.

Useful for international studies.
URL: gopher://israel.nysernet.org:71

Slovakia Document Store (SDS)
Clickable map leads to many images

The Slovakia Document Store (SDS) offers information about the geography, history, culture, politics, and economy of the Slovak Republic. For tourists, there's also advice about attractions, currency exchange rates, and a small English-Slovak dictionary. The Web site offers a variety of images, including a clickable map that leads to more than 100 pictures depicting Slovakian landscape and life. SDS links to other Slovakia-related sites on the Internet.

Useful for international studies.
URL: http://www.eunet.sk/

South African Politics
Copy of the constitution plus information on the political scene

Provided through the Rhodes University gopher, this directory will bring you up to date on recent political events in South Africa. In addition to news reports, you'll find a copy of the constitution of South Africa, electronic copies of *South Africa Watch* magazine from Oxfam Canada, an electronic image of a ballot from the 1994 general election, and the texts of speeches by Nelson Mandela,

Useful for international studies.
URL: gopher://gopher2.ru.ac.za:70/11/South African Politics

State Fact Sheets
Profiles on jobs, population, income and farming across the U.S.

From the Economic Research Service (ERS) of the U.S. Department of Agriculture comes updated e-mail information on population, jobs, income and poverty, and farms for all 50 states as well as a summary for the entire country. The two-page profiles contain tables of information, and are updated as new information becomes available from such agencies as the Bureau of Labor Statistics, Bureau of Economic Analysis, the Bureau of the Census, and ERS.

Useful for reference; social studies.
To subscribe: LISTSERV@ERS.BITNET
Message body: GET Two-letterStateName DATA

State of Washington Information
Facts and figures on government and education

Text, images and sound clips that provide information about the government and resources of the State of Washington are available at this prototype Web page. Included here are daily updates on bills, amendments, bill reports, bill digests, roll calls on bills, legislative and committee schedules, and online informational files from the state legislature; and links to educational servers statewide.

Useful for government studies.
URL: http://olympus.dis.wa.gov/www/wahome.html

Statistics Canada Talon Service
Lesson plans, mailing list on Canada

Statistics Canada's Talon gopher — named for Jean Talon, Canada's first official statistician — provides information about the products and services it offers based on the statistics it collects relating to Canadian society and economy. Its mailing list provides electronic copies of the Statistics Canada *Daily*, a bulletin summarizing new data and publications available from the agency. The gopher, available in English and French, also offers detailed lesson plans for grades 7 and higher that are included in its educational CD-ROM *E-Stat*. These deal with such topics as Canadian business and industry, labor, economics, demographics, health and welfare, crime and justice, and multiculturalism. Full-text documents in the gopher are searchable by keyword.

Useful for activities and projects; mailing lists (listservs) and newsgroups.
URL: gopher://talon.statcan.ca
E-mail: daily@statcan.ca
To subscribe: listproc@statcan.ca
Message body: subscribe daily YourFirstName YourLastName

Stockholm International Peace Research Institute
Conflict and cooperation

This institute founded by the Swedish government conducts scientific research on the issue of conflict and cooperation among nations. The Web site includes chapter summaries of the organization's yearbook.

Useful for government studies; international studies.
URL: http://www.sipri.se/

SummitNet
Background and details on meeting of Western Hemisphere leaders

The Summit of the Americas, held in Miami, Fla., in December 1994, brought together the democratically elected leaders of the Western Hemisphere to discuss such issues as trade, investment, environment, and government reform. On the SummitNet server, based at Florida International University, you'll find articles in English and Spanish about the summit from *The Miami Herald,* U.S. State Department documents on the Americas, profiles and images of the heads of state attending the summit, and related materials.

Useful for international studies.
URL: http://summit.fiu.edu.

Supreme Court Decisions
Actions and biographies of justices

Cornell University Law School provides hypertext copies of Supreme Court decisions from 1990 on, as well as biographies of the Supreme Court Justices and a hypertext publication on civil rights. You will also find a hypertext copy of the landmark Roe v. Wade Supreme Court decision, which legalized abortion in the United States.

Useful for law and legal issues.
URL: http://www.law.cornell.edu/lii.table.html

Tables of Contents for the Federal Register
New rules and regulations

If you're looking for information about the executive branch of the U.S. government, these files from the National Archives and Research Administration may interest you. Each table of contents file includes a descriptive entry and page number for every document published in a single day's *Federal Register*, the legal newspaper of the Office of the Federal Register. The register contains regulations, orders, and other documents of the executive branch, grouped by agency. The files are usually only one day behind, and you can search them by keyword. Archives for the current year are also available.

Useful for government studies.
URL: gopher://gopher.nara.gov

TALKNOW Mailing List
Forum lets Arab and Jewish children form friendships

TALKNOW provides a moderated forum to encourage K-12 Israeli and Palestinian children as well as Arab and Jewish children worldwide to get to know one another by "talking" electronically. Its organizers hope that by communicating at an early age, these children will become friends, and work toward a more peaceful world.

Useful for mailing lists (listservs) and newsgroups.
URL: gopher://jerusalem1.datasrv.co.il
E-mail: mkragen@access.digex.net

To subscribe: listserv@jerusalem1.datasrv.co.il
Message body: subscribe Talknow YourFirstName YourLastName

Treasures of the Czars
History and art of the Russia's dynasties

Treasures of the Czars, an online exhibition presented by the St. Petersburg (Fla.) Times, gives visitors an inkling of the splendor of the Russian royal dynasties. Among other activities, you can click on a timeline, and hyperlink to images and text about the emperor of a particular period and his family. In an archive containing messages from other online visitors, several commented that they preferred the virtual exhibition to the real one which they had actually seen in Russia.

Useful for international studies.
URL: http://www.times.st-pete.fl.us/treasures/TC.Lobby.html

U.S. Agency for International Development
Aid to developing countries

The U.S. Agency for International Development (USAID) offers nonclassified information about its programs for building political, economic, and social stability in developing nations. Information is arranged both by sector (economics, health, etc.) and by region or country. You can also find background information about USAID, Congressional reports, information about business opportunities in the developing world, and links to related servers.

Useful for international studies.
URL: gopher://gopher.info.usaid.gov

U.S. Bureau of Justice
Statistics on many aspects of the justice system

The U.S. Bureau of Justice offers a wealth of statistics on its server. You'll find data on crime rates, drug use among jail inmates, race and crime, capital punishment, DNA testing, firearms use, probation and parole, and many other aspects of the justice system in the United States.

Useful for law and legal issues.
URL: gopher://uacsc2.albany.edu/1/newman/crjbjs

U.S. Census Bureau Data
Statistics on the country's people and economy

The U.S. Census Bureau offers a variety of statistics about the nation's people and economy. You'll also find Census Bureau news releases, news and analysis of census data from the Center for Economic Studies, and statistical briefs (summary articles). Of special interest is a data extraction system, available via TELNET, that lets you download data from the Census Bureau's huge databases to your own site.

Useful for government studies.
URL: http://www.census.gov/
E-mail: gatekeeper@census.gov

U.S. Congress
E-mail your elected representatives in Congress

By following the e-mail address format below, you can reach any member of the U.S. Senate or House of Representatives. Or try looking them up in the directory of Congressional e-mail addresses housed at the University of Michigan. To contact Speaker of the House Newt Gingrich, write to: georgia6@hr.house.gov

Useful for government studies.
URL: http://thomas.loc.gov
E-mail: FirstInitialLastName or LastNameFirstInitial@hr.house.gov

U.S. Federal Government World-Wide Web Servers
Indexes scores of sites

This page offers an index to World-Wide Web sites and other Internet resources maintained by the U.S. government. Compiled by the Federal Information Exchange, it includes descriptions and links to Web servers that offer both information about multiple federal agencies and tools to search for information across all listed sites; servers at single agencies, offices or sites in the executive, legislative and judicial branches, with links to other related sites; and servers with information about federal government-sponsored consortia.

Useful for government studies.
URL: http://www.fie.com/www/us_gov.htm

U.S. Food and Drug Administration
Congressional testimony, consumer news

The U.S. Food and Drug Administration (FDA) offers news releases, transcripts of congressional testimony, details about FDA programs, consumer information, and information about its various programs.

Useful for agriculture; consumer information.
URL: http://www.usda.gov/

U.S. Government
Searchable data on the federal, legislative, judicial branches

This site, maintained by MCI Corp., offers a cornucopia of links and pointers to information about the government of the United States. It includes a searchable index of World-Wide Web sites maintained by the federal government in addition to reference material on the executive, legislative and judicial branches of government. Of note are the profiles on members of Congress and the Supreme Court.

Useful for government studies.
URL: http://www.gov.mci.net/fed/fed.html

U.S. Government Printing Office
A yearbook featuring the members of Congress

Images of the president, vice president and members of the 104th Congress from the *Congressional Pictorial Directory* are available from the U.S. Government Printing Office (GPO). The GPO also offers information about the White House, the federal budget, congressional hearings, and other federal matters, much of it on a paid subscription basis.

Useful for government studies; images.
URL: http://www.access.gpo.gov/picdir/title.html

U.S. Holocaust Memorial Museum
Teaching aids help in answering kids' questions

The U.S. Holocaust Memorial Museum in Washington, D.C., uses its Web site to provide information about its onsite and outreach educational activities. Its educational section also has a variety of practical aids to learning about this dark chapter in history, including a short account of the Holocaust, answers to frequently asked questions about it, and an article about children in the Holocaust. An annotated bibliography of videotapes used in teaching about the Holocaust and a teacher's guide full of tips on teaching about this period could prove especially useful to those trying to explain it to youngsters..

Useful for history; museums on the Web.
URL: http://www.ushmm.org/index.html

U.S. House of Representatives
Keep up with the activities of members, committees

Through its server, the U.S. House of Representatives offers
access to legislative information and data about House members, committees, and organizations. You can find out here what's happening on the House floor and about how individual members have voted on specific measures; who's who in the House and how to contact them; How the House is organized and operates; as well as links to the home pages of House members and other government servers..

Useful for government studies.
URL: http://WWW.HOUSE.GOV
E-mail: congress@hr.house.gov

U.S. Senate
Committee reports and news about the Upper House

In the U.S. Senate's gopher server, you can find news releases and general information from individual senators and from the following Senate committees: Agriculture, Nutrition, and Forestry
- Bipartisan Commission on Entitlement and Tax Reform
- Democratic Policy
- Environment and Public Works
- Indian Affairs
- Labor and Human Resources

- Republican Conference
- Republican Policy
- Rules and Administration
- Small Business

You can do full-text searches on all documents in the server. This service is provided by the Office of the U.S. Senate Sergeant at Arms and the Senate Committee on Rules and Administration.

Useful for government studies.
URL: gopher://Gopher.Senate.GOV/11

United Nations Children's Fund (UNICEF)
Focus on welfare of youngsters

The United Nations Children's Fund (UNICEF) focuses on the welfare of children around the world. Materials here include information about UNICEF programs and several archived publications, such as a *State of the World's Children* report and UNICEF's annual report.

Useful for international studies.
URL: gopher://hqfaus01.unicef.org/

United Nations Development Programme
The agency and its role

At this United Nations gopher, students can learn what the U.N. is, how it works, and what it's doing. press releases and other documents offer information about various U.N. branches and programs. This site links to additional U.N. gophers and related resources.

Useful for government studies; international studies.
URL: gopher://gopher.undp.org

University of North Carolina EXPO
A free ticket to online exhibitions

EXPO at the University of North Carolina gives you a free ticket to a number of online exhibitions, many of them organized by the Library of Congress. You'll find exhibits (including both text and graphics) on the Vatican, Soviet archives, the Dead Sea Scrolls, and the Christopher Columbus expedition. You can reach exhibits at other sites as well. When you're ready for a rest, you can drool over menus and photos of dishes from Le Cordon Bleu cooking school in Paris, or learn how to order a recipe book from Le Cordon Bleu, and books about the Library of Congress exhibitions.

Useful for international studies.
URL: http://sunsite.unc.edu/expo/ticket_office.html

Valley of the Shadow: Living the Civil War in Pennsylvania and Virginia
One war, one valley, two sides

This innovative Web site at the University of Virginia, Charlottesville, looks at the American Civil War from the perspectives of two neighboring communities: one in Pennsylvania, the other in Virginia, both sharing the same valley but supporting opposite sides in the conflict. It includes photographs, records, maps, and newspaper clippings.

Useful for history.
URL: http://jefferson.village.virginia.edu/vshadow/vshadow.html

Vietnam Historical Archive
Background and an excerpt on the nation's longest war

The information at this Web site is based on CD-ROM material published by Medio. It also includes an excerpt, *Enough, But Not Too Much: Johnson's Decisions for War, 1963-1965* from the book *America's Longest War*, by George C. Herring.

Useful for history; international studies; Vietnam War.
URL: http://www.medio.net/Mediocom/Demos/Vietnam/

Vietnam Vetrans Home Page
Tributes and memories of the Vietnam War

This Web site provides many personal stories and pictures as part of its collection of information about the Vietnam conflict. It also contains a glossary of terms associated with the war. Some parents may consider some of the language in the memoirs to be inappropriate.

Useful for history; Vietnam War.
URL: http://grunt.space.swri.edu/index.htm

Viking Network
Fact sheets show impact of ancient explorers on local life

The Viking Network is a resource students can turn to for information about these ancient explorers from Scandinavia. History teachers and others from the many regions where the Vikings traded and explored post fact sheets about the influence of the Vikings on local languages and customs. Also available are back issues of *Vnet News*, research results, and information about conferences and projects about the Vikings.

Useful for history.
URL: gopher://gopher.bbb.no:72/11/vnet

Volunteers in Technical Assistance
Reports on international emergencies

The Volunteers in Technical Assistance (VITA) provides the latest information about natural disasters and other international emergency situations, such as those in Rwanda and Haiti. The information is compiled by the Office of U.S. Foreign Disaster Assistance and United Nations representatives in these countries from reports by other emergency aid and disaster relief agencies, such as the World Health Organization, UNICEF and USAID. This gopher also offers weather, hurricane and earthquake reports from a variety of sources. A link to the Alliance for a Global Community provides a list of volunteer opportunities, such as collecting books for schools overseas and working for student exchange programs.

Useful for international studies.
URL: http://www.vita.org/
E-mail: incident@vita.org (to request reports by e-mail)
Message body: Your address and reason for request.

Voter Information Services (VIS)
U.S. presidents and members of Congress rated

Voter Information Service, a nonprofit, nonpartisan organization, publishes ratings of U.S. Presidents and Congress members for the benefit of voters. The VIS ratings — hosted by Software Tool & Die, an Internet services provider — show each politician's level of support for various causes.

Useful for government studies.
URL: gopher://ftp.std.com:70/11/periodicals/voteinfo

Washington D.C. Sightseeing Map
See the sights of the U.S. capital

Anyone interested in the history and heritage of the United States will enjoy a virtual stroll through the nation's capital. By clicking on any of the highlighted sites on the street map of Washington, D.C., and you'll find an image, description and bit of history at the very least. The Web page at Arlington National Cemetery, for instance, also gives information, such as advisories on any upcoming refurbishing or construction, and the frequency of tours for those who may be able to make a personal visit.

Useful for activities and projects; history; images.
URL: http://sc94.ameslab.gov/TOUR/tour.html

Welcome to the White House
Learn about the U.S. government and the First Family

Welcome to the White House: An Interactive Citizens' Guide provides a single entry point to all government information on the Internet, It gives a glimpse into the lives of those at the White House, with information and photos of the president, vice president and their families, including Al Gore's favorite political cartoons; and takes visitors on a virtual tour of the White House. This Web site also offers links and detailed information about Cabinet-level and independent agencies; a searchable index of federal government information; and a map of Washington, D.C. When you e-mail the president, you'll even receive a reply — not from him but an assistant.

Useful for government studies.
URL: http://www.whitehouse.gov

E-mail: president@whitehouse.gov or vice.president@whitehouse.gov

White House Archives
Press releases, other news about the Clinton Administration

The Texas A&M University server offers this folder of press releases and other documents from and about the Clinton Administration. It includes recent information from the Massachusetts Institute of Technology White House server as well as older materials (dating back to 1992) from the clinton@marist.bitnet mailing list and the alt.politics.clinton Usenet newsgroup. The directory can be searched by keyword.

Useful for government studies.
URL: gopher://gopher.tamu.edu/11/.dir/president.dir

White House Summaries
Documents detail daily activities of the Executive branch

The U.S. Department of Agriculture (USDA) offers this daily summary of White House press releases on briefings, executive orders, appointments, visits and other activities. If you are looking for specific information, you can try searching the archives by keyword vie e-mail; send a message to the address below with the instructions: search white-house keyword keyword. You can also request the full text of current and past press releases (up to two months old) and other White House documents.

Useful for government studies; mailing lists (listservs) and newsgroups.
URL: http://www.esusda.gov/wh/whsum.html
To subscribe: almanac@esusda.gov
Message body: subscribe wh-summary

Window-to-Russia
Rich history and culture revealed

Operated in Moscow by Relcom Corp., Window-to-Russia offers World-Wide Web access to online resources in and related to Russia. It includes images of the Kremlin and of contemporary Russian art, as well as materials in such subjects as Russian history, business opportunities, and science and technology. Some resources (particularly those based on Russian servers) are in the Russian language and require Cyrillic font support.

Useful for international studies.
URL: http://www.kiae.su/www/wtr/

Women's Resources on the Internet
From sports to social issues

From information about America3, the first all-women's team in the 143-year history of the Americas Cup, to a collection of online articles about women and computing, this Web site at the University of North Carolina provides pointers and direct links to all sorts of electronic resources about women. Some of these resources do deal with issues that may not be suitable for younger students, such as sexuality and abortion.

Useful for sports and hobbies.
URL: http://sunsite.unc.edu/cheryb/women/wresources.html

World Bank Population, Health, and Nutrition
Focus on the developing world

The World Bank PHNLINK network focuses on issues in population, health, and nutrition — with a particular eye to Africa, Asia, and Latin America. One of the network's mailing lists, PHNFLASH, provides a weekly electronic newsletter and article archive with project updates and other information about health, nutrition and population issues.

Useful for international studies.
E-mail: PHNLINK@worldbank.org
To subscribe: Listserv@tome.worldbank.org
Message body: subscribe PHNFLASH YourFirstName YourLastName

World of the Vikings
Learn about the age of these ancient sea-rovers

The World of the Vikings offers a number of links to online resources on the topic of Vikings, and more generally Norway and Scandinavia, in literature and history, sources for the Runic font, and mailing lists. It also links to some images and information about a CD-ROM project of the same name, led by the National Museum of Denmark and the York Archaeological Trust.

Useful for history.
URL: http://www.demon.co.uk/history/index.html

WWW Paris
See the Eiffel Tower and other famous sights

If you can't travel to Paris in person, then you can at least tour it in cyberspace. An interactive map leads visitors to famous museums and monuments, with images and histories of each with such details as founding dates and, in the case of the Eiffel Tower, how far it can sway. Other links take you to shops, cafes and calendars of events, as well as other Internet sites that offer information about France and French culture. Although most of the information here is in English, you can find a glossary of basic French terms helpful to tourists.

Useful for international studies.
URL: http://meteora.ucsd.edu/~norman/paris/

Sports and hobbies

19th Hole
Rules, records and results for golf fans

This Web page provides resources for golfers and for enthusiasts of the professional golf tours. It includes golf records, tournament schedules, and results, information about tournaments, clubmaking materials, information about golf courses, handicap files, a collection of golf images, and the like.

Useful for images; sports and hobbies; travel and recreation.
URL: http://dallas.nmhu.edu/golf/golf.htm

Bicycling Information from rec.bicycles
From buying a bike to riding it safely

rec.bicycles, a Usenet newsgroup, offers articles, glossaries, mailing lists, images and collections of articles and columns about bicycling. You'll find information for all levels of expertise, covering such topics as buying a bicycle, building and repairing bikes, places to tour, and safety tips.

Useful for sports and hobbies; travel and recreation.
URL: gopher://draco.acs.uci.edu:1071/

Carlos' Coloring Book Home Page
A rainy day activity for preschoolers

No need to find the crayons to use this interactive coloring book. Just select the color you want from the onscreen menu, then click your mouse on the appropriate part of the picture on the screen. Choose from images of a birthday cake, Christmas tree, crown, flower, house or snowman, all taken from *Coloring Book 2.0* by Jim Allison. If you have a Macintosh, you can even download a copy of *Carlos*, named for its creator, Carlos A. Pero, a graduate student in the Department of General Engineering at the University of Illinois, Urbana-Champaign.

Useful for activities and projects; entertainment.
URL: http://robot0.ge.uiuc.edu/~carlosp/color/

CricInfo
A sticky wicket, you say?

CricInfo is a database about the game of cricket. You'll find statistics and score-cards, articles about cricket, and information for the uninitiated. Contributions are encouraged.

Useful for sports and hobbies; travel and recreation.
URL: gopher://cricinfo.cse.ogi.edu:7070

Fencing: Federation Internationale d'Escrime
Articles, contacts and images

The Federation Internationale d'Escrime maintains a fencing page on the Web. It includes a collection of drawings and photos (with thumbnails as well as full-size color images), a hypertext archive of a fencing newsgroup, frequently asked questions and answers about fencing, articles, book reviews, information about clubs and associations, an events calendar, and links to other fencing resources.

Useful for images; sports and hobbies.
URL: http://www.ii.uib.no/~arild/fencing.html

Fish Information Service (FINS)
Information and advice for aquarium enthusiasts

Anyone interested in aquariums should check out this Web site. You'll find catalogs of marine and freshwater fish (with pictures), several other images and movies, a glossary, a list of frequently asked questions and answers, information about diagnosing and treating fish diseases, suggested do-it-yourself projects, and links to related Internet sites. You can also post your questions and ideas on a discussion page.

Useful for biology; images; sports and hobbies.
URL: http://www.actwin.com/fish/index.html

Global Cycling Network (VeloNet)
Find friends and free information

The Global Cycling Network, also called VeloNet, is a cooperative server that invites cycling enthusiasts everywhere to share their knowledge and ideas. In addition to the e-mail conversations, you'll find links to other bicycle resources on the Internet.

Useful for sports and hobbies.
URL: http://cycling.org
E-mail: (? — Jay)

GolfData Web
All you need, on the green or the couch

Maintained by David Kearns at GoldData Corp., this home page includes not only scores and tournament news, but links to programming schedules for the Golf Channel, and information about golf-related travel, real estate opportunities, publications, equipment vendors, associations, clubs and courses.
URL: http://www.gdol.com/

Hang Gliding Mosaic Picture Server
Get the hang of the sport online

Hang gliding and paragliding enthusiasts will find a variety of interesting images and documents on this Web server. Included are photos and movies, a list of questions and answers about hang gliding, archived mailing-list messages, and links to other aviation-related servers.

Useful for images; sports and hobbies.
URL: http://cougar.stanford.edu:7878/HGMPSHomePage.html

IGA World Youth Baseball
Scores, schedules and standings

The IGA World Youth Baseball Web page is an unofficial collection of scores, schedules, and standings of various youth baseball leagues. Compiled by Neil Enns of Brandon, Manitoba, it also gives information about the history of the World Youth Baseball Championship and its stars who now play in the major leagues.

Useful for sports and hobbies; travel and recreation.
URL: http://www.brandonu.ca/~ennsnr/WYB/.

Internet Movie Database
Profiles, ratings, reviews and more on films, filmmakers

Movie buffs can use this extensive database from Cardiff University of Wales to
find profiles, ratings, reviews, images and sounds on films, actors, and directors,
most of it contributed by users of the database. You can search by film title, actor,
character name, genre, even by quote. A search, for example, of characters called
"Luke" provides a lengthy list, including Harris Gordon as "Dr. Luke Morrison"
in *Hollywood* (1923) and Mark Hamill as "Luke Skywalker" in *Star Wars* (1977).
Other items of interest here are lists of rec.arts.movies top 100 films and bottom
100 films from the rec.arts.movies Usenet newsgroup; top 20 lists of busy people;
and lists of some famous celebrity marriages. A file of frequently asked questions
and answers tells you how to download a copy of the database, which spans si-
lent films period to movies currently in production.

Useful for entertainment; images.
URL: http://www.cm.cf.ac.uk:80/Movies/moviequery.html

InterNETional Scouting Page
Leads to information about Scouting internationally

Like the World-Wide Web, Scouting is about exploring, says Webmaster David
Jansen. This Web site provides pointers or direct links to pages about national
Scouting organizations and home pages for individual groups and units world-
wide; information about the 1995 World Jamboree; lists of mailing lists and newsgroups; FTP sites; collections of Scout logos, frequently asked questions about
the Scouts, and Scouting bulletin boards; and downloadable images.

Useful for sports and hobbies.
URL: http://www.strw.leidenuniv.nl/~jansen/scout.html
E-mail: David.Jansen@strw.leidenuniv.nl

Kids Soccer Page
Stories from young players

The Kids Soccer Page encourages kids across North America to share their soccer
experiences.
URL: http://www.cts.com/browse/jsent/kid.html

National Hockey League: Hawaii's NHL Home Page
Links, lists, latest news

This Web page dedicated to the National Hockey League (NHL) is based,
strangely enough, at the University of Hawaii. You'll find schedules and standings for the current season, statistics, a list of award and trophy recipients, links
to the home pages of several NHL teams, and so on.

Useful for images; sports and hobbies.
URL: http://maxwell.uhh.hawaii.edu/hockey/hockey.html

Nautical Bookshelf
Boating tips, book descriptions and a bulletin board

The Nautical Bookshelf is an information center (and mail-order shop) for boaters and anyone interested in reading about the sea. It includes descriptions of hundreds of nautical books; if you want to purchase one, you can order via e-mail or phone. In addition, the server offers free boating tips and a nautical bulletin board.

Useful for literature; sports and hobbies.
URL: gopher://gopher.nautical.com:2550

Orienteering and Rogaining Home Page
A primer on cross-country navigation

Orienteering and rogaining enthusiasts—and anyone who wonders what those sports are all about—should take a look at this Web page. Included are definitions of orienteering and rogaining (the sport of long-distance cross-country navigation), a list of mailing lists, news, club information, results and rankings, and links to related servers.

Useful for images; sports and hobbies.
URL: http://www2.aos.Princeton.EDU:80/rdslater/orienteering/

Our Family Museum
One family's history

This *Collection of Family History Notes* traces the past 250 years of the Churchyard family's history, giving information on 360 family names and 835 individuals. This is a well-done example of how an individual can publish material on the Web.

Useful for genealogy; history.
URL: http://uts.cc.utexas.edu/~churchh/genealgy.html

PetBunny Discussion List
Ask about rabbit care here

This open forum is for anyone interested in keeping rabbits as pets. The home page answers frequently asked questions related to rabbit care, and links to other forums where you can find more information. In addition, there are links to other Internet resources with images, stories and veterinary information about bunnies.

Useful for mailing lists (listservs) and newsgroups; sports and hobbies.
URL: http://www.mit.edu:8001/people/klund/bunny/bunny.html
E-mail: PETBUNNY@UKCC.UKY.EDU
To subscribe: LISTSERV@UKCC.UKY.EDU
Message body: SUBSCRIBE PETBUNNY YourFirstName YourLastName

Railroad Resources Page
From models to metro schedules

This Web page provides pointers to railroad resources of every kind — documents, databases, mailing lists, FTP sites, and more. Traveling families can get rail and transit schedules, rail fans can find out about interesting places to visit, and model railroaders can reach newsgroups and club bulletin boards. Some of the linked sites include photos and illustrations.

Useful for trains; travel and recreation.
URL: http://www-cse.ucsd.edu/users/bowdidge/railroad/rail-home.html

Railways Home Page on Mercurio
Pictures, histories, even paint schemes

If you have a question or simply want to browse, you can find just about anything you've ever wanted to know about European trains at this site, such as: one-line descriptions of all European locomotives and shunters; back issues of railway journals; paint schemes for some systems; images; and schedules for some European railways. Operated by a group of European train enthusiasts, it includes e-mail addresses to obtain further information from them about the railway systems in specific country.

Useful for sports and hobbies; trains; travel and recreation.
URL: http://mercurio.iet.unipi.it/home.html

Rockhounds
Discussion group, databases and more on minerals

Besides joining a discussion list for those interested in rocks and minerals, you can browse through lots of related information at the Rockhounds' home page. Starting with the group's archived messages, you can examine images from mineral collections at museums worldwide. locate mineral identification and other mineralogy software, view (with the appropriate software) a movie about minerals, even search a database on the subject.

Useful for images; mailing lists (listservs) and newsgroups; sports and hobbies.
URL: http://www.rahul.net/infodyn/rockhounds/rockhounds.html
E-mail: rockhounds@infodyn.com
To subscribe: rockhounds-request@infodyn.com
Enter in subject line: subscribe

Rollercoasters
Just for fun!

This site contains just about anything you could possibly want to know about rollercoasters or about amusement parks in general, including fees and hours. You'll also find images of rollercoasters.

Useful for entertainment; travel and recreation.
URL: ftp://gboro.rowan.edu.

Running Page
No need to keep chasing around

The Running Page offers news and information for runners of all distances and skill levels. You can find out about upcoming races and marathons, pick up training tips, learn about running clubs around the country, read running-related publications, and link to other servers offering materials for runners.

Useful for sports and hobbies; travel and recreation.
URL: http://sunsite.unc.edu/drears/running/running.html

Southland Ski Server
Interactive reports from skiers

The Southland Ski Server, an admitted "labor of love" by Mark Bixby, offers a unique feature: interactive ski reports based on information provided by skiers of Southern California's ski resorts plus Mammoth and June. Using a forms browser, you can select the resort you're interested in and then view multiple recent reports submitted by fellow-skiers. A lengthy version of each report indicates such factors as the type of equipment used, surface, number of moguls, the skier's age, sex, ability and the rating he or she gave the run, as well as what the skier loved and hated, and a brief overall review by the skier. A short version presents everything except the overall review in tabular form. Also available here are trail maps, rate sheets and other resort information, as well as road and weather reports, most provided by the resorts.

Useful for sports and hobbies; travel and recreation.
URL: http://www.cccd.edu/ski.html

Subway Navigator
"Virtual trips" through some of the world's best-known cities

The Subway Navigator is an interactive service that lets you take "virtual trips" on the subway or metro system of 14 major tourist cities — Vienna, Paris, Munich, Athens, Hong Kong, Milan, Amsterdam, Madrid, Stockholm, London, Boston, New York, Chicago, and Washington. You choose a starting or stopping point, and the Subway Navigator maps out a route and tells you the length of the trip.

Useful for activities and projects; travel and recreation.
URL: gopher://gopher.jussieu.fr

Tennis Server
Tips for playing plus tour rankings and results

The Tennis Server on the World-Wide Web offers materials for players and fans alike. You'll find professional tennis results (with a focus on the major tournaments), rankings for the pro tour, images of top players, tips on playing the game and choosing equipment, tennis rules, an online tennis store, and links to other tennis resources.

Useful for images; sports and hobbies.
URL: http://arganet.tenagra.com/Racquet_Workshop/Tennis.html

U.S. Scouting Service
General information on Scouts, Cubs, Explorers

An unofficial home page for the Boy Scouts of America, provided by HyperInfo Solutions, links to information about the organization's activities and those of some member units across the United States, such as the Cubs and Explorers. It provides addresses; details about ranks, merit badges and awards; and links to other Scouting resources, including Web pages and Usenet newsgroups.

Useful for sports and hobbies.
URL: http://www.scouting.org/scouting/
E-mail: hyper@iquest.com

Unicycling
For novices and experienced riders

Based on the Kent State University Web server, the Unicycling page includes tips on riding a unicycle (for everyone from beginners to experts), a file of frequently asked questions and answers about unicycling, tips on buying a unicycle, a roster of unicyclists around the country, and images and movies.

Useful for sports and hobbies; travel and recreation.
URL: http://nimitz.mcs.kent.edu/~bkonarsk/index.html

Virtual Railroad Atlas
All aboard!

Based at the University of Alberta in Edomonton, Yves Beaudoin's Virtual Railroad is the hub for Internet resources associated with railroading, especially those relating to steam locomotives. Its Atlas provides lists and links to the other HTTP, gopher and Anonymous FTP sites that archive train-related material.
URL: http://gpu.srv.ualberta.ca/~ybeaudoi/Virtual_Railroad/home.html

World Wide Webs
Learn to make string figures from around the world

At his Web site, Richard Darsie teaches visitors not only how to make a series of "cat's cradle"-like figures with a loop of string, but what this art form meant to a variety of cultures. He follows a fascinating essay about the history of string figures with more than two dozen illustrations of different figures and instructions on how to create them.

Useful for activities and projects; entertainment.
URL: http://www.ece.ucdavis.edu/~darsie/string.html

Starting point

AMI, MountainNet Inc.
Up-to-date education, economic development information

AMI, the work of Internet service provider MountainNet Inc. of West Virginia, offers an extensive body of information, particularly for those interested in education and economic development. The links and pointers are up-to-date, thanks in part to the information AMI gleans from David Riggins' Gopher Jewels and Gleason Sackman's Net-Happenings mailing lists. Connections are indexed by subject and then alphabetically by the name of the institution or server at which the information is found.

Useful for starting points.
URL: http://www.mountain.net/Pinnacle/amiwww/amiwww.html
E-mail: INFO@MOUNTAIN.NET

BBN National School Network Testbed
A K-12 index and some suggestions

The server at Bolt, Beranek and Newman (BBN) Systems and Technologies leads to some useful collections of Web resources for K-12 students and teachers, It also suggests some sites with lots of graphics that are both educational and entertaining, such as the San Francisco Exploratorium. The testbed is a prototype full-service educational network funded by the National Science Foundation. Its other instruction-related services are only open to experimental schools in California and New England.

Useful for images; starting points.
URL: http://copernicus.bbn.com

Big List
Virtual fieldtrips, cyberspace tools and resources for high-school instruction

The Big List was compiled by art teacher Karen Hellyer of University Laboratory High School at the University of Illinois as a starting point on the Internet for high-school teachers, but anyone looking for educational resources should find it useful. It covers all K-12 subject areas, including athletics and counseling services. Around the World in Eighty Nanoseconds is a section that takes you on virtual fieldtrips to a variety of cultural, spatial, conceptual, and geographical locations, while Tools and Technology is a page that links to sites on the Internet where you can learn the ins and outs of how things in cyberspace work.

Useful for starting points.
URL: http://www.uni.uiuc.edu/Jan13biglist.html

Canada SchoolNet
Links to the best resources in Canada and other countries

Funded by the Canadian government as well as many private companies, SchoolNet is an educational network linking hundreds of schools across Canada — and open to the general public worldwide. The system includes resources for students, teachers, parents, and researchers. Highlights include newsgroups on a variety of subjects, an Internet help database that answers questions written in plain English or French, monitored discussion groups for students, and a guide to the 100 best science and technology resources available on the Internet. SchoolNet also offers access to libraries and other online resources around the world.

Useful for school resources; starting points.
URL: http://schoolnet.carleton.ca/schoolnet/hmpage.html

Canadiana, the Canadian Resources Page
Data in French and English

Canadiana, the Canadian Resources Page, offers links to a wide variety of Internet-based information (both text and graphics) about Canada. Topics include facts and figures, tourism, government data, history, politics, science and technology, business, education, and entertainment. You can also get news and weather forecasts and link to Canada-related newsgroups. Materials are in English and French.

Useful for international studies; mailing lists (listservs) and newsgroups.
URL: http://www.cs.cmu.edu:8001/Web/Unofficial/Canadiana/README.html

Clearinghouse of Subject-Oriented Internet Resource Guides
Lists evaluate and describe resources in many disciplines

The University of Michigan's Library and the School of Information and Library Studies (SILS) maintains these lists of Internet resources, which are prepared by experienced Internet users and SILS students. Each guide offers an evaluation of available resources on a particular topic, and provides an Internet address but no direct link. Lists cover topics in the humanities, sciences and social sciences, such as bereavement support, cancer patient information, citizens' rights, "cyber-preneurship," employment opportunities, public services and nonprofit organizations, travel, and women's health.

Useful for Internet and computing; starting points.
URL: http://www.lib.umich.edu/chhome.html

Consortium for School Networking (CoSN)
Projects entwine Internet, curriculum

The Consortium for School Networking (CoSN), an organization promoting the use of computer network technology in K-12 education, offers this server for CoSN members as well as the general public. You'll find lesson plans and project ideas you can use to incorporate the Internet into classroom activities.

Useful for activities and projects; starting points.
URL: http://cosn.org
E-mail: info@cosn.org

The daily news — just the links
A list of news sources on current events

A university in the Netherlands keeps tabs on sources of current events information as well as a list of daily newspapers on the Web.
URL: http://www.cs.vu.nl/%7Egerben/news.html

Education Online Service (EOS)
Projects, guides for high-school students

The Educational Online Service, based at Brown University, is attempting to consolidate at one site information available across the Internet for high-school students and teachers. For now, this site links to education-oriented Webs, gophers and Usenet newsgroups, as well as specific research projects, guides, lists of online resources, and other specific pointers.

Useful for Internet and computing; starting points.
URL: http://archive.phish.net/eos1/main_plain.html
E-mail: eos@brown.edu

Educational Online Sources (EOS)
Hundreds of resources for education and kids

Brown University's Educational Online Sources (EOS) provides pointers to, and lists of, hundreds of Internet resources for education and kids. You can reach Web and gopher servers, browse a list of Usenet newsgroups, and find out about electronic texts and software archives. Resources are categorized by subject. EOS also provides information about using the Internet, including introductory-level materials.

Useful for starting points.
URL: http://netspace.students.brown.edu/eos1/webs_image.html

Educational Resources Information Center (ERIC)/AskERIC Service for Educators
Electronic libraries, mailing lists and Q&A services

The federally funded Education Resources Information Center (ERIC) offers an extensive body of resources related to education through its AskERIC project.

- *ERIC Clearinghouse on Information and Technology (ERIC/IT):* This is the sponsor of the AskERIC Project. It also is one of 16 ERIC Clearinghouses nationwide which provide a variety of services, products, and resources at all education levels.
- *AskERIC:* This is an Internet-based question-answering service for teachers, library media specialists, administrators, and others involved in education. AskERIC staff personally select and deliver information resources within 48 working hours to the client.
- *AskERIC Virtual Library:* This site contains selected resources for education and general interest. These include lesson plans, digests, publications, reference tools, Internet guides and directories, information from government agencies, AskERIC InfoGuides, archives of education-related mailing lists (listservs), and access to other library catalogs and gopher sites.

Useful for online "tutors"; starting points.
URL: http://eryx.syr.edu/
E-mail: askeric@ericir.syr.edu
Message body: Your request; indicate topic of interest.

EI Net Galaxy
Highlights include information about community service, veterans affairs

While it doesn't specifically point to educational resources, the Galaxy provides a well-organized launch pad for Internet exploration. Its Community section, in particular, offers some links and pointers not usually highlighted at other Internet "starting points" that might be helpful to some families, such as information on charity and community services, veterans affairs and parascience.

Useful for health and social services; starting points.
URL: http://galaxy.einet.net/

Florida Institute of Technology Education Gopher
Links from far and wide

The Florida Institute of Technology's server offers a wide range of resources, with a focus on education. From its main menu, it provides a subdirectory of links to educational sites around the Internet. You'll also find information and links in subject areas other than education.

Useful for starting points.
URL: gopher://fit.edu/

Global Network Navigator
Focus on the Internet

Developed by book publisher O'Reilly and Associates, this page contains a lot of Internet-related information. It tends to be slow, however.
URL: http://gnn.com/gnn/GNNhome.html

Go MLink: The Electronic Library
Emphasis on Michigan and library science

Go MLink, based at the University of Michigan, is a jumping-off point for hundreds of online servers. The connected servers cover a wide range of fields, but two are particularly emphasized:

- *The state of Michigan.* Go MLink accesses important resources for residents of Michigan and for people seeking information about the state.
- Library science. Another goal of Go MLink is to provide a professional development tool for librarians, including electronic journals in library science, news affecting the library profession, and the like. Links take you to other library services around the world.

Useful for starting points.
URL: http://mlink.lib.umich.edu

Gopher Jewels
Lists and e-mail services highlight treasures of gopherspace

Gopher Jewels is not only a list of what its maintainer David Riggins considers great finds but a mailing list service that keeps subscribers up-to-date on gopherspace. Begun as a personal list that Riggins, it has grown into a searchable subject tree with pointers to more than 1,800 categorized sources. Its moderated gopherjewels mailing list allows gopher developers and users to share information about interesting gopher sites. The unmoderated gopherjewels-talk gives gopher users a forum in which to ask questions, post inquiries for locating information, and discuss information quality and content, gopher features you would like to see, and other related topics.

Useful for Internet and computing; mailing lists (listservs) and newsgroups.
URL: gopher://cwis.usc.edu/11/Other_Gophers_and_Information_Resources/ Gophers_by_Subject//Gopher_Jewelshttp://galaxy.einet.net/gopher/gopher.html (searchable form)
E-mail: gopherjewels@einet.net or gopherjewels-talk@einet.net
To subscribe: listproc@einet.net
Message body: subscribe ListName YourFirstName YourLastName

Janice's K-12 Cyberspace Outpost and Big K-12 Gopher
Resources, school sites

Compiled by Janice Abrahams of the Clearinghouse for Networked Information Discovery and Retrieval, this server includes both the K-12 Outpost (a collection of Web pointers) and Big K-12 Gopher (pointers to gopher sites). Both will lead you to a variety of interesting sites for K-12 students and teachers, such as examples of using the World-Wide Web for educational purposes and schools with their own Web pages.

Useful for school resources; starting points.
URL: http://k12.cnidr.org/janice_k12/k12menu.html
E-mail: janice@k12,cnidr.org

Kids Internet Delight (KID)
Something for everyone

The Kids Internet Delight started life as a list of resources for families which Webmaster John S. Makulowich used at an Internet seminar. Sites were drawn from suggestions he sought from other network users, and offer resources ranging from consumer and science information to entertainment and literature for youngsters,

Useful for starting points.
URL: http://www.clark.net/pub/journalism/kid.html

Kids on Campus
Graphics, activities teach how to use the Internet and find information

To encourage students of all ages to learn to use the Internet and find the information they need, the Cornell Theory Center has linked its Kids on Campus home page to resources rich in graphics and activities. These range from the solar system and sounds to online expositions and dinosaurs.

Useful for activities and projects; Internet and computing; starting points.
URL: http://www.tc.cornell.edu/Kids.on.Campus/KOC94/

Kids Web
An online library specifically for school kids

Kids Web is a prototype of a comprehensive digital library for school children. The project aims to catalog material found on the World-Wide Web that will be interesting, understandable and navigable to kids in kindergarten through Grade 12. KidsWeb is developing links to documents and images in a wide range of subjects, from art and astronomy to computers and drama to sports and weather. This project grew out of a computer multimedia class based on the World-Wide Web that was taught to eighth-graders at Syracuse University. Funded by the State of New York, it is being developed as part of The Living Textbook, a project which applies high-performance computing and communications to K-12 education..

Useful for starting points.
URL: http://www.npac.syr.edu/textbook/kidsweb/
E-mail: kidsweb@npac.syr.edu

Kids' Web
Internet sites, activities, software reviews for parents of younger children

Kids' Web, designed by Phoenix attorney Steven Burr and his 5-year-old daughter Emma, has special appeal for parents of younger children. It includes Emma's favorite Internet sites, as well as links to kid-oriented home pages, children's poems, and the family's software recommendations. Many of these have online activities for youngsters, such as coloring, puzzles and tours of space ships.

Useful for software; starting points.
URL: http://www.primenet.com/~sburr/index.html

Mitch's Internet Resources by Topic
Links useful to teachers, students

This list of over 500 Internet resources was compiled by Mitchell Sprague, a teacher in the Mendocino (Calif.) public schools, originally for the benefit of teachers in his own district. You'll find descriptions and addresses for gopher sites, World-Wide Web pages, and TELNET and FTP servers. All sources are organized by subject area — agriculture, art, astronomy, biology, business, chemistry, and so on.

Useful for reference; starting points.
URL: gopher://quest.arc.nasa.gov:70/11/resources/mitch

E-mail: mitch@tcsgi.mhs.mendocino.k12.ca.us

More Education Gophers, Rice University
Regularly updated subject trees

Rice University's gopher is a good jumping-off point for anyone exploring the educational resources available on the Internet. The directories of several major gopher sites—comprising more than 100 gophers in all—are merged into one set of menus, organized by subject. The menus are updated weekly. This site also posts information for Rice University students, faculty, and staff.

Useful for reference; starting points.
URL: gopher://riceinfo.rice.edu/11/Subject/Education
E-mail: riceinfo@rice.edu

Smithsonian's Information Servers
One-stop access

The Smithsonian Institution isn't short on valuable information, nor is it short on servers on which to dish out this information. Until the museum builds a full-blown home page, it is providing here a list of what the resources it makes available via the Internet, with links to the Web, gopher and FTP sites where these educational materials, photo archives and software are kept.

Useful for astronomy and space exploration.
URL: http://www.si.edu/sitoc.html

Teaching and Learning on the Web
Resources and applications for instruction

Provided by the Maricopa Center for Learning and Instruction, this Web site gives pointers to Internet applications and resources that can be used for instruction. In addition to these links, the server offers Mosaic documents created by Maricopa faculty and students. For example, there's one called "A 21st-Century Approach to 20th-Century Physics," which provides an introduction to relativity, cosmology, particle physics, and other topics.

Useful for education; Internet and computing; school resources.
URL: http://hakatai.mcli.dist.maricopa.edu/TL/index.html

Technologies de Formation et Apprentissage
Effects of technology in education

Based at the University of Geneva, Technologies de Formation et Apprentissage (TECFA) is an academic team exploring the applications and effects of technology in education. This Web server not only provides information about TECFA projects, but also serves as an excellent starting point for any search of educational resources on the Internet—it provides subject-specific pointers to hundreds of Web and gopher servers, mailing lists, and archives.

Useful for education; Internet and computing; starting points.
URL: http://tecfa.unige.ch/

Uncle Bob's Kids' Page
Something for all the family

From science to sports, you can probably find a link here to something interesting or unusual. "Uncle Bob" (Bob Allison) provides an annotated collection of Internet resources for kids of all ages. This extensive list is well worth browsing.

Useful for starting points.
URL: http://gagme.wwa.com/~boba/kids.html

webNews
Announcements and links to new Web sites, services and software

webNews contains hundreds of hypertext announcements on new Web sites, services and software, taken from selected Usenet newsgroups. Not only can you read each announcement, but a hypertext link lets you move to the resource itself. Articles are archived monthly, and can be browsed by subject.

Useful for Internet and computing; news sources; starting points.
URL: http://twinbrook.cis.uab.edu:70/webNews.80

WWW Virtual Library
Specialists in each subject offer lists of Internet resources

The Virtual Library points to Internet resources, arranged by subject by specialists in each field. It is supported by the developers of the World-Wide Web itself at CERN. Subjects range from Aboriginal studies and aeronautics to whale-watching and wine growing, with links to the sites maintaining each library. From here, for example, you can connect to the WWW Virtual Library: Education at Charles Sturt University, which in turn provides links in this subject to online information, such as tutorials, lesson plans, reference books, guides, and software.

Useful for Internet and computing; reference; starting points.
URL: http://www.w3.org/hypertext/DataSources/bySubject/Overview.html
E-mail: vlib@mail.w3.org

Yahoo
Index is current and comprehensive

This is considered to be one of the premier starting points on the World-Wide Web. Compiled by two PhD candidates at Stanford University, this index is not only searchable, but also rates the more than 20,000 sites that are categorized here by subject. The index is updated at least twice a day

Useful for starting points.
URL: http://www.yahoo.com

Travel and recreation

Cape Town 2004
Any vacation plans for 2004?

This is the World-Wide Web site of the South African city that is applying for the 2004 Summer Olympics.
URL: http://www.aztec.co.za/aztec/capetown.html

Kites
Images and interaction from kite lovers

This site is for kite enthusiasts. You can browse the newsgroup rec.kites and view color thumbnail sketches (downloadable in JPEG format) of a variety of kites.

Useful for images; travel and recreation.
URL: http://www.latrobe.edu.au/Glenn/KiteSite/Kites.html

Vocational studies

Advanced Technology Information Network
Agricultural curriculum, career data

The Advanced Technology Information Network offers resources relating to agriculture and biotechnology. It includes curriculum and career information designed for high-school students enrolled in agricultural education programs in California, but possibly of interest to others outside that state. You'll find national and worldwide agricultural news, market reports, schedules, weather, exporter information, a publications index, and information about ongoing research in biotechnology.

Useful for agriculture.
URL: gopher://caticsuf.csufresno.edu

America's Job Bank
An easy way to look for a job

This U.S. Department of Labor Web site lists over 100,000 jobs in governement and the private sector. The server can perform searches according to several criteria, including job codes and geographic areas.
URL: http://www.ajb.dni.us/

California Agriculture Teacher's Project
Curriculum for high-school program

This server posts the curriculum for a two-year agricultural program in California secondary schools. The material covers eight basic areas: California Agriculture, Animal Science, Plant Science, Agricultural Business Management, Leadership, Supervised Occupational Experience, Employability, and Careers.

Useful for agriculture.
URL: gopher://caticsuf.csufresno.edu

Career Magazine
If you're hunting for a job or just planning for the future

If you are changing jobs or building career contacts for the future, Career Magazine's database offers a starting point. You can customize your criteria by location, job title and major skills and search through hundreds of job openings drawn from postings in job and contract-related Usenet newsgroups. Published by National Career Search, which helps employers find qualified candidates, the magazine is building on its Web site a section that will profile major corporate employers; a forum for users to exchange information; a searchable "classifieds" section of products and services; and articles from the magazine itself, such as tips on improving your memory and preparing for an interview. Also available are selections from *The Wall Street Journal's National Business Employment Weekly* with advice and opinions on job hunting and career management as well as listings of professional and technical job openings worldwide.

Useful for jobs.
URL: http://www.careermag.com/careermag/

CareerMosaic
Find out what employers are looking for

The CareerMosaic page indicates the level and type of education and experience sought in employees by a variety of employers, such as Philips Semiconductor, Sprint International, and others in the high-technology, finance and health-care industries. Its College Connection section provides younger job-seekers with information on co-op opportunities, entry-level openings, and tips on how to prepare a resume. The Jobs Offered section lets you search, by keyword, the top Usenet "jobs offered" newsgroups from across the United States, as well as in certain specialized fields. CareerMosaic is operated by Bernard Hodes Advertising, part of the Omnicom Group, the largest agency specializing in employee recruitment, designing on-campus programs and placing help-wanted ads.

Useful for jobs.
URL: http://www.careermosaic.com/cm/

DO-IT
Career connections for high-school students

The University of Washington's Disabilities, Opportunities, Internetworking, and Technology (DO-IT) program, primarily funded by the National Science Foundation, encourages Pacific Northwest high-school students with disabilities to explore careers in science, engineering, and mathematics. In addition to live-in summer programs, DO-IT offers programs to connect students with mentors—college students, professors, and professionals, most of whom have disabilities themselves—via the Internet. On the DO-IT server, you'll find resources related to disabilities, science, engineering, mathematics, post-secondary education, and careers, as well as background information on the DO-IT educational programs. DO-IT also sponsors several e-mail discussion lists.

Useful for health and social services; jobs.
URL: gopher://hawking.u.washington.edu

FederalInformation Exchange,Inc.
Job opportunities with the federal government

If you're looking for a job with the U.S. government, the World-Wide Web page of the Federal Information Exchange is a good place to start. From here, you can link to the pages of several agencies—such as the Department of Energy, the Federal Aviation Administration, and the National Aeronautics and Space Administration—that offer Internet job postings.

Useful for jobs.
URL: http://web.fie.com/web/fed/

Microsoft Corp.
Career opportunities, internship programs

This Web page provides information about landing a job at Microsoft Corporation—which, according to *The Wall Street Journal,* offers one of the nation's best internship programs for young people. The site also offers a general overview of the direction in which computer software technology is moving, and information on the latest Windows software applications for the Internet.

Useful for jobs; software.
URL: http://www.microsoft.com/at-jobs/default.htm

Preparing Youth for Employable Futures
Prognosis and programs

Preparing Youth for Employable Futures is a report from the National 4-H Council and the U.S. Department of Agriculture (USDA) Extension Service. It offers a summary of the employment future facing today's youth, including such topics as family breakdown, declining education standards, the benefits of mentor systems and apprenticeships, and models for work force preparation. The report also provides background on several USDA Extension programs designed to educate and prepare young people for future careers.

Useful for jobs.
URL: gopher://cyfer.esusda.gov:70/00/CYFER-net/resources/workforce/work1

Lexicon of the Net

Adapted from The Internet Users' Dictionary, by William H. Holt and Rockie J. Morgan © *Copyright William H. Holt (Resolution Business Press, 1995).*

The Internet has a parlance all its own. Here are some of the terms you're likely to encounter as you surf the Internet:

American Standard Code for Information Interchange (ASCII) Defines a standard set of characters. Computers send files to one another in ASCII to avoid conflicting file formats. E-mail messages are composed of ASCII text, so you can't use bold, italic, or underlined text, or other fancy formatting.

article A message posted to a Usenet newsgroup.

bits per second (bps) A measurement of the speed at which data is transferred over a modem. To determine the number of characters a modem is capable of transferring per second, divide the bps rating by 10, e.g. a 4800 bps modem is capable of transferring 480 characters per second.

body The section of an e-mail message that contains the actual information that you are receiving or sending (the message itself).

bookmarks Also called hotlists in some World-Wide Web browsers. These electronic pointers let you store the addresses of Web sites you plan to use frequently.

browser Also called a browsing program. A program for navigating and downloading information from the World-Wide Web. A browser translates information coming from a Web server so that you can view it on your computer. Popular browsers include Mosaic and Netscape Navigator.

case-sensitive Describes a software program or programming language that can distinguish between uppercase and lowercase letters, and usually means that you should be diligent in how you type in an Internet address.

cruising "Cruising the Net" has several possible meanings, such as sending an e-mail message directly to one person, browsing a newsgroup and posting a message to everyone who browses that group, or tapping into an informational server via the World-Wide Web or gopher.

default home page The first page that appears on your screen when you load your World-Wide Web browser.

dial-up As in dial-up SLIP account, describes a temporary (versus dedicated) connection to a computer or network using a modem and phone line. It's usually cheaper, but slower, than a dedicated connection.

discussion group A type of electronic mailing list or Usenet forum.

discussion list A type of electronic mailing list that encourages subscribers to exchange ideas and information. It may be monitored by the person or persons who administer the list so that discussions stay on track.

distribution list A type of electronic mailing list that acts more like a newsletter or bulletin. It compiles and edits notices and news items from subscribers and others about a particular subject, then e-mails this information to subscribers.

domain name The mnemonic address used to make the Internet (or IP) addresses used by computers more intelligible to humans. The IP address 198.137.240.100 becomes *whitehouse.gov* — the home of the President of the United States. To explore the White House server, you type whitehouse.gov, not the IP address. Your Internet service provider's computer usually maintains a database of domain names and their corresponding IP addresses. Internet programs like Mosaic know where to find this database and convert the domain name to an IP address quickly.

domain type Refers to the type of organization (in the United States, government, military, educational, commercial, non-profit or network). It is shown as the three letters at the far right of a domain name (*whitehouse.gov*).

download To move data or software packages from one computer to another, usually from a host computer to a client (your computer).

electronic mail (e-mail) The oldest and most widely used form of communication on the Internet. Using an e-mail program, you can send messages, documents, and even pictures, to other computer users around the globe.

File Transfer Protocol (FTP) A protocol that lets you transfer files from a host computer on the Internet to your computer, using a specialized program. You can download software, images, sound files, and electronic texts from several FTP archives around the Internet. Certain FTP archives are now "wrapped" in World-Wide Web pages, letting you download files just by pointing and clicking.

forms Electronic questionnaires that are found on home pages on the World-Wide Web, including those that help you search for information. They also are found at Web sites that have some kind of interactive feature so that you can set parameters or choose items, like building a wildlife migratory map or coloring a picture. Forms are graphical, so you need a Web browser like Mosaic or Netscape to view them

freeware Software written by people for their own use and then distributed free of charge to others.

globe The icon in the upper right corner of the screen in Mosaic and some other browsers. (Netscape Navigator uses a capital "N" instead.) When the globe is turning, it indicates that the program is either retrieving or waiting for data.

gopher A software program developed at the University of Minnesota (and named for that school's mascot). When you run gopher, you can "burrow" to thousands of informational servers just by clicking on folders and file names — your screen resembles Windows File Manager and the Macintosh Finder. Gopher files contain only plain text, with no graphics or sound. Many World-Wide Web browsers now also give you gopher access.

Graphics Interchange Format (GIF) A graphic file format, developed by the CompuServe online service, that is widely used on the World-Wide Web because it reduces the amount of time required to transmit an image over phone lines.

header The part of an e-mail message similar to the address on the front of an envelope. It contains information mainly for the computer, such as where the message came from, where it's going and its format.

home page The opening page of a Web site. When you enter a site, you usually start at the home page, which may branch off to other pages.

host address Commonly called an Internet Protocol (or IP) address. See Internet Protocol (IP) address.

hotlist Also called bookmarks in some World-Wide Web browsers. See bookmarks.

hotspot Underlined text or an images surrounded by blue or green borders on the World-Wide Web. By clicking on the text or image, you are linked to another page on the same server or to a different server entirely.

hyperlink A link between two related pieces of information. By clicking the link, which is usually displayed as underlined text by a World-Wide Web browser, you can move electronically to another document that may be located anywhere in the world.

hypertext A document that contains links to other documents or media, including sound, graphics, and video files. Links can point to items within the same document or anywhere else in the world on the Internet.

HyperText Markup Language (HTML) The language used to create documents for the World-Wide Web. HTML lets an author lay out a Web page, place graphics, set the size of text elements, install links to other documents, and so on. Web browsers take arriving HTML information and build the page onscreen.

HyperText Transfer Protocol (HTTP) The language computers speak to each other to transfer World-Wide Web data.

Information Superhighway The term used by Vice President Al Gore for the National Information Infrastructure (NII), the Clinton Administration's vision of a huge, high-speed, interactive data network that would encompass even the Internet.

inline graphic An image that is embedded in text or appears on a line beside text.

Integrated Services Digital Network (ISDN)A technology offered by some telephone companies that allows data to be transferred at a minimum speed of 64,000 bps. In some areas, it is being used to access the Internet, and phone companies in the future may use it to transmit video and other complex data over phone lines.

interactive Describes any electronic resource that allows you to do more than passively read information. More and more home pages on the World-Wide Web are creating interactive features to allow users to play games, create maps, color pictures, ask questions, and so on.

Internaut An experienced user of the Internet.

Internet (or Net) A worldwide network of computer networks that enables people who connect to it to do research and to communicate online.

Internet access The right to use software programs on a host computer which is connected to the Internet. These software programs provide Internet services, such as file transfer (FTP), remote computer access (TELNET) and newsgroups (Usenet).

Internet account Personal space on a host computer, which is connected to the Internet through the organization that provides your Internet access. Having your own Internet account means that you can browse or search the Internet using various software programs and services, send and receive e-mail, and store personal files.

Internet Protocol (IP) address Also called a host address. The numbered address used to identify computers on the Internet. Your computer is usually assigned an IP address when you log on to your Internet service provider's computer. For home accounts, the address generally changes every time you connect. When you try to access another computer, such as the one at the White House, you enter that computer's domain name (*whitehouse.gov*) which is translated into its IP address (198.137.240.100).

Internet service A means of communicating and/or accessing the information resources of the Internet. Services include e-mail, the World-Wide Web, gopher, FTP, TELNET and Usenet newsgroups. To use a service you need a specific type of software program, such as a browser for the World-Wide Web. With the Web's rapidly growing popularity, many Web browsers are beginning to build in access to some other services as well, eliminating the need for multiple programs.

Internet service provider The organization that provides you access to the Internet. For home computer users, this is usually a commercial entity.

Joint Photographic Experts Group (JPEG) A standard for compressing graphic images, named for the committee that developed it. JPEG is typically used to compress photographs. Not all Web browsers can directly display JPEG images — you may need a second software application.

keyword The particular word or phrase you enter in a questionnaire-type form onscreen to tell a search tool, such as Lycos, what you want it to look for on the Internet.

listserv An electronic mailing list, especially one that uses one of the LIST-SERV mailing list management programs.

log on (or log in) Generally, to establish a connection with a computer system. Specifically, to give a command that identifies the user to the computer and starts a process of validating the user's password.

lurking Monitoring a mailing list or Usenet newsgroup to learn more about the tone and topics of discussion before you post a message or article. Does not imply sinister behavior.

mailing list A group of people with a common interest who sign up to regularly exchange messages by e-mail or receive a periodic summary of the messages. Some mailing lists serve as discussion forums for a particular topic; they may be moderated, but most are not. Other lists serve more as bulletins or newsletters that compile messages submitted by subscribers. Lists are founded and often maintained and moderated by listowners. Each list develops its own customs and rules, and it's often a good idea to monitor a list before posting a message. Mailing lists usually have a smaller but more focused following than Usenet newsgroups.

megabyte (MB) A measurement of storage (of a storage device, such as a hard drive or diskette), memory (of a computer) or communications transmission capacity. It actually equals 1,048,576 bytes.

modem A device used for data communications over telephone lines. It converts analog (telephone) signals to digital (computer) signals, and vice versa. Modems come packaged internally with most new computers, but can be added either internally or externally to older computers.

Mosaic The first World-Wide Web browser, developed by the National Center for Supercomputing Applications (NCSA) at the University of Illinois. Released in 1993, Mosaic has become the standard tool for browsing the Web. NCSA continues to develop free versions of Mosaic, but several commercial software developers have licensed the program and sell modified versions of it.

Moving Picture Experts Group (MPEG) A method of digitizing video and audio, named for the committee that developed it. MPEG allows computers to store and display motion pictures or animations. Most Web browsers don't include built-in MPEG viewer programs. While MPEG movies tend to be jerky, the technology will improve, and many expect MPEG to prevail over competing standards, such as QuickTime and AVI.

Netscape Navigator A popular World-Wide Web browser developed by Netscape Communications Corp., the company that hired many of the NCSA programmers who developed Mosaic.

network A group of computers that are interconnected to allow data to be exchanged.

newbie A newcomer or inexperienced Internet user.

newsgroup A forum on Usenet to which people with a common interest post messages (or articles) containing questions and comments. There are more than 10,000 Usenet newsgroups.

newsreader A software program that enables you to read and post articles (or messages) to Usenet newsgroups.

online service A commercial entity, such as CompuServe, America Online and Prodigy, that offers various services to its paid subscribers, such as e-mail, discussion forums, information resources, and, to varying degrees, access to the Internet.

packet switching A method of transmitting data over telephone lines on a communications network. The data is bundled and sent in packets, or envelopes, over multiple routes. The data can be switched from one path to another if a "traffic jam" occurs or a more direct route becomes available.

Point-to-Point Protocol (PPP) A method used by computers to communicate with one another over phone lines. PPP is a newer and faster system than Serial Line Protocol (SLIP), and if you're offered a choice, take this type of connection from your Internet service provider.

post To send a message or article to an electronic mailing list or newsgroup.

query The request that you send through your computer to an online database. By setting parameters, you can specify the type of information you want the database to find and display.

QuickTime A standard for digitizing video and sound developed by Apple Computer, Inc.

robot A search tool used to comb the World-Wide Web for files containing specific words or phrases.

Serial Line Protocol (SLIP) A method used by computers to communicate with one another over phone lines. SLIP is an older and slower system than Point-to-Point Protocol (PPP), but is still widely offered as a way of connecting to Internet service providers.

server A computer system that provides services, such as a database sharing, e-mail routing and file transfer, or controls the devices that it makes available for use by client computers (like yours).

shareware Software made available for general use without charge. The developer may ask those who use it to pay a nominal fee

signature file (sig file) A file that you may create, store, and automatically attach at the end of your outgoing e-mail messages. It can contain your job title, postal address, Internet addresses (such as e-mail and home page addresses), phone and fax numbers, and even a quotation or ASCII drawing that sums up your personal philosophy of life.

snail mail Describes letters delivered relatively slowly by the U.S. Postal Service and the post offices of other countries, as opposed to the rapid delivery of electronic-mail messages.

spider A type of search tool that you can use to find information on the Internet.

subject line The line in the header of an e-mail message that indicates what the message is about.

surfing Another word for cruising, meaning using any or all of the multiple services of the Internet.

Teletype Network (TELNET) A protocol developed by the Defense Advanced Research Projects Agency that allows you to connect to a computer at another location. That computer (the remote host) lets your computer act like a terminal, or part of its own system. This enables you to access library catalogs. electronic bulletin boards and other information files that some organizations, such as universities, normally only make available to their staff. students and users in their local area. TELNET, a text-based technology, was a forerunner of Internet services like gopher. It is rapidly losing ground to faster and more graphical services like the World-Wide Web.

thumbnail graphic A small image used on World-Wide Web home pages that represents and hyperlinks to a larger image. The thumbnail can be a miniature, a portion, or simply something symbolic of the larger image. It gives you an idea of what the larger image will show without forcing you to spend time downloading that graphic. If you do want to view the larger image, just click on the thumbnail with your mouse.

Transmission Control Protocol/Internet Protocol (TCP/IP) The common "language" spoken by the millions of computers that make up the Internet. It is the program that you run first, before you can load programs to read your e-mail or access the World-Wide Web.

Uniform Resource Locator (URL) An identification system that provides the protocol and address of any Internet resource. Every page on the Internet has a unique URL. The basic syntax of URL consists of the protocol, host name, port number and directory path—for example, the URL for Resolution Business Press is: *http://www.halcyon.com/ResPress/*

UNIX The operating system used by most of the large computer systems connected to the Internet. A registered trademark of X/Open Co. Ltd.

Users Network (Usenet) Also called Netnews. A worldwide bulletin-board system that includes more than 10,000 forums (or newsgroups) focusing on different topics. You can use a newsreader program to read other people's messages (or articles), and post questions and comments.

V.32bis A data compression standard for 14,400-bps modems.

Web server A computer connected to the Internet that can take requests from World-Wide Web browsers, such as Mosaic, and return files to the browsers.

Webmaster The person who maintains a World-Wide Web site.

Wide Area Information Server (WAIS) A networked information retrieval system used by many servers on the Internet that allows you to search for information by keyword. A WAIS computer indexes the data it stores not just by file names, but by specific words in each file. When you enter a keyword, the server hunts for files that come closest to matching what you're looking for.

wide-area network (WAN) Multiple computer systems networked over a large geographic area—for example, NSFnet.

World-Wide Web (Web or WWW) The most rapidly growing service on the Internet. It is a network of informational servers that features formatted text, graphics, animated "movies," and sound. Some Web sites (or home pages) let you read and post messages, and others let you download files using FTP. The Web features hypertext links, letting you click on a highlighted word to call up more information—even if it's based on another server halfway around the world. To access the Web, you need a software program called a browser.

worm Originally, a worm was a program that could damage a computer by consuming all the machine's memory, causing it to crash. The newer worm is a type of search tool that you can use to find specific information on the Internet.

Index

D

E

F

G

H

I

N

Q

R

S

T

How to install *Mosaic in a Box*

Mosaic in a Box is a simple-to-install World-Wide Web browser package developed by Spry, Inc., the Internet division of CompuServe. Spry developed the award-winning *Internet in a Box* package.

Mosaic in a Box will give you immediate access to the Internet and World Wide Web through CompuServe's Internet on-ramp. Most users in North America should have local telephone access to the network, avoiding long-distance charges.

Mosaic in a Box will only work with the CompuServe network. When this book went to press, the monthly service fee was $9.95 a month for three hours of access. That price may be lower when you sign up.

The process is simple and should only take a few minutes to complete. All you need is a PC that uses the Microsoft Windows operating system and a modem.

The following instructions presume your hard disk is drive **C** and your floppy disk is drive **A**. If these are not the correct designations of your drives, please make the appropriate substitutions.

To install *Mosaic in a Box*

1. Turn on your computer and start Windows.

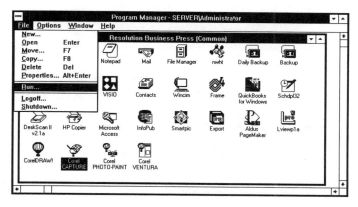

2. Insert the *Mosaic in a Box* disk in drive A.

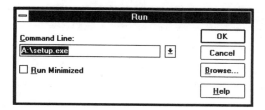

3. Select **Run** from the Program Manager's File menu.
4. Type the path command line **A:Setup** and click **OK**.

The Setup program may ask for permission to modify the AUTOEXEC.BAT file, which generally should not pose a problem. The default directory should be satisfactory.

You may need to know the make of your modem as well as the communications port it utilizes. Most are configured for Com 2.

The setup process should take less than 10 minutes. The setup program will install a *Mosaic in a Box* icon group, which will include documentation on Mosaic. Spry is expected to release an e-mail program for *Mosaic in Box*, which you can download for free. See the Products page on the Spry Web server for more details.

SPRY, Inc. Software License Agreement

THIS IS A LEGAL AGREEMENT BETWEEN YOU AND SPRY, INC. ("SPRY"). CAREFULLY READ ALL THE TERMS AND CONDITIONS OF THIS AGREEMENT PRIOR TO OPENING THIS PACKAGE. OPENING THIS PACKAGE INDICATES YOUR ACCEPTANCE OF THESE TERMS AND CONDITIONS. IF YOU DO NOT AGREE TO THESE TERMS AND CONDITIONS, RETURN THE UNOPENED PACKAGE AND ANY OTHER COMPONENTS OF THIS PRODUCT TO SPRY FOR REFUND. NO REFUND WILL BE GIVEN IF THIS PACKAGE HAS BEEN OPENED OR COMPONENTS ARE MISSING.

1. License: This License Agreement grants the purchaser of this package one License to use one copy of the specified version of the enclosed SPRY product ("Software") on any single computer. You may transfer the Software from one computer to another so long as it is not used on more than one computer at a time. You may not transmit the Software from one computer to another in a network or to serve multiple users. Solely for your own backup purposes, you may make a single copy of the Software in the same form as provided to you on the enclosed diskette. You may not copy any of the enclosed books or printed material (the "Documentation") for any reason.

2. Transfer: You may transfer the License to another party if the other party agrees to the terms and conditions of this Agreement and completes and returns to SPRY a Registration Card available from SPRY. If you transfer the License, you must also transfer or destroy all copies of the Software in any form, including the original and backup copies. You have no right to sublicense or loan the Software.

3. Copyright: You may not remove, obscure, or alter any notice of patent, copyright, trademark, trade secret or other proprietary rights.

4. Term: This License is effective until terminated. This License and your right to use the Software terminate automatically if you violate any part of this Agreement. You agree upon termination to return or destroy within 5 days all copies of the Software and to affirm in writing to SPRY that you have done so.

5. Limited Warranty (Disclaimer and Limitation of Liability): SPRY warrants the enclosed diskette on which the Software is provided to be free from defects in materials and workmanship at the time of delivery to you.

SPRY has made reasonable checks of the software to confirm that it will perform in normal use on compatible equipment substantially as described in SPRY specifications for the Software, as published most recently prior to the delivery of this package to you. However, due to the inherently complex nature of computer software, SPRY does not warrant that the Software or the Documentation is completely error free, will operate without interruption, is compatible with all equipment and software configurations, or will otherwise meet your needs. ACCORDINGLY THE SOFTWARE AND DOCUMENTATION ARE PROVIDED AS-IS AND YOU ASSUME ALL RISKS ASSOCIATED WITH THEIR USE.

AS YOUR SOLE REMEDY FOR ANY BREACH OF WARRANTY, you may return to SPRY the original copies of the Software and Documentation, along with proof of purchase and any backup copies, for replacement of (at SPRY's choice) for a refund of the amount you paid for this package, provided the return is completed within 90 days following the delivery of this package to you.

SPRY MAKES NO OTHER WARRANTIES EXPRESS OR IMPLIED, WITH RESPECT TO THE SOFTWARE OR THE DOCUMENTATION, THEIR MERCHANTABILITY, OR THEIR FITNESS FOR ANY PARTICULAR PURPOSE. ALL WARRANTIES, EXPRESS OR IMPLIED, WILL TERMINATE UPON THE EXPIRATION OF 90 DAYS FOLLOWING DELIVERY OF THIS PACKAGE TO YOU. Some states do not allow limitations on how long an implied warranty lasts, so the above limitation may not apply to you.

IN NO EVENT WILL SPRY BE LIABLE FOR INDIRECT, INCIDENTAL, OR CONSEQUENTIAL DAMAGES, INCLUDING, WITHOUT LIMITATION, LOSS OF INCOME, USE, OR INFORMATION, NOR SHALL THE LIABILITY OF SPRY EXCEED THE AMOUNT PAID FOR THIS PACKAGE. Some states do not allow the exclusion or limitation of incidental or consequential damages, so the above limitation or exclusion may not apply to you. This warranty gives you specific legal rights, and you may also have others which vary from state to state.

6. General: This Agreement constitutes the entire Agreement between you and SPRY and supersedes any prior written or oral agreement concerning the contents of this package. SPRY is not bound by any actions or statements of its independent distributors, nor by any provision of any purchase order, receipt, acceptance, confirmation, correspondence, or otherwise, unless SPRY specifically agrees to the provision in writing.

7. U.S. Government Restricted Rights: The Software and Documentation are provided with RESTRICTED RIGHTS. Use, duplication, or disclosure by the Government is subject to restrictions as set forth in subparagraph (c)(1)(ii) of the Rights in Technical Data and Computer Software clause at DFARS 225.227-7013 or subparagraphs (c)(1) and (2) of the Commercial Computer Software Restricted Rights at 48CFR 52.227-19, as applicable.

8. SPRY Address: Contractor/manufacturer is SPRY, Inc., 316 Occidental Ave. South, Seattle, WA 98104, (206) 447-0300.

Using the Internet for Education and Recreation

Coming in Fall 1995
from Resolution Business Press

Internet for Teachers, by Teachers

Written by a team of teachers for other Kindergarten through Grade-12 classroom teachers. Through it, teaching professionals will discover why they should use the Internet, how they can do so effectively, and which Internet resources are especially useful to teachers. **Douglas Steen, Mark Roddy PhD, Michael Bryan Stout and Derek Sheffield / $24.95 / ISBN 0-945264-19-4**

Secrets of The Webmasters

Answers from the experts on how to hang up your shingle in the fastest-growing corner of cyberspace, the World-Wide Web. Several dozen Webmasters of successful home pages share their insights and design strategies with individuals and institutions who are ready to create home pages of their own. **Charles Deemer / $24.95 / ISBN 0-945264-20-8**

The Internet Users' Dictionary

Clear, concise definitions and illustrations of more than 3,000 technical and colloquial terms and concepts that have proliferated in cyberspace. **William H. Holt and Rockie J. Morgan / $18.95 / ISBN 0-945264-16-X**

Now Available

UNIX: An Open Systems Dictionary

An authoritative reference book filled with jargon-free definitions for nearly 7,000 common and uncommon UNIX terms. Filled with examples, illustrations and diagrams. For anyone who uses UNIX and its look-alike operating systems, from managers to maintenance personnel, novice to advanced users. **William H. Holt and Rockie J. Morgan / $24.95 / ISBN 0-945264-14-3**

Internet for Parents

For busy parents (and grandparents) who aren't sure about the Internet and what's in it for their family. Shows how the Internet is being used at home and at school—and why it's important to get connected to it. Comes with free software to help you access the hundreds of educational online resources described in the book. **Karen Strudwick, John Spilker and Jay Arney / $24.95 / ISBN 0-945264-17-8**

To Order Our Books

Check local bookstores or order direct with your credit card by calling 1-800-397-4612 (or 206-455-4611 locally). We accept VISA, MasterCard and American Express.

You may also send a check or money order (in U.S. funds) to Resolution Business Press. Please add $3 per order for shipping in the United States and Canada, and $12 per order for other countries.

Booksellers and libraries may order direct or through Baker & Taylor and Pacific Pipeline.

Resolution Business Press, Inc.

11101 N.E. Eighth St., Suite 208

Bellevue, WA 98004

(206) 455-4611 / Fax: (206) 455-9143 / 1-800-397-4612 /

e-mail: rbpress@halcyon.com

World-Wide Web: http://www.halcyon.com/ResPress/